ADVANCE PRAISE

The voices of Holocaust survivors, preserved in print by Samuel Cox in *I Will Give Them an Everlasting Name: Jacksonville's Stories of the Holocaust*, is a valuable source of both historic preservation and inspiration.

Cox's well-crafted narratives make ample use of primary source material, including interviews with, and personal recollections of Holocaust survivors. He provides readers with brief, yet richly detailed stories of men and women who survived the most indescribable horrors in human history who made new lives for themselves in a small southern city far from their ancestral homeland.

As a Holocaust educator the value of individual testimonies cannot be overstated. The wealth of primary and secondary documentation covering the Holocaust is vast, however it is the personal stories of men and women who emerged from the Shoah and rebuilt their lives in a land far from home that provides us with a true and terrifying glimpse into the past, juxtaposed against a hopeful view of the future. Local students of the Holocaust will learn how these survivors contributed in inestimable ways to the community they called home for many decades.

On a more global level, Cox's work preserves the stories of a small segment of the population of Holocaust survivors who arrived in the United States in the years following World War II and contributes to the catalog of testimony that is integral to understanding and appreciating the scope of the Holocaust and its impact on survivors, their families, and their communities.

Patrick Nolan, M.A., Holocaust Educator, Duval County Public Schools; Adjunct Professor of History, University of North Florida

---

The chronicle *I Will Give Them An Everlasting Name*, crafted by Samuel Cox, is a remarkable effort in documenting a history that is now all but forgotten. The preservation of these life histories is itself an incredible and desirable achievement, but there is something special that many will not notice or understand about this compilation of stories.

Samuel Cox, as a part of his own fascination with history, was able to create an environment of absolute trust with these incredible people. As a second-generation child of a survivor, I know how difficult it is for many Holocaust survivors to speak about the ugly, desperate circumstances they endured. The fact that Sam was able to enlist so many of these folks to speak to his classes and then to divulge their life experiences in such detail is a feat beyond remarkable.

The book is prescient and timely in this age of political turmoil, where antisemitic attacks are at an all-time high and democracy itself hangs in the balance. It is unfortunate that there is not a Samuel Cox in each city across America. There are so many stories untold from this era. Let this chronicle serve as an important reminder of what mankind is capable of both in kindness and horror.

Mark Friedemann, Son of Holocaust survivor Richard Friedemann

---

This valuable book centers on the testimony of six women and four men, each of whom during the 1990s spoke to high school students in Jacksonville who were studying the Holocaust under the direction of Samuel Cox. Eight of the speakers were Holocaust survivors, including four who had endured Auschwitz. The accounts of their wartime existence are conveyed by Cox with sympathy but also with blunt honesty, for the camps were blunt in what they imposed: the constant threat of death, by gas or other means; the long days of heavy labor; the tiny amounts of food that prisoners were given to sustain them; the filthy conditions and overcrowding that prompted disease; and the forced marches, especially common in the last months of the war, as sick and famished prisoners were compelled to plod from camp to camp, and those who fell behind were shot.

First is the narrative of a former officer in the United States Army, a man who had taken part in the liberation of Dachau and had then served as deputy commandant at Landsberg Prison, where many high-ranking Nazis, some of them heavily involved in the Holocaust, were confined after the war, and a number were executed. His recollections of what he saw at Dachau, and his impressions of the notorious Nazis whom he encountered at Landsberg, are particularly riveting.

Cox's book concludes with the account provided by a Danish physician, who participated in the best-known rescue of the war, the evacuation to Sweden of almost all Jews living in Denmark, this action taking place just as German occupiers were preparing to deport them to the camps.

Of the ten individuals featured, only one was still alive when Cox completed his book in 2023. Inevitably, the last members of the generation that endured the Holocaust, as well as those who combatted it or otherwise witnessed it, are passing on. Yet, this is coming at a time when interest in teaching young people about the Shoah and its lessons is at unprecedented levels. The subject, not widely taught prior to 1980, is now a fixture in most European countries, and a considerable majority of states in the US either mandate or promote Holocaust education in their schools. Many hundreds of colleges and universities worldwide offer courses on the Holocaust.

Since the number of survivors is declining rapidly, those who teach about the Holocaust must grapple with the issue of how best to provide immediacy to students who will never have the opportunity to attend a talk by someone who was there. Among the resources that instructors may find useful in compensating for this loss are anthologies of testimony.

The book that Samuel Cox has added to the field includes a range of accounts, each of which offers its own perspective on Holocaust-related issues, while none is more than 30 pages in length. It is a work that will be of interest to a wide readership, but it may have a particular appeal in high school or college courses that include units on the Holocaust, for it has the virtue of covering a great deal of ground in a short space.

Paul E. Kopperman, Professor Emeritus of History, Philosophy and Religion, Oregon State University

---

Samuel Cox did as he vowed. He gave everlasting names to some of the most amazing and surely the bravest human beings that God ever created. Sam's stories of Holocaust survivors were not written with the detachment that exists in some works of historical non-fiction. While accurately captured, the accounts were told with the compassion and depth of understanding that could only be achieved by many painful face-to-face and heart-to-heart

conversations with individuals about the most horrific and darkest moments which exists in any period of our world's history. The unimaginable cruelty of Hitler and his Third Reich, along with the unwavering courage and resilience of his victims have begun to dim in today's environment of preoccupation with other pursuits. But people of all ages, education, interests, and lifestyles will be able to read Sam's unforgettable narratives in *I Will Give Them An Everlasting Name: Jacksonville's Stories of the Holocaust*, and they will never again be able to forget the horrors of Hitler's hell and those who lived to tell the story.

Susan Clark Armstrong, writer, journalist, and former columnist for the *Florida Times Union* newspaper. Her work has appeared in numerous publications

I WILL GIVE THEM AN EVERLASTING NAME

JACKSONVILLE'S STORIES OF THE HOLOCAUST

SAMUEL COX

a|p

ISBN 9789493322547 (ebook)

ISBN 9789493322530 (paperback)

ISBN 9789493322554 (hardcover)

Publisher: Amsterdam Publishers, The Netherlands

info@amsterdampublishers.com

I Will Give Them an Everlasting Name is part of the series Holocaust Survivor True Stories

CONTENTS

INTRODUCTION

I will give in my house and within my walls
a monument and a name
better than sons and daughters;
I will give them an everlasting name
that shall not be cut off. – **Isaiah 56:5**

Those who do not remember the past are not worthy of their
future. – **Maksym Rylsky**

Remember what the Amalekites did to you along the way when
you came out of Egypt. When you were weary and worn out, they
met you on your journey and attacked all who were lagging
behind; they had no fear of G-d. When the Lord your God gives
you rest from all the enemies around you in the land, He is giving
you to possess as an inheritance, you shall blot out the name of
Amalek from under heaven. Do not forget! – **Deuteronomy 25:17–
19**

The Holocaust, planned, initiated, and directed by Nazi Germany
from 1933 to 1945, was among the most horrific atrocities – indeed,
arguably *the* most horrific – in modern history. More than ten

million innocent and blameless Europeans were murdered: Roma and Sinti (Gypsies), Jehovah's Witnesses, communists, homosexuals, mentally or physically handicapped, Christian martyrs, those who resisted the Nazi totalitarian regime, and – representing the highest total of any group – six million Jews. Two-thirds of Europe's nine million Jews were murdered before the Germans were ultimately defeated.

After coming to power in January 1933, Nazi leaders quickly moved from instituting antisemitic laws to using Jews as slave labor in concentration camps throughout Germany. Soon after invading Poland in September 1939 to start World War II, Nazi subjugation of the Jews spread throughout Europe as the Germans overran one nation after another. Now, with millions more Jews under their control, the Nazis expanded their network of concentration camps and simultaneously created dozens of ghettos throughout Eastern Europe to contain them. Soon, the German government created mobile killing squads and, finally, death camps. The enormity of the ghastly systemized torture and murder of the Jews of Europe is unparalleled in history. The fortunate few who emigrated early, those who outlasted the Nazis by hiding, and the ones who miraculously survived the ghettos and camps carried with them the permanent scars of survival and the nightmares of pain and persecution. They also bore the existential guilt of surviving when most family, friends, and neighbors did not.

And yet, amid the horrors, there were myriad instances of the triumph of the human spirit that serve as examples to all. Many victims of the Holocaust, both the survivors and the millions who perished, along with rescuers and liberators, demonstrated amazing resilience, resistance, and courage that often defies description. Although tormented, the survivors triumphed with legacies of lives well lived and filled with a moral vigor that often was passed on to their children and grandchildren.

In this book, however feeble my attempt, I aim to describe in small measure the bravery and tenacity of a handful of survivors I have known personally in one city – Jacksonville, Florida. Their lives and those of their descendants are shining testaments that Hitler and Nazi Germany did not succeed in their grisly goal to eliminate the Jews of Europe. The survivors had long and successful lives and families that contributed to the cultural, professional, economic, social, and religious fabric of communities around the world. Jacksonville was enriched and shaped by these survivors and others impacted by the Holocaust who ultimately called the city home. Indeed, Jacksonville became a city that represented the American dream that these individuals chose to pursue in different ways. They all remained linked there by the Holocaust and their post-Holocaust life and were a light unto a city that welcomed them.

The chapters that follow are unique history lessons. You will meet survivors and witnesses. When reading about their personal experiences, the facts and figures of the Holocaust become more real than what any textbook or secondary scholarship can describe. These testimonies teach us how their experiences impacted them. The stories also encourage reflection on fundamental issues: good versus evil, solidarity versus indifference, and respect for one's fellow man, along with faith, persistence, and hard work. Restoration of their belief in humankind in and around Jacksonville ultimately became celebrations of life.

For five years, from 1994 to 1999, I taught a yearlong high school elective course on the Holocaust in the bedroom community of Orange Park, just south of Jacksonville, at St. Johns Country Day School. Designed for juniors and seniors, the course was intense. We covered content related to various genocides in history, with a concentration on the Holocaust. We were privileged to have a number of guest speakers over this period, many of whom spoke to the classes several times. The worthy group included Holocaust scholars, local rabbis, concentration camp liberators, a rescuer who helped save the lives of hundreds, if not thousands, of Danish Jews, and more than a dozen Holocaust survivors. Over the years, I developed close relationships with many of these speakers. Now, two-and-a-half decades later, I have chosen to highlight the stories of ten whom I came to know, respect, and love and whose stories are powerful examples of the nearly incomprehensible genocide. At the time of this writing, all but one are deceased, but their stories must live on and the world must remember through them. These intrepid friends of mine displayed incredible physical, emotional, and often spiritual strength, along with intellectual cunning, to resist, evade, outthink, and outlast the utter wickedness of the Nazis. Haunted by the past, each still exhibited an unquenchable passion for life. For eight of the ten you will soon get to know, surviving the almost unsurvivable was miraculous and often heroic, yet their lives over the decades that followed showed that survival was only the beginning.

My research included personal interviews with each of these friends, along with video recordings of their testimonies to my students, followed by face-to-face and virtual interviews with many of their children and grandchildren in 2020 and 2021. I also combed newspaper articles, television interviews, and the lengthy Shoah Foundation interviews conducted with many of them. Additionally, I consulted other primary and numerous secondary sources to complete the research, corroborate details, and provide context. In an attempt to give proper credit without the burdensome plethora of footnotes, I have chosen to summarize many of the testimonies and interviews in my footnotes and bibliography.

The late Auschwitz survivor and Nobel Prize winner Elie Wiesel once said, "If you were in the camps, if you smelled the air and heard the silence of the dead, then it's your duty to be a witness and tell the stories."[1] The people you are about to meet answered that call. They are no longer able to share their stories, yet my hope is they will never be forgotten. Their lives stand as collective testimony. May we recall the imperative from Moses, found in Deuteronomy: "*Zachor!* Do not forget!" This book is their story.

1

ELLA LUCAK ROGOZINSKI
SVALYAVA, CZECHOSLOVAKIA

Ella Rogozinski, Auschwitz prisoner A-5674 (From The Faces to Remember Project. Copyright : Agnes Lopez)

Ella Rogozinski was a pleasant, kind woman with a jovial sense of humor, ready with a smile, and a direct demeanor. She tended to say just what she thought. One word that comes to mind is zesty. She was short and stocky – "plump" as she sometimes described herself – and in her seventies when I knew her. Ella would bounce around my classroom of high school students, brown eyes sparkling yet intense, sharing her story. It was one they so desperately wanted – and needed – to hear. Self-deprecating and winsome, she would light up a room. Her warm, convivial spirit and the power of her story drew her listeners in as they yearned to know more about this dignified lady who had experienced so much horror and tragedy. At one point near the end of each testimony,

Ella would hold out her left forearm, roll up her sleeve, and show us the number A5674 tattooed there and still readily visible 50 years later. The number was a constant and permanent reminder of the 18 months she spent in Auschwitz when she was the same age as the students she was addressing.

Now in her mid-nineties (96 at the time of this writing in 2023), sadly, Ella's mind is riddled with Alzheimer's. She may have lost some zest, but her long, full life has indelibly impacted her children, grandchildren, and great-grandchildren, along with a generation of students with whom she shared her story. She left a deep impression on a young history teacher who had the privilege of getting to know her in the 1990s. Ella spoke several times to my Holocaust Studies elective classes, each time as engaging and powerful as the last. A couple of times, I picked her up from Underwood's, the jewelry store where she worked for decades. Once we went to lunch afterward, although it took some coaxing; she didn't want to miss any more work than necessary. Her work ethic, in her seventies, when she had no financial reason to have a job, continued to be irreproachable.

When my wife and I were preparing to marry in the summer of 1998, we went to Ella at Underwood's to ask her help in picking out wedding bands. We made this decision partly because of my great trust in her but perhaps more because I wanted my soon-to-be wife to meet this friend I admired and loved so much.

Ella Rogozinski was born Ella Lucak in Svalyava, Czechoslovakia (now part of Ukraine) on February 11, 1927. She was born to Adolph Lucak, a city government worker, and Freida Mermelstein Lucak, who owned a mercantile business with her family. Ella was one of four children. She had an older brother, Otto (Chaim was his Yiddish name), and two older sisters –Helga was seven years older than Ella, followed by Olga, who was four years older. She enjoyed a wonderful childhood – she called it "idyllic." Svalyava was close to the Ukrainian border and had a population of about 15,000. Ella recalls there were about 450 Jewish families in the town, along with

Czechs and Ukrainians. She remembers having a blissful youth with many friends, both Jewish and Christian, and a loving family.

Materially, she and her siblings wanted for little. The family lived an upper-middle-class life, with familiar closeness a central theme in their daily routine. The Lucaks spoke Yiddish at home, but Ella began studying both Russian and German at school in second grade. She also learned to speak Hungarian, Czech, and Hebrew and later learned English after immigrating to the United States. She attended Hebrew school twice weekly. She said her fluency in seven languages was later instrumental in her survival.

In school, Ella loved not only languages but history. About one-third of the students in her public school were Jewish. Ella had Jewish and Christian friends growing up, both in her classes and her neighborhood, and rarely experienced antisemitism in her early years. Religiously observant, the Lucak family observed all the Jewish holidays and kept kosher. Ella grew up in a family where religious faith and traditions were central to their lives, and her family was instrumental in both her social and moral development. As a child, Ella also loved flowers, which have continued to bring her joy throughout her life.

Life changed dramatically in 1938, however, once the Nazis began to occupy the Sudetenland, the western part of Czechoslovakia. By March 1939, all of Czechoslovakia was occupied. Suddenly, fewer and fewer Christians came to the family store, the gentile children stopped coming over to play, and the school was no longer the friendly, safe place it had been. In addition to the economic consequences of the German occupation, the Jews of Svalyava lived in fear. By 1941, life had deteriorated for the Jews of Svalyava, including the Lucak family.

After several years of antisemitic discrimination and increasing hardship, Ella and her family were transported to the Kolomyia Ghetto in 1941. The occupying Germans began establishing ghettos throughout conquered Eastern European cities. The ghettos were holding centers for large numbers of Jews from each city and area villages and *shtetls*. They were held there before being sent to concentration camps. They lived in the Kolomyia Ghetto for about four to six months before being sent to a forced labor camp in Budapest late in the year. For more than a year, Ella and her family were in the Budapest Ghetto. They were in Dohany Street Synagogue – the "Doheim Jeutze" – while working in the nearby labor camp. The next year, she and her family were on a train to Kolomee, on the border of Poland and Czechoslovakia. There they waited for six weeks, unsure of what was next. Suddenly, in January 1944, they were told to pack one suitcase each, leave everything else behind, report to the local train station, and await further instructions. They and other Jews were deported to the Múnkacs Ghetto in southwestern Ukraine. Again, they were herded inside cattle cars, with no windows or seats. For days, the Jewish prisoners could only stand as there wasn't enough room to sit. There was no room even to move or lean on one another, and sleep was often futile. Their only source of water was the occasional rain that might seep into the cattle car. Many of the prisoners died en route, and when they did, their corpses were used as cushions. The air was stale and smelled of rotting flesh and human excrement.

Once they finally arrived at the Múnkacs Ghetto, the family spent one month there. Then they were ordered to leave once again and bring their meager possessions to the local train station. It was nighttime when they arrived and the Lucak family was met by chaos. Confusion reigned, and fear was palpable. Young Ella was 16 and her world was again being turned on its head, though this time in utterly incomprehensible ways. Ella and her family, along with the other Jews there at the station, were receiving mixed communication coupled with circulating rumors. They were told initially that they were being sent westward to Germany to work, then that they were being sent east and out of the war zone. They weren't sure where they were going, why they were being deported, and their fate once they got to their destination.

Ella, her parents, and her siblings ultimately were handed two pails for the family and herded from the station platform onto an overcrowded cattle car, much like they had when deported months earlier to the Múnkacs Ghetto. Within minutes, the train pulled out of the Budapest station and disappeared over the horizon, leaving the city behind. Ella and her family began an eight-day-long train journey with little food or water. The stench from the now-full buckets, used by the dozens of crammed-together occupants as their bathroom, was so intense it sickened her. Approximately 250 people were packed into each rail car for the arduous journey deep into Poland. The ride seemed to take longer than anyone expected, and with the confusion about their destination, no one really knew what lay ahead. They began to realize that the train had been going "around and around and around," as Ella recalled.

Finally, the occupants – exhausted, ill, and filthy – felt the train slow to a stop. As the wheels squealed to a halt, Ella and the others realized they were not in Germany, nor had they been evacuated out of harm's way. Though they did not know it initially, the trainload of Jews had been transported to the notorious Auschwitz-Birkenau death camp in Oświęcim, Poland, 41 miles [66 kilometers] west of Kraków. Auschwitz, a former Polish army barracks on a marshy plain just outside of Oświęcim, consisted of 22 brick "blocks" arranged in three lines, surrounded by a double perimeter of 13-foot-tall electrified barbed wire. Even in the dark of night, the gas chambers and crematorium were chillingly visible.

Hundreds of German guards yelled *"Schnell!* [Quickly!]" Blinding light illuminated the night. Dogs were barking, and confusion prevailed. The doors of the long line of cattle cars were pulled open and the hundreds of Czech Jews were quickly unloaded into the bedlam of chaos and death.

"Dogs. Noise. *'Raus! Raus!* [Out! Out!]'" Ella said. "And from that moment on everything was fast. *Schnell! Schnell!* Everything had to be done *schnell* Just amazing, and pushing and screaming, and the train was high. We had to jump down, and little children, two-years-olds, five-years-olds, older people, everyone had to jump down! Everything went very fast. And the men had blue and white stripes, with big sticks. They were Jewish people, and they made those people go down, down, down."

Ella remembered some guards ripping babies from the mothers' arms. The women screamed and hollered, and there was shooting. Many were terribly upset because the guards took their children from their hands. Why would a young mother be told by fellow Jewish prisoners to give the child away? It made no sense to Ella. She soon learned, however, that the old and infirmed, along with the young children, and anyone escorting a child such as a young mother, would be immediately selected for the gas chamber. Auschwitz, she came to quickly realize, was about survival, and few were fortunate enough to do so.

Briskly, the men and women were separated into two lines and the selection process began. A tall, good-looking man in uniform with a leather coat and perfectly polished boots – Ella later learned he was the infamous Dr. Josef Mengele – did the selecting. Ella described Mengele as "the big German king." Ella and her sisters were sent to the right – chosen to work at the camp and live.

Ella, Helga, and Olga were led to a stark, cold holding room. Then they were stripped, their clothes taken, and their heads and other parts of their bodies shaved. They stayed overnight. In the morning, they were given blue-and-white-striped "dresses" – a camp uniform – and wooden clogs [klompen], or as Ella described them, "Holland shoes," and taken to another temporary barracks. In the chaos, Ella was separated from her sisters. When they found each other in the holding room, naked and shaved, each one looked the same. Ella barely knew her sisters. The girls realized their mother, two aunts, and a young cousin were not with the group. They presumed they had been sent to the other line, to the left.

The girls were already famished upon arrival, having little or no food for days. Still, food was withheld for another two or three days. Hunger would continue to be with them for many more months.

7

Several members of the group asked a female German guard where their parents were. "See that smoke? Over there!" came the terse reply.

The next day, confused and not yet able to fully comprehend what was going on, the young girls repeated the question to a prisoner from Slovakia who had been at Auschwitz for a while: "Where are all those people? Where are our parents?"

The Slovakian prisoner responded matter-of-factly, "See the smoke? Don't you smell it? Don't you see? They're in the smoke. They're in the sky. They're in heaven."

"Like big, black clouds," one observer remarked afterward, "the smoke of the crematorium hung over the camp. Sharp, red tongues of flame behind the sky, and the air was full of the nauseating smell of burning flesh."

Fifty years later, Ella quietly, hesitantly recalled, as her sparkling eyes grew distant, dim, and misty, "You know, it took us maybe two months before we believed it. We didn't believe it until we convinced ourselves that every day people go in ... and nobody came out." Ella could never forget the pungent smell of burning flesh that hung in the air that night and in the nights and days that followed. She soon came to learn this was the smell of the crematorium. She recalled, even after five decades: "You don't know how flesh burns. But sometimes, if you put margarine on the stove ... *Ach!* Terrible! It stays in your throat for months and months, that smell!" She couldn't cook on a barbecue grill because the smell of burning beef reminded her of the burning flesh of Auschwitz, including that of her own family.

When Ella finally received food, her diet often consisted of one potato or cabbage daily and occasionally a cup of watery soup. Soon, it was not even that; she was given a single piece of bread and a bowl of water to be shared by eight. Ella began to approach death by starvation.

She and her sisters were soon told by the prisoners to stay away from the electric barbed-wire fences. All three were in the same barracks. Their work assignment was to put clothes taken from the murdered prisoners into boxes to be sent back to Germany. The building where the young women worked was located near one of the crematoria. They sorted and cleaned the clothing that the gassed prisoners had left behind in the disrobing rooms. Twelve or more hours a day, over 540 days, they combed through the mounds of Jewish wallets, purses, and clothing. Their job included looking for money that might be hidden in buttons or hems. These were the clothes taken from the Jews immediately prior to them gasping for their final breaths in the Auschwitz gas chambers. "Everything went into boxes," Ella said. "Day after day, big trucks came with everything: with pillows and shoes, thousands and thousands of glasses, and everything. Everything went away for Germany."

There were 350 or so young women in her work group. For reasons unknown to her, it was not until about two months after their arrival that the three sisters were finally tattooed. Ella had A-5674; her two sisters had A-5672 and A-5673. As she was being tattooed, Ella asked the guard in German to make the tattoo smaller because she thought it was ugly. Impressed by her proficiency in German, the guard consented. After being tattooed, they said, "Well, you know everybody with a number never gets out of here."

Their work went on for months and months. "I never saw anyone coming out," she recalled. "It was a terrible, terrible thing. One father worked there and put his own son in the oven." Jewish musicians were ordered to form an orchestra, and they would play beautiful music designed to keep the prisoners calm before they went to work or were sent to the gas chambers. Ella and her sisters withstood the imprisonment nightmare at Auschwitz for 18 debilitating months. Early on, after about two months, Ella got very sick and could barely speak. Her loss of speech lasted until nearly one year after her liberation – all told, nearly two-and-a-half years. As the Nazi killing machine murdered thousands of her people day after day, Ella said she "died a million times." Yet she remained

9

stoic, bottling up her anger and sadness inside, never crying. They were grisly days for everyone, and for a teenage girl, the experience was truly horrific.

Not long after her arrival, a German guard, a driver who transported the goods they had sorted and cleaned back to Germany, displayed compassion and kindness. He told Ella her father and brother were still alive and working in a coal mine outside the camp. The guard even brought Ella a note from her father. To receive a handwritten note from her father defied all odds and brought Ella and her sisters hope. He wrote simply, "*Liebe Kinder* [Dear children], I am fine. Your father." The guard, however, told Ella and her sisters that their father was "very frail ... and he's very sick ... and your brother is also terrible."

After a few weeks, the kindly guard said he had to leave the camp and return to Vienna for a new assignment. Communication with her father and brother was severed. It was only later that she learned their fate. News ultimately came that their father had died. He had been forced to work in back-breaking slave labor, and despite the efforts of his son, who worked alongside him and helped him with the punishing toil, he was unable to maintain the routine. Ella's grief-stricken brother then threw himself onto the electric perimeter fence, dying just moments after his father's death. Chaim was 21 years old, a time that should have been the prime of his life.

Ella tried to ignore the reality of the crematoria, and yet, even before she heard the official word that they had died, deep down she knew her parents and brother were likely gone. She also knew that if she and her sisters were going to survive, they would need to not only be strong and courageous but smart. They kept it secret that they were sisters because they knew they would likely be separated – or worse – if the information got out. The three sisters shrewdly disciplined themselves by rationing the little food they received, looking out for one another. Every morning, each prisoner in the barracks was given a slice of bread for the day. Most of the starving prisoners immediately devoured their small portions, but Ella and her sisters divided one slice for breakfast, one for lunch, and one for dinner to have at least minimal nutrition spread throughout the day. Their self-discipline and selfless love helped keep them alive. For their constant thirst, they were given a "big bowl" of tea that 20 people had to drink from, and the rest of the day they had nothing to drink. After the four o'clock morning wakeup call, they had to stand in line at five o'clock for their tea, a piece of bread, and maybe, if they were lucky, a bowl of soup to share with the others. The soup sometimes had the bonus of old potato peels and perhaps bits of beets.

Occasionally, Ella would hear the screams of children being used for the horrific medical experiments conducted by Mengele and his staff. She saw them being taken inside the medical building, yet she never saw any of them leave. She didn't know any details of what was going on until after the war. She knew enough to understand it had been a place of evil and death. While she was fortunate not to be a victim of such depraved experimentations, Ella surely endured her own hell. She recalled that often she and the others hoped the person in the bunk next to them in the barracks would die in the night so they could have their bread. They were treated like animals and ultimately began to act like animals themselves. The Nazis tried hard to dehumanize the prisoners, particularly the Jews. "I would see birds flying and think, G-d, why couldn't I just be a bird?" she said.

Periodically, the Nazi doctors would come to the barracks to draw blood from the prisoners that would help save the lives of wounded German soldiers on the front. The Nazis believed the Jews were subhuman but thought nothing of infusing Jewish blood into the wounded soldiers. Of course, losing blood placed emaciated Jewish prisoners at greater risk, further weakening their atrophied bodies. Ella said she always hid so she never had to give blood. "One time they took my middle sister, but she screamed and hollered and made such a thing that they let her go," Ella said.

Ella's granddaughter, Dana Rogozinski, recalled her grandmother telling her that "every Sunday, the German officers played a game where they lined up the prisoners and counted them off by a random number. Those selected, like every third or every fourth, were shot and killed. This went on for hours at a time." She added: "My grandmother said she died a million times. Not only was she nervous and holding her breath that she didn't get shot, but she couldn't turn her head and look to see where her sisters or her aunt were."

The guards also used female prisoners as prostitutes. "They came around and they chose very pretty girls for the German soldiers," Ella said. "So you lived always with fear. You don't know what you do right, you don't know what you do wrong. You were ugly it wasn't good, you were pretty it wasn't good. So that's how life was." Ella said the Nazis created a camp where "you became an animal. I don't even know if you understand, but sometimes a mother and child or sister, if she died, you kept it a secret for a day, and you can have her bread. And the minute she died, if she had better shoes or something, you took it off." Ella paused, then continued, "And it was no tears. You know it was, like, 'Oh, thank G-d, she died.'" Even Ella, the kind, gentle, and loving teenager, was reduced to a survival-of-the-fittest mode, and the nightmare impacted her long after the hell of Auschwitz was over.

Ella and her sisters had endured more than two years in two debilitating ghettos and survived 18 long months of hell at Auschwitz-Birkenau, where more than one million were murdered in the gas chambers. The test of their endurance was not yet over, however. More trials were to come, most perhaps even more difficult than the abyss of Auschwitz.

In January 1945, the Soviet army invaded Poland and began to defeat the occupying German army. On January 18, the prisoners were herded onto a cattle car for a short train ride before being forced off for a long and arduous walk westward on foot. Another journey awaited.

Near the war's end, as Germany's military force collapsed, Allied armies began closing in on Nazi concentration camps. Soviets came from the east, the British, French, and Americans from the west and south. The Germans frantically began to move the prisoners out of the camps near the front, particularly in Poland, as Soviet troops advanced. The prisoners were taken to camps inside Germany to be used as forced laborers. Prisoners were first taken by train and then by foot on "death marches," as they became known. The already-high death toll of the prisoners grew ever more alarmingly horrific over the next few months.

The largest death marches took place in the winter of 1944–45, as the Soviet army began its liberation of Poland. Nine days before the Soviets arrived at Auschwitz, the Germans marched tens of thousands of prisoners out of the camp toward Wodzisław, a town 35 miles away, where they were put on freight trains, or force-marched to other camps. About one in four died or were murdered on the way there. Ella and her sisters were among those forced to march west.

The Nazis often killed large groups of prisoners before, during, or after these marches. During one march, 7,000 Jewish prisoners – 6,000 of them women – were moved from camps in the Danzig region bordered on the north by the Baltic Sea. On the ten-day march, 700 were murdered. Those still alive when the marchers reached the shores of the sea were driven into the water and shot.

The *Schutzstaffel*, or SS, were the Nazi's elite, powerful paramilitary organization that administered the network of hundreds of concentration and death camps throughout German-occupied Europe. The SS, particularly sadistic in its treatment of the Jews, began evacuating Auschwitz and its satellite camps on January 17, 1945, as the invading Russian soldiers rapidly approached. All told, nearly 60,000 prisoners were forced on these death marches from the Auschwitz camp system. Thousands were killed in the days immediately before the death march, and tens of thousands of prisoners, most of whom were Jews, were forced to march to

Wodzisław in the western part of Upper Silesia before going further west. More than 15,000 died during the death marches from Auschwitz. In Wodzisław, the prisoners were put on unheated freight trains and cattle cars and deported to concentration camps in Germany, mainly to Flossenbürg, Sachsenhausen, Groß-Rosen, Buchenwald, Dachau, Bergen-Belsen, and Mauthausen. On January 27, 1945, the Soviet Army entered Auschwitz and liberated the few remaining prisoners, most of whom had been too weak to make the journey west to Germany.

Ella was not there when the Soviets arrived. She went on the unthinkably cruel death march from Auschwitz to Bergen-Belsen, which took about three months and was 450 miles long. When they left on January 18, they were markedly malnourished, underweight, sick, and weak. They had no warm clothes and wore camp-issued wooden clogs with no socks while marched through subzero temperatures, snow, and ice. Ella recalled "walking, walking, walking ... weeks and weeks and days and days with nothing on. Freezing snow, hungry, no food, no nothing. We just eat the snow. ... Daytime we didn't walk ... just nighttime. They didn't want the German people to see. ... It was terrible."

At one point in the long journey, Ella's sister, 22-year-old Olga, developed severe frostbite on several of her toes after losing her clogs and having to continue barefooted in the snow for days on end. One foot turned blue, then black, from the frostbite. Her sisters knew she couldn't survive if they didn't take drastic action. Either the infection would quickly kill her, or her inability to walk would mean the guards would shoot her. "Helga took off [Olga's] shoe," Ella recalled, "and the toes were black. So, somebody said, 'Helene [which Helga sometimes was called], you have to do something' ... because if the Germans saw that she cannot walk fast enough, they would shoot her." They determined that they had to cut off her middle toes.

The 25-year-old Helga walked ahead for half a day and found what might be a solution. She was able to borrow a pair of rusty scissors from another prisoner who was a nurse. "My sister walked one way," Ella said, "brought the scissors, took off the two [toes] ... we put snow on, and she had to take back the scissors to that lady." Cutting off Olga's infected toes prevented gangrene. There was no anesthesia, penicillin, antibiotics, or medicine of any sort to numb the pain or help prevent infection. Ella recalled that if a prisoner slowed down, they would be "put on the side of the road to die" or shot on the spot. So Ella and Helga carried Olga for the rest of the long, grueling walk. "That's how we walked, miles and miles to that camp," Ella said.

They trudged through the snow as if in a daze, putting one frozen foot in front of the other, starving and weak. She said she envied the dogs and wanted so badly to eat as well as they did. "We were freezing to death." After a while, all three sisters were walking without shoes. Although thousands died, the Lucak trio once again fought for their lives. After their long journey – cold, frail, and barely alive – the sisters arrived at yet another concentration camp.

Ella described Bergen-Belsen as hell. That was a strong description after surviving 18 months at Auschwitz. After the prisoners made it to Bergen-Belsen, they were not fed for five days. Then, ten or more people were forced to drink a few ounces of filthy water from the same bowl. Their one small daily meal – watery soup or stale bread – was shared by a group as well. When the meager rations were distributed, mothers and children fought each other for a single piece of bread. Prisoners were filthy, covered with lice, often running high fevers, rife with disease, malnourished and starving, and alarmingly underweight. What little strength was left after leaving Auschwitz was all but depleted by the time they got to Bergen-Belsen. Ella stayed there for weeks and was very sick. "I almost died," she said. As at Auschwitz, she "felt like an animal."

During those weeks, they did little but listen to the cries and screams of the dying. "It was terrible. Like herrings, one next to the other on the floor ... dirty, filthy, wet, coughing, crying, screaming. People had diarrhea, people had terrible fevers, typhus. We had typhus. It was terrible." The bodies of hundreds upon hundreds of the dead piled up since the ground was too frozen to bury them and the crematoria were no longer operable to burn them.

One day, one of her sisters went to the gate and asked a guard for some fresh water for Ella and was willing to do whatever the guard wanted so that she could help keep Ella alive. She persisted for two days but still received no water for Ella. Finally, Ella said, "One day, we heard big tanks coming and cars. It was the American soldiers." Actually, the soldiers in the tanks who would soon liberate Bergen-Belsen were British, from the 63rd Anti-Tank Regiment and the 11th Armored Division, along with some Canadian units. Just before liberation, however, the fleeing German guards told the prisoners that they had poisoned the wells so, out of fear, the inmates drank no water for ten days. The inevitable dehydration meant death for many so soon after their long-awaited liberation.

As the British 11th Armored Division entered Bergen-Belsen on April 15, 1945, its soldiers were unprepared for what they found. Inside the camp's fences, they discovered more than 60,000 emaciated, feeble prisoners in dire need of immediate medical attention. They soon came upon more than 13,000 corpses in various stages of decomposition scattered all around the camp. One member of a British Army Film and Photographic Unit described the scene of unburied bodies: "The bodies were a ghastly sight. Some were green. They looked like skeletons covered with skin – the flesh had all gone. There were bodies of small children among the grownups. In other parts of the camp, there were hundreds of bodies lying around, in many cases piled five or six high."

Another British soldier, a corporal of 15th/19th The King's Royal Hussars, described the scene of survivors: "We weren't expecting to see anything – we didn't know there was such a place. We had been going ahead without any idea there was anything there. I think that was the worst part." What he and other liberators saw was incomprehensible. "I couldn't believe what I was seeing – I couldn't believe ... people could sink to that level, and treat people the way they treated these prisoners," the former corporal recalled 75 years later. "When you see a person who is a living skeleton, as these people were, it's difficult. It's astonishing that any human being could survive the terrible torture. ... Anybody who didn't see the place as we saw it would find it very difficult to believe what we actually saw. Bodies stretched out on the ground. Nobody had the strength to move them. The people on the other side of the barbed wire didn't know who we were – they just stared as we approached."

Bergen-Belsen had no gas chambers; it was a slave labor concentration camp. The mass murders in gas chambers were confined to death camps farther east in Poland. Still, estimates place the number of Bergen-Belsen deaths at more than 50,000 Jews, Czechs, Poles, anti-Nazi Christians, homosexuals, Roma, and Sinti. The rate at which prisoners died rose dramatically after a mass transport of inmates from other camps began in December 1944. From 1943 until December 1944, the estimated death total was about 3,100 in Bergen-Belsen. From January to mid-April 1945, that number rose to around 35,000. An additional 14,000 died between April 15 and the end of June 1945, after liberation, because of their weakened state.

Ella and her family, now made up of only Helga, Olga, and their Aunt Lea, at long last were liberated just two days after the British and Canadian troops stumbled upon Bergen-Belsen, on April 17, 1945. The Lucak girls were finally free and had survived the Nazi death grip. Nevertheless, the happiness was bittersweet. They had to acknowledge the sorrow they felt about the deaths of their brother, parents, and other family members who perished at Auschwitz.

Though she survived the effects of her years in two ghettos and two concentration camps, 18-year-old Ella stood only five feet tall and weighed a mere 52 pounds. She was close to death, little more than a skeleton and barely strong enough to walk, unable to speak, yet she was alive.

"Soldiers liberated us, cleaned us, and yet still more than half of us died," she said. The troops immediately gave the prisoners bread. "People died just grabbing bread!" Ella exclaimed. Others died from eating more than their malnourished, emaciated bodies could immediately handle, such as the rich chocolate some soldiers gave them. Of Ella's barracks of 800 women at Bergen-Belsen, only 50 survived, about six percent. Ella and her sisters got sick devouring a jar of peanut butter – her first time tasting the rich North American concoction. Ella, Helga, and Olga, however, never left one another's side and, miraculously, all three survived, their loving solidarity letting them persevere together.

Ella recalled seeing an "important American general" at the camp soon after liberation. She thought later it may have been General Dwight Eisenhower himself. Her eyes lit up as she fondly recalled the soldiers' kindness. "Let me tell you, those ... soldiers!" They provided food and baths, and sprayed them with white powder, since "we had lice all over. I mean lice you couldn't even pick off from your skin. It was 10, 20 lice just eating your skin. ... For weeks, the soldiers, unbelievable what they did to us."

For a while after liberation, Ella said she hated everybody, but soon found the hate "was eating on me." Ella had lost both of her parents, three aunts, two uncles, her brother, and multiple cousins, along with most of her childhood friends. Altogether, she estimated, she lost about 60 relatives. Ella lamented half a century later, "I hope I die before something bad happens again to children – Jewish or non-Jewish."

The three Lucak girls were soon transported to a displaced persons (DP) camp somewhere in Germany. It was there that Ella met Jakob Rogozinski, a Holocaust survivor from Poland. Ella and Jakob quickly fell in love, finding strength in an emotion that the Nazis had tried to rip out of their hearts. Despite what the Nazis thought of them and the Third Reich's many attempts to dehumanize them, Ella and Jakob said they always knew they were not animals but human beings, each with a heart and soul, able to find love in the ruins. A few short weeks after meeting in the DP camp, Jakob asked Ella to marry him. They wasted little time. They married immediately in the camp, finding tenderness amid the ashes. Ironically, all three sisters' weddings were held within weeks of one another. And they were all married wearing the same wedding dress.

The newlyweds spent about three years in the DP camp before immigrating to Israel to be with Jakob's surviving brother. They lived in Israel for seven-and-a-half years. Their first two sons, Chaim and Abraham, were born there. Israel disappointed the young couple. It was "not what I expected," Ella recollected. They endured another "battlefield of hate" during the Suez Crisis in 1956. She was ready for the bombs, tanks, and sirens to stop. The fear of war and terror reminded her too much of Europe; she dreamed of moving to the United States. Olga and Helen had immigrated to Jacksonville, Florida, so finally, in early 1959, Ella and her family moved there. Though Ella spoke seven languages by this time, she and Jakob spoke not one word of English between them. She and Jakob came to the United States with $8.50. Ella recalled that she couldn't read or write English. "I had no profession. I was [just] a little girl from Czechoslovakia." They knew, nonetheless, that America would be their home.

Because of the language barrier and her being Jewish, Ella encountered prejudice, this time in her new homeland. But this proud, strong, and courageous little Jewish woman knew nothing could be harder than what she already had endured. America was where she finally felt she could live freely despite any obstacles she and Jakob might face. Their lives in their new home would not be easy, but the resilience from what they had withstood would help them find success living an American dream of their own. Ella and Jakob's third son, Sam, was born in Jacksonville in 1960.

When the immigrant Rogozinsky family moved there in 1959, they were dirt poor, Ella said. Unable to afford an apartment, they lived briefly in what she called a "little shack." From there they moved into a tiny apartment – and antisemitism struck again. They were forced into a new home after only two weeks because the landlord learned they were Jewish. To help support a family of five, Ella worked in a bakery, washing large pots for 35 cents an hour; her take-home pay was $18. She had two more jobs, cleaning a hotel and houses, which meant a few more dollars. Jakob was an auto mechanic, earning $42 a month. With sheer determination and hard work, the couple finally saved enough money to purchase what would be their first home, a modest one, with a mortgage of $50 a month. After they paid the mortgage on their tiny home each month, they had little left for anything else, but they enjoyed the bounty of their new home and new life. "America was a dream for me," Ella declared.

For decades, Jakob was a mechanic at Al Sager Volkswagen, moonlighted at United Parcel Service, and had a third job cleaning a post office. In 1980, Ella polished silver at Underwood's Jewelers and, later, repaired jewelry. She drew pictures of the pieces she worked on until she taught herself to speak and write English. She was at Underwood's for years, even after her finances improved and she no longer had to work. Dementia finally forced retirement when she was in her mid-eighties.

Ella was determined not only to succeed but to prove that she and her family were just as good as everyone else. While the boys were growing up, Ella would take them to the library, with the much-appreciated air conditioning, so they could escape the wilting Florida heat. The family was unable to afford such luxury in their modest home. It was in the library that Ella began to learn English as she read with her young boys and later studied one son's first-grade lesson book. "He came home every day, 'Momma, look, I have homework ... apple, dog,'" she reminisced. "I would sit with him every night. One day he says, 'Mom, you have the paper upside down!'"

Ella and Jakob's three boys were their greatest joy. By working multiple jobs and "eating a lot of chicken bones," Ella and Jakob said they were able to send their boys to the best colleges. Love was plentiful, although the parents were watchful and, sometimes, exacting. They instilled good work ethics in their progeny and expected much from them in return. All three sons received college scholarships and earned straight A's.

Ella admitted she was a taskmaster, always pushing them toward excellence. She wanted each one of them to appreciate the remarkable opportunities they had in what she called "America: the best country in the world!" The Rogozinski home was no democracy. "We never got a vote; things were never discussed or negotiated," son Abe recalled with a smile. "It was a constant give-and-take between us wanting to become very Americanized. We were the new kids, immigrants, and our parents were holding onto Old World values. And I have to admit, they won. All three of us are grateful for that."

Chaim and Abe became prominent orthopedic surgeons, and Sam earned a business degree; he managed the medical practice. Along with one of Ella's grandsons, they own and operate the thriving Rogozinski Clinic in Jacksonville, specializing in spinal injuries and surgery. Doctors told Ella and Jakob they wouldn't be able to have children after what their bodies had been through. But the Rogozinski clan includes their three sons, 11 grandchildren, and 12 great-grandchildren. Ella and Jakob's descendants have not only embraced the American dream, they have contributed, enjoyed, and flourished in the cultural fabric of this nation. The family has successfully defied and defeated the Nazi goal of eradicating the European Jews.

They had many chances to return to their hometowns or countries, but Ella and Jakob never did, nor did her sisters. "Every time I see something nice about Czechoslovakia, I think 'Let's go!'" Ella said in her seventies. "And then, I don't." She still owned a home and property there, which had belonged to her parents, but she said, "Who cares? It's just a house, just a house. America is my home." Even after many years, Ella never took her life here for granted. She is thoughtful, yet absolute, about her adopted homeland:

"If people would know ... if people would know what America is. If Jewish people, American Jewish people, or Catholics, who grow up in America, do they know what they have? They don't. They don't appreciate ... they complain about taxes, they complain about everything. America is beautiful! I'm just afraid it can happen again. You see the skinheads ... it's terrifying. It can happen. That people can do that to people. Why? People can do that to people; they make an animal out of you. ... I had so much hate in me [after the war]. So much hate. And I still do. I try to forget. But I cannot forgive. I cannot forgive...

My children are so successful. People come back and they talk to me, 'Ella, what a wonderful life you made for yourself.' Sweetheart, nobody gave us a penny. We put penny and penny together. My son was already a doctor; he drove a ten-year-old car because he paid off the loans. He said, 'Mom, America gave me a chance. I'm gonna pay back every penny.' And they showed on TV that so many people owe money. Not my children. They paid back the money. The first dollar they made. I don't have to make 'em, they had the responsibility. All three of them ... they are very plain children. Even though they bought beautiful homes, they still go trick-or-treat with their children, go to the beach. They don't belong to a club, they don't golf. They [are] just plain people. They give [to] charity, they do a lot of beautiful things. Their name is not in the paper."

For more than two decades after arriving in the United States, and more than three decades after their liberation, Ella and Jakob didn't speak of their experiences in the Holocaust. They tried to put their painful past behind them and focused instead on creating new lives, raising a family, and enjoying the fruit of living in freedom and hope. Yet they still carried their scars internally, and for years their religious faith was lost. They didn't attend services at a synagogue for 20 years while they wrestled with their pain. Like

Jacob in the Bible, they wrestled with G-d and questioned His goodness and mercy. How could G-d have allowed His chosen people to be nearly annihilated from the face of the Earth, with more than six million murdered, while survivors like Ella and Jakob withstood unspeakable horrors and then lived on, suffering from survivor's guilt?

Ella eventually returned to her faith, unable to deny her cultural heritage or her G-d any longer. She and Jakob began attending synagogue once again, taking some comfort in coming back to their faith tradition. English became her seventh language; ultimately, she claimed she could spell in English better than any of her coworkers at Underwood's. She came to believe that G-d worked in her life despite the harshness she had experienced. As evidence, she pointed to their children and her part in their successes. "You wouldn't believe it, but I have two surgeon sons here in town," she exclaimed in a 1998 interview. "They've traveled the world to teach other doctors different kinds of surgery with the things that they invented. Don't you think G-d chose me for a purpose?!"

Until beset with dementia in recent years, Ella continued to fix breakfast for her three boys every morning. Ella is proud of her sons, and they have great love and respect for her. They have referred to her as a benevolent dictator, but they insist they very much appreciate their proud Jewish upbringing and the disciplined work ethic example of both parents. Their father, Jakob, passed away in 1995.

Ella's sister, Helga, died in 2010 at the age of 87, and Olga passed away in 2017 at 93. The three sisters came close to perishing on several occasions during the Holocaust, yet all three lived long lives in their adopted country of the United States, filled with the love of family and joyful successes.

Ella and Jakob rarely spoke of the world they left behind and the incredible hardships they experienced. Ella never wanted Chaim, Abe, or Sam to hate. That was all in a life past and America was their home now, a land of opportunity and hope and freedom. She called the United States a storybook and said she had enjoyed a wonderful life being married to Jakob for 47 years. "I know what hate is" and "I know what hunger is," Ella said. "And I have been very lucky to be in America."

When I knew Ella in the mid- to late 1990s, her eyes were vibrant and piercing, her smile frequent, as were her laughter and self-deprecating humor. She referred to herself as "a fat, old Jewish woman." More than once she shared that her sons bought her expensive dresses. Laughing her delightful laugh, she'd ask, "What's an old fat Jewish lady needing with such nice dresses?" She said she donated the dresses to the poor who needed them much more than she did! Perhaps this aptly captures Ella's life in a short example: She didn't take herself too seriously, enjoyed a life filled with laughter, and still set high standards for her family, pushing them to attain those goals. She has never forgotten from whence she came and constantly sought to help those less fortunate than she.

Still, Ella Rogozinski, number A-85674, never forgot. Her days in the ghettos, in Auschwitz-Birkenau and Bergen-Belsen, and on a death march remain forever etched in her mind and eternally burned into her soul, as well as on her forearm. "You don't believe what people do to people," she periodically reminded those who listened. "A lot of times, I am still very sad." If people ask how she survived, Ella responded, "There's always a better day. There's always a better day, and you eat a little piece of bread." [1]

Ella Rogozinski as a child

Ella Rogozinski and her siblings as young children in the 1930s

Ella Rogozinski wedding photo

Ella Rogizinski, 1995, Orange Park, FL.

2

CARLA NATHANS SCHIPPER
GRONINGEN, THE NETHERLANDS

Carla Schipper in the 1990s in Jacksonville, Florida.

Carla was about 80 years old when she addressed my students. She spoke softly, her voice occasionally trailing off, her eyes reflecting long-ago memories still vivid half a century later. Her gentle demeanor did not disguise her testimony's power. Nor did her mild traits dampen the fire burning in her still. She held a strong conviction that all the accounts, facts, and experiences of the Jews in Europe, including her own, should be shared with the next generation.

Born August 13, 1917, in Groningen, Netherlands, Carla was the only child of Joseph and Johanna Nathans. After graduating from high school, Carla trained to be a nurse. She married Andre Andriesse in 1938 when she was 21. The next July, their first daughter, Channa, was born. The couple settled in Enschede, a sizable Dutch city near the German border. Carla and Andre lived comfortably in a large home adjacent to the synagogue. As a young mother, she enjoyed life in the city with her husband and newborn daughter. Andre, dark and handsome, was born in Cuijk aan de Maas, a small town in the Netherlands. His devoutly religious family adhered to the beliefs and practices of Orthodox Jews. His parents, Eufemia and Joshua Andriesse, had three children – two sons and a daughter. When Andre was five years old, his father died, leaving Eufemia to raise three children alone. Emotionally distraught and struggling financially, she made the difficult decision to send a young Andre to a Jewish orphanage in Utrecht. It was heart-wrenching for her but good for Andre. He had a positive experience there and it was his home for the next 13 years. At 18, he left the orphanage and joined the military. When he had completed his obligatory stint, he returned to Cuijk aan de Maas to pursue a career as a cantor. In 1936, he was hired to be the cantor in the small village of Aalten. He frequently visited an aunt and cousins in Apeldoorn, a nearby town. It was there he met Carla Nathans.

Carla's parents didn't want her to date Andre. However, after a somewhat tumultuous courtship, they wed on August 26, 1938. Andre had a job as assistant cantor in Enschede and they settled into a new home beside the synagogue. It was the center of every aspect of their busy lives – professional, religious, and social.

The next year, on July 20, 1939, daughter Channa was born. The little family was comfortable and content. However, there was unrest brewing after a particularly horrific event, *Kristallnacht* (Night of Broken Glass), on November 9–10, 1938, in Germany. Many German Jews began immigrating to the Netherlands to escape Nazi persecution. There were rumors of war, and anxiety increased day by day, particularly for the nation's Jews. Then, on

September 1, 1939, a little more than a month after Channa came into the world, the German army invaded Poland and World War II began. The young Andriesse family's happiness was short-lived; their comfortable lives were forever changed.

Eight months later, on May 10, 1940, Germany invaded the Netherlands, its northwestern neighbor. The German Luftwaffe [Air Force] bombed the country with frequent air raids. Decades later, Carla said, "I can still see it happening," pointing up at the sky. "We could hear planes dropping bombs. It was scary." After a scant five days, the Netherlands surrendered. For the next five years, German military forces occupied the small nation as the war raged around them.

The occupation soldiers were everywhere in Enschede and throughout the Netherlands. With hostile forces controlling the economy and food supply, food soon became scarce for the Dutch, particularly the Jews. The Germans wasted no time ordering landlords and banks to evict many Jews from their homes.

On a cold winter night in February 1941, less than a year after the occupation began, German soldiers, with rifles and bayonets, banged on the Andriesses' front door. Carla was terrified and begged Andre not to answer. Andre said he had to, so he did while Carla remained upstairs with Channa. It was the Gestapo. The soldiers demanded to be taken next door to the synagogue. Carla could hear a loud commotion while Andre stalled for time, suspecting they wanted to confiscate the sacred Torah. Clad in only a nightgown, Carla grabbed baby Channa and another little girl who was living there and rushed to the cold, icy rooftop, where they hid for several hours. "We had a flat roof," Carla recalled. "It was covered with ice and snow two feet high, but I went out with the girl who was staying with us. I thought to myself, *Maybe I can jump down*. But there was no way. There were searchlights and Gestapo everywhere. ... We just stood in the cold. And stayed for several hours."

Andre was badly beaten by the Nazi soldiers but survived. After hiding most of the night on the rooftop, dodging searchlights, Carla heard her husband quietly call, "We have to get out of here." The Germans stole jewelry and more and hauled off the baby carriage before leaving, and the Andriesses feared they would return. That night, they hid in the synagogue.

"We crouched in the miserable freezing cold under the balcony [where women prayed] and sat there until the sun rose the next morning," Carla recalled. It was very cold. Before dawn, still in nightclothes, they went next door to the head cantor's house, shared with his housekeeper. They spent the night, never again to sleep in their own home.

After a fitful sleep at the head cantor's home, Carla and Andre found temporary quarters with some cousins for three days. The conditions were crowded, so they sought a less crowded option, which they found across the street with friends, the de Leeuw family. For the next seven months, they lived in an attic room in the house of the de Leeuwses, which proved a safe haven for a short while. But a little more than six months later, the Nazis returned.

On Saturday, September 13, 1941, a mass roundup of Jews was ordered for Enschede. Because Andre was in *shul* for Shabbat praying rather than at home, he wasn't captured. Early the next morning, however, Carla and Andre were sleeping in their attic room when they heard the bell ring at the house across the street. The Gestapo were calling on their neighbors! They knew they would be next. Carla warned Andre against going out or even going next door to the synagogue. She begged him: "Don't go to shul. They are coming for you."

"No, I have to go," he said. "I belong to the congregation. They count on me." As cantor, he was vital to the daily worship service. So Andre went, and the Nazis entered the service and arrested him. Carla went outside and saw the Gestapo taking Andre down the street. Their eyes failed to meet. She never saw him again.

Andre and the other men in the synagogue were marched into the street that day. Pregnant and holding their two-year-old daughter, Carla watched in agony as he was led away. Soon after his arrest, Andre was deported to Mauthausen concentration camp, outside of Linz, Austria. Life would never be the same for Carla and her soon-to-be two children – they began a perilous life on the run that would last nearly five years. The small family hid from the Nazis in myriad ways and multiple locales, defying capture and death over and over, enduring significant physical discomfort and great emotional trauma that would haunt them for decades. Despite a life ultimately well lived in the United States, 50 years later, the pain of her ordeal was still visible.

The purpose of the mass roundups was to imprison, enslave, and ultimately annihilate the Dutch Jewish population. All over Nazi-occupied Europe, Jews were systematically taken from their homes and neighborhoods and put in a system of concentration camps, mostly in Germany and Poland. In Eastern Europe, because of the millions of Jews living there – far more than in Western Europe – they were usually transported first to the ghettos, which were essentially holding centers, before eventual deportation to either a work or death camp. In the Netherlands, a smaller country with fewer Jews, they were rounded up, arrested en masse, confined in a large public area, and then deported to a transit camp instead of a ghetto, often Kamp Westerbork.

The camp was built by the Dutch government in 1939 as a refuge for Jews fleeing from the Nazis. Now, as Nazis controlled the Netherlands, they took over Kamp Westerbork and repurposed it into a holding station for Jews being shipped to Auschwitz, Bergen-Belsen, Sobibor, Theresienstadt, or Mauthausen, where they were most likely to be murdered or worked to death.

Sometime later, Carla found that Andre, after his September arrest, was killed at Mauthausen on October 17, 1941. She learned the news from Siegfried Menko, a successful local businessman and president of Enschede synagogue's congregation. The Nazis forced

Menko to serve on the local Jewish Council, the *Judenrat*. One assigned responsibility was to contact family members of those who had died. The Nazis ordered him to bring relatives of those who had been rounded up to Gestapo headquarters so the grieving kin would hear the names of the dead out loud publicly. Carla refused to go and subject herself to something so cruel and humiliating. "I'm a very religious person; G-d was with me at that moment." She recalled, adding that G-d's presence was "what I lived by, and still live by ... I would not give them the satisfaction." So Menko delivered the sad news.

Just a few weeks after learning of Andre's death, Carla found out she was pregnant with their second child. However, she could feel no happiness about it, still suffering from profound grief, living day-to-day in severe depression. "I never thought about being pregnant," she recalled. "I never thought of the child. Never. Not until I was seven months pregnant."

Carla and Channa shared two rooms in their home; she was now reluctantly allowing another family to live there. They got by on very little – Andre's meager pension. Soon she would have another mouth to feed as accommodations grew even more crowded.

In April 1942, Carla moved into her own place just outside Enschede. The arrangement did not last long. With her baby due any day, she moved back to the city to live with friends of friends, the Palache family, to be closer to the hospital. Just before giving birth, she arranged for her father and stepmother (her mother had died several years earlier) to come and care for Channa. Later that month, on April 12, a new daughter was born. Carla's father named the baby Jedidjah, meaning "beloved by G-d" in Hebrew. Very soon after Jedidjah was born, Carla's father was captured and deported to Auschwitz. She never saw him again.

At only 24 years old, Carla was already a single parent of two young children: a toddler and a newborn. Her mother was dead, her young husband had been murdered, and her father was gone. During her two-week hospital stay after the birth of Jedidjah, Carla was issued the yellow Star of David that the German government required to be worn by every Jew in the various Nazi-occupied nations. She was forbidden to leave the hospital without displaying it, so she sat up in her hospital bed and sewed it on her jacket. "I remember it was a brown jacket with wide lapels and a matching brown skirt," she said, adding, "You didn't think much about it because everyone had to do it. And no one would talk about the star."

After her release from the hospital, Carla and her two little girls returned to their small apartment. Quarters were cramped and Carla moved through each day as if in a daze. Within a couple of months, by summertime, Carla had heard from friends that the Nazis were preparing to round up the women in the city. "I didn't want to be caught," she recalled. So, Carla considered going into hiding. Her fears had been amplified as she recently learned her brother had been killed at Auschwitz. One by one, her family was losing the fight against the Nazis and she didn't want what was left of the little Andriesse family to perish. Channa, now two-and-a-half, kept asking for "Daddy," and Carla couldn't bear the thought of losing yet another family member, especially one of her children.

Carla found out that a local Lutheran pastor was organizing a rescue operation to hide Jews. She went to the minister, Leendert Overduin, at his home in August 1942. "It was kind of known in Enschede that he could be trusted," yet, she said, she was still "scared to death. After Andre was taken, I was scared all the time." The minister told her he would try to help.

He succeeded in finding a home for Channa. "I had to take my daughter to a train station and give her to someone I'd never seen in my life!" Carla exclaimed in recalling the painful memory. The stranger took Channa's tiny hand and the two of them boarded a train – destination and fate unknown to Carla. At the time, she wasn't told where Channa would be hidden. "I didn't know if I'd ever see her again," Carla said.

Two weeks later, Carla was notified that Channa had been placed with a childless couple, a kind Christian family living in Veenendaal, a small city of about 50,000 in the central Netherlands. The father was a local high school principal. Carla was told that the couple quickly fell in love with Channa, though Channa constantly asked for her mother. The couple had also asked for baby Jedidyah, but Carla refused to relinquish both of her daughters.

Several weeks passed and then, in November 1942, a couple living in a small rural village offered to take Jedidyah and, reluctantly, allowed Carla to live in their farmhouse in the village of Marle as well. Carla soon figured out the couple just wanted her baby because it was a dangerous business to hide Jews. If they were to be caught, the Jews would be immediately killed or sent to a concentration camp, and the family giving shelter to the Jews would suffer the same fate. Despite these perils, the couple, Jan and Pauline Mulder, took in both Jedidyah and Carla.

The tiny town of Marle was barely a dot on the map, with only a few farms and a small elementary school. The population 80 years later was still a meager 70 people, and there were just a few families living and working in scattered farmhouses. The Mulders owned one of the farmhouses, which was next to the elementary school where Jan was the principal and Pauline was a teacher. Although Jedidyah and Carla were in the same home, Carla lived alone in an unheated attic bedroom upstairs in the farmhouse, rarely seeing her daughter. The room had a single small window, a bed, a chair, and a small dresser. Jedidyah lived downstairs with the couple, who raised her as if she were their own child.

Carla had nothing to do day after day, sitting all by herself, living largely on rye porridge. She had virtually no contact with anyone outside the home and rarely was even able to go downstairs by herself because of the risks of being discovered. She had to wait to use the bathroom until Pauline came to get her at a safe time. This inability to use the bathroom at natural intervals ultimately led to a serious intestinal illness that plagued Carla for the rest of her life.

Carla and Jedidyah lived in the farmhouse with the elderly couple for two years. Carla said she "was going crazy." Most of her family was dead, she had no friends or social support network, and she was kept apart from her children. She was no longer motivated to live. "I wanted to go to the camps," she said softly, decades later.

On the rare occasions when Pauline felt it was safe for Carla to venture downstairs to use the bathroom, eat, or help in the kitchen, there were occasional conversations that offered a bit of respite from the gloomy, isolated environment in which she lived. Pauline, though, became increasingly more paranoid that Jedidyah, as she began to learn to talk, would tell some rare visitor to the home that Carla was hiding in the attic even though the toddler was just 18 months old. Carla became convinced Pauline was unstable. By January 1943, Carla was not allowed to see Jedidyah at all. Pauline had taken the baby as her own and pushed the young mother from the toddler's world. Carla was forced to endure the unbearable situation for two long years.

Five or six times, people from the resistance organization who had helped place Carla and Jedidyah in the Mulder home came to visit and check up on Carla and the living situation. On these occasional visits, the organization would bring food ration stamps for butter, sugar, and flour. However, Carla was allowed to see the visitors only once or twice because Pauline considered it unnecessary. Carla was deeply hurt by these missed opportunities for human interaction and to connect with the Underground. She was miserably lonely, deeply despondent, and living in fear every single day. The inability to meet with members of the Resistance only deepened her despondency. Decades later, she took a more charitable view of the Mulders. She understood the fear that the Mulders must have felt and appreciated the risks they took. Despite the Mulders' failure to emotionally relate to or sympathize with Carla or to forge a real relationship with her, they did have the courage to hide her in their home, knowing the grave consequences. By carrying out that brave deed, their own lives were at stake.

Historically, although many of the Dutch did little to help the Jews of their nation, it has been estimated that perhaps as many as 25,000 non-Jewish Dutch families opened their homes to hide Jews. There is also the well-known story of Miep Gies who, along with husband Jan, helped hide the family of Anne Frank along with four others in an annex above her father, Otto Frank's, company. By a miraculous turn of events, Miep was not sent to a concentration camp when the Franks were caught, but that was unusual. Such Righteous Gentiles, as the State of Israel has pronounced these non-Jews who risked their lives to hide or rescue Europe's Jews and had no desire for financial gain or harbored ulterior motives, were relatively few in Europe. Nonetheless, those who did such noble things were indeed righteous. Perhaps the Mulders hid Carla and Jedidyah because they wanted a child, but, regardless, they risked their lives to hide them. The Mulders were not recognized by Israel as Righteous Gentiles, but they certainly deserve a debt of gratitude.

Pauline Mulder's family members were Christian Scientists. Carla recalls that most of them were lovely people. Various relatives would, on occasion, come by the home; they knew Carla was hiding there. They even went to talk with Carla a couple of times. She described them as intelligent and respectful despite their religious differences. "They did a lot of good for me," Carla said.

However, one Mulder family member wasn't so lovely – Pauline's mother. She visited for several weeks in the spring of 1943. Pauline told Carla her mother was a Nazi and unsympathetic to the Jewish plight. So Carla was sequestered in her attic room during the entire visit. Once, during Pauline's mother's visit, in the middle of the night when everyone was sleeping, Carla had to sneak downstairs to use the bathroom. Pauline's mother got out of bed to go to the bathroom, too. After praying about how she should respond with Pauline's mother at the door, Carla decided to pretend she was Pauline, disguising her voice. She said she was in the bathroom and the older woman could go to her room and return in a short while. The mother was in her eighties, and it was a dark night, so she did as she was told. It was a close call that truly frightened Carla, but she had faith in G-d's plan.

With both Carla and the Mulders fearing discovery, Jan built a tiny hiding space within the attic room where Carla would sometimes hide for hours at a time, alone in a small, dark space, when the Gestapo were in the area.

In early 1943, Carla was visited by a woman from the Underground. Carla confessed to her that she was at her wit's end and that she "didn't care anymore. I would go to the camps. I could be killed. I couldn't take it anymore." The resistance worker suggested another Jewish woman might be brought to live in the attic room with Carla to help alleviate her exasperation and provide some human interaction. The Mulders agreed to accept another Jew, which, of course, increased their own risk substantially. That spring, a 54-year-old woman came to live with the Mulders, sharing the small attic hideaway with Carla. The new roommate, Mrs. Wijnberg, was rather provincial. She and Carla had little in common yet had to share cramped quarters and a small single bed. Unfortunately, the woman did little to alleviate Carla's dire situation.

The eventual kindness of others, however, ultimately gave Carla the will to survive. At one point in June 1943, shortly after Mrs. Wijnberg's arrival, the Mulders went out of town to attend a wedding. They sent Carla and Mrs. Wijnberg to stay with nearby neighbors – a sheriff and his wife. They took Jedidyah along with them to the wedding. The forlorn and lonely Carla, perhaps at the point she most needed it, was received warmly, treated kindly, and fed well. The couple told her they were always available to help if she ever needed anything. "When we left, the lady of the house said to me that anytime I would get into trouble, I could come back to them," Carla recalled." The Mulders returned home in less than a week, so Carla and Mrs. Wijnberg came back "home," but the words from the sheriff's wife "sustained me to the end of the war," Carla said.

While sustaining her will to live, the words could not sustain Carla's patience with her living situation. Finally, in early 1944, Carla had reached her breaking point and decided she could no longer continue hiding in the Mulders' attic. She learned through a contact with the Underground that close friends, who had also been kept out of sight, had come out of hiding, received false identification papers, and were posing as a minister and his wife. The dark-haired woman had dyed her hair blonde. Carla was so fed up hiding that she decided to do the same – change her appearance and leave her hiding place.

At first, the Mulders were not supportive of Carla's decision because a drastic change in appearance increased the risk of discovery. Carla had made up her mind, though, despite the risks. "I didn't care. I wanted out," she said. "There comes a time that you don't care anymore and that is a dangerous time. Your judgment is not clear. You see no future. You become depressed and distressed that nothing matters anymore. But that's how I was. I didn't care."

Jan agreed to buy some peroxide for Carla to gradually begin dying her hair so she might appear less Jewish. It took several months of daily use, but slowly her hair turned much lighter. Someone from the Resistance was able to get her a false identification card, though she would need to be photographed so that a picture could be used for the card. The organization arranged for Carla to go to a beauty salon to get a perm, but because of her poor health and nutrition, her hair was brittle and unhealthy and came out in large clumps during the process. So instead of a perm, she had a new style of closely shorn hair. Despite the hiccup with her hair, she was photographed and, after waiting a few more months, her new identification paperwork was complete. She was ready for the next chapter in her harrowing, life-and-death escape from the Nazis.

The Mulders told Carla she'd have to leave young Jedidyah with them. The decision was not easy for Carla, but she felt she had no choice. In two years with the Mulders, from the fall of 1942 until October 1944, she had seen very little of her child. She had already been deprived of being a mother. In addition, with the loss of her family, her home, and the privilege to raise Channa, she now faced the prospect of assuming a new identity and losing Jedidyah, too. Living with the Mulders had quite likely kept the two of them alive, but the physical and emotional price was more than Carla could pay. She was physically ill, weak, distraught, and depressed. She had to leave even if it meant going solo, without her precious child. Grief-stricken, she would leave Channa in the Mulders' arms.

Carla recalled her last meal with the Mulders before leaving. Jan read aloud from Psalm 121 in the Bible: "I raise my eyes upon the mountains; whence will come my help? My help comes from the Lord, Maker of Heaven and Earth. He will not allow your foot to falter; your Guardian will not slumber. Behold, He neither slumbers nor sleeps, the Guardian of Israel. The Lord is your Guardian; the Lord is your shade at your right hand. By day, the sun will not harm you, nor the moon by night. The Lord will protect you from every evil; He will guard your soul. The Lord will guard your departure and your arrival, from this time and forever."

Carla greatly appreciated Jan and what she felt was a most appropriate reading and sendoff. The reading from the Ketuvim, one of the books of the Bible, galvanized her faith and gave her hope and courage. She went off into the great unknown.

In mid-October 1944, Carla left Marle and the Mulders, bound for Utrecht. She arrived quite alone, with no children and a new name, Henriette Andriesen, the name on her forged identity document. She had been given the address of a woman who lived in a large, three-story boardinghouse, where she was to work as a maid. Carla, though, was not destined to work there for long because she was too weak and sick to do what was required. She had been hiding for close to two-and-a-half years, malnourished, with serious digestive problems and other illnesses. "I looked as though I came out of a concentration camp," she said years later. "I couldn't function properly, attending to three floors with three flights of stairs. After a week or ten days, I got very sick, but I never went to a doctor, of course."

A fellow boarder in the room beside hers recommended that Carla leave work as a boardinghouse maid; the friend found her a place to live and work in Maarssen, close to Utrecht. Her new job was with a doctor and his wife; she was their maid. The home was smaller, which was less physically demanding, and there weren't boarders around who might pose risks to Carla. At first, the doctor and his wife provided food for Carla, but after a couple of weeks, their rationed food was not sufficient to feed her; she ate at a nearby soup kitchen. There, sugar beets were the only sustenance available, so Carla didn't get enough calories or nutrients to properly sustain her. Her stomach problems grew worse. Still living in fear, with significant depression, a weakened state, and separated from Channa and Jedidyah, Carla realized her living situation had to change.

She remembered what the sheriff and his wife had told her before she left their home. She decided to take them up on their offer of help. Carla wanted so badly to be near Jedidyah that she made the difficult decision to return to Marle. She told the doctor and his wife she must leave and was able to catch a truck ride back east in the direction of Marle. On the night of February 1, 1945, riding in the back of the truck with 14 or 15 others, she made the dangerous journey. At one point, the truck was halted by the Gestapo at the entrance to a bridge. When they asked for her identification papers, Carla spoke to them in German and told them that they were going to find food. Miraculously, they were allowed to continue on the drive. In addition to her native Dutch, Carla spoke fluent German, as well as French, Greek, and Latin. Her education and proficiency in languages saved her life that night.

The truck dropped her off in the village of Zwolle, nearly 65 kilometers from Marle. She walked all day, covering part of the journey – about 30 to 50 kilometers – to Nijverdal. She hoped to stay with the minister who had helped her get her identity papers and her new hairstyle. Unfortunately, when she knocked at his door, tired and weak and in desperate need of a place to rest for the night, he refused to let her in. Her pleas fell on deaf ears and she had to walk the remaining miles to Marle. Carla arrived that night, February 2, 1945. Altogether, she had walked nearly 70 kilometers in a single day, through snow and ice and brutal subfreezing temperatures, with only a light jacket over her emaciated frame, and no food or water. Her body had been fragile before her long, cold trek and it truly was a miracle that she was able to survive. Carla, however, persevered with the hope that the generous offer extended months earlier by the sheriff and his wife would still be available. It was a dangerous risk, but she felt she had no other choice.

Finally, after she passed the Mulders' house, she arrived at the sheriff's home in Marle. With barely enough strength to even knock on the door, she tapped feebly. The door was opened by an unfamiliar woman, closely followed by the highly pregnant sheriff's wife. "Oh, you were sent by God," the sheriff's wife exclaimed on seeing Carla. She knew that Carla had trained as a nurse, and since she was due to deliver any day, it was an answer to a prayer that Carla just showed up. She was immediately invited inside and given a beautiful and clean room where she could stay. Exhausted and weak, Carla prayed that the baby would not come during the night so that she could get some sleep. She quickly fell fast asleep and did get a day's respite. The baby arrived early on the morning of February 4. Fortunately, a physician was there for the delivery, so Carla assisted rather than take charge.

Following the delivery, Carla returned to her room, exhausted. The doctor accompanied her and diagnosed a painful disease, erythema nodosum, a blood infection. He ordered her to rest and said it would take six weeks for her to recover. She endured a high fever and painful aches in her legs, which were covered with red blotches and sensitive to the touch. Carla offered to leave to try to find a bed at the local hospital since she did not want to infect the newborn baby in the house. The family refused, letting her stay while they nursed her to health, simultaneously caring for their newborn child. The sheriff's wife told her not to worry, and that they would take care of her.

Carla stayed with the generous couple, resting and recuperating. As a precautionary measure to protect the sheriff and his family, she never knew their names. She did know that they showered her with love and kindness and gave her nourishing food and a warm, safe bed. They had saved her life.

After six weeks, she had regained some strength and her health had improved markedly. The sheriff told her it was time to leave because it was too dangerous for them to let her continue to stay. The sheriff found a young couple who lived on a nearby farm and agreed to take Carla in. They had a radio and, because of that, Carla soon learned that the Germans were close to defeat. Three weeks later, on May 7, 1945, Carla listened to the radio broadcast. The words she heard she would never forget – the Germans had surrendered!

The war was finally over. Two-and-a-half years after she had left Enschede, Carla no longer had to hide. She was 28 years old, her mother was dead, and presumably her father, too, and her husband and brother had met the same fate. She was now a young widow with no home, no money, and without her two children beside her. She desperately wanted them back in her arms.

As soon as she was free, she walked straight to the Mulders to retrieve Jedidyah. However, instead of returning Jedidyah to Carla, the Mulders began questioning Carla's plans for the future. They didn't want to give up the child. Instead, they offered the young mother a place to stay in exchange for letting her be with her daughter. Regardless of her pleas, the Mulders still adamantly refused to return Jedidyah to her. Overcome with emotion, Carla borrowed a bicycle with wooden wheels – the Germans had stolen every bit of rubber they could find – and quickly pedaled from Marle to her hometown of Enschede. Once there, she went to plead her case with Pastor Overduin, the Lutheran minister who headed the resistance organization that had found the hiding place for Carla and Jedidyah. He agreed to intervene, but when he did, the Mulders made excuses as to why the child could not be returned to her mother. The Mulders first said the child was sick and couldn't leave, and then they contended that Carla was not really the mother. Finally, after about a month of exasperating arguments, the Mulders capitulated and agreed to return little Jedidyah to her mother. With her baby back in her arms at long last, Carla again pedaled from Marle to Enschede – this time with her child riding on the back.

Yet when she returned to her Enschede, Carla had no place to live. She went to her former apartment beside the synagogue, but it was already occupied by friends, the de Vries family. They invited Carla and Jedidyah to stay with them until the mother and daughter could find permanent housing. Now that she had at least temporary quarters, Carla began her quest to get Channa back. She learned that Channa was at the home of Jan and Ellie Thoomes in Veenendaal. At the end of May, she made her way there. Upon arriving at the Thoomes family's home, Channa, now six years old, came running to greet the mother she barely remembered. Channa was terribly thin, "almost a skeleton ... it was terrible," Carla said. "Oh, she looked so bad."

The couple explained to Carla that food was hard to come by during the war. Because of the food shortage, they had to send Channa to live with various families who were unable to feed her well. Channa was malnourished and suffering from dysentery and poor vision. The Holocaust and the war had taken a detrimental toll on the girl and physically and emotionally impacted her for the rest of her life. But on her first night reunited with her mother, she and Carla slept together in a single bed holding one another tightly the whole night long. At long last, after what had seemed like an eternity, Channa and her mother were finally together again.

The long nightmares called World War II and the Holocaust were over. Although Carla had lost so much at the hands of the Nazis, she was alive and free and reunited with her two precious little girls. She learned many years after the war that her father was killed at Auschwitz on July 7, 1942, and she already knew of her husband's murder. Carla's emotional state was fragile, and her physical health still hung in the balance, but with her daughters, she was ready to live and look to the future.

After her liberation, Carla had no immediate contact with the various people besides the Mulders who had been involved in hiding her. She was unable to thank them for their courageous efforts.

At the war's end, the community in Enschede had lost relatively fewer of their members than the death toll in the general Jewish population of the Netherlands: 500 Jews out of Enschede's population of 1,300 were saved (38.5 percent); the survival rate in the Netherlands overall was less than 20 percent. (However, the survival rate of Jews in most of the other Nazi-occupied nations was far less than in the Netherlands.) Three leaders of the Jewish Council in Enschede deserve much of the credit, along with the prominent minister Overduin. The Jewish leaders had taken the initiative, against the advice of the Jewish Council of Amsterdam, and urged their community to go into hiding and not to answer the call-up of the Germans for "labor in the East." They were in a position to issue these directions to their flock since they had access to funds, leaders in the community, and a well-developed underground movement headed by Overduin.

Overduin helped to save more than 1,000 Jews between the fall of 1941 and the spring of 1945. In addition to keeping so many alive and on the road to recovery, he also found homes for orphaned children after the war. He survived the war, living until 1976. His heroic rescue efforts eventually led to his arrest late in the war, and he was imprisoned until the war's end. He refused to accept any honors or commendations for his wartime activities, but the hundreds of Dutch Jews who survived because of him, including Carla, Channa, and Jedidyah, are proof of his courage and compassion.

Carla never knew the names of the helpful sheriff and his wife. There was a documented "heroic police officer" named Dick Mos in Enschede who, along with his wife, Rie, although officially serving the Nazis covertly cooperated with Overduin to find homes for Jews in which to hide. They were recognized by Yad Vashem in Jerusalem in 1977 as Righteous Gentiles. This may have been the same "sheriff" and his wife who had helped Carla, or even a different courageous policeman; it may never be determined. Still, Carla was grateful for the rest of her life to the couple.

After the war, Carla began to try to pick up the pieces of her life. She, with her two little girls, lived in Enschede with the de Vries family until she was able to secure accommodations in a large villa owned by the Serphos family, a mother and her two daughters who had allowed several families to live in the villa. Carla's quarters included two bedrooms and a small kitchen. She and Jedidyah shared one bedroom and Channa slept in the other. The large villa was full of survivors in communal living, with barely any furniture, linens, or towels, and few clothes. Food was scarce. Survivors, in the villa and in town, scrounged for furniture and food the best as they could.

Among other guests in the villa were two brothers, Bernard and Henry Schipper, who shared a third-floor room. The brothers helped some people find furniture; Carla was impressed by their magnanimity. Communal dinners were held in the kitchen in shifts – it just so happened that Carla and her girls were assigned to a shift with Bernard Schipper. Carla and Bernard quickly became friends; it was a mutual attraction.

Bernard ("Bernie" to friends) Schipper was a German Jew, born in 1919 in Braunschweig, Germany, to a middle-class family that had emigrated to Germany from Poland just before World War I. In the spring of 1939, at age 19, Bernie and his 18-year-old brother, Henry, fled Germany for the Netherlands. Bernie found a job in Enschede in a textile factory, where he worked until early 1942. The persecution of the Jews in the Netherlands had markedly increased by that time, so he and Henry left Enschede and found work on a farm, which was a bit more isolated and protected from the Nazi roundups. By the fall of 1942, however, they were notified about an upcoming roundup and hid themselves in a burned-out barn. The brothers stayed hidden there for three years under the care of a kind farmer and his family.

Carla liked Bernard almost from the start. Their courtship moved quickly. Within several months, Carla, her girls, and the Schipper brothers were able to obtain a small house that they shared. In 1946, Henry found work in Amsterdam, and soon thereafter, Bernard and Carla decided to get married.

The Schippers stayed in Enschede, trying their best to form the bonds of a blended family in every sense. Channa and Jedidyah suffered from the trauma of their early lives. They barely knew their mother and kept their emotional distance from her, while Carla remained very ill. Now they suddenly had a new father; Channa barely remembered Andre. Jedidyah had never known him and had been raised mostly by the Mulders as their own daughter. After the war, the Mulders visited Jedidyah often, which was confusing and difficult for her and Carla. Though the fighting was over, their lives were full of transitions and continued hardships.

In 1947, Carla found out she was pregnant, and in August that year, Ruthie was born. Three years later, in 1950, the Schippers moved to Amsterdam to be closer to Bernie's work. While in Amsterdam, Carla worked as a seamstress. Life was full in Amsterdam, with work and active social lives filled with many friends. The girls were active with school, piano lessons, private Hebrew lessons, and their friends. Despite their busy lives in Amsterdam, by 1951 they began thinking of moving to the United States. With the Cold War heating up, the thought of remaining in Europe frightened them. They knew little about life in America, but they did speak a bit of English, and Bernie's brother and his uncle were already in the States. So the Schipper family decided to make the big move across the Atlantic.

On November 11, 1953, the Schippers arrived in the United States. Channa was now 13, Jedidyah was 11, and Ruthie was six when the family sailed into New York harbor. They moved into the home of Henry and his wife Rose temporarily until they could get settled and find a place of their own. Henry and Rose had one child, with another on the way, in their tiny New York apartment. The Schipper family of five being added to the mix made for extremely cramped quarters. Bernie got a job as a mechanic in Manhattan at American Business Machines. After just a week of living with Henry and Rose, the Schippers were able to move to a place of their own. Bernie earned $60 a month; Carla supplemented their income doing freelance sewing. Their monthly rent for the apartment was $90, so even with the two incomes, they could barely make ends meet. The following year, the family moved to a less expensive apartment.

In early 1957, the family welcomed Carla's fourth child and Bernie's second, a son they named Jonathan. The entire family was thrilled to have a little boy added to the clan, though Jonathan was born with Down syndrome. The challenge added to the family dynamics, and Carla needed to devote considerable time to him. Physicians advised Carla and Bernie to place Jonathan in an institution, but they refused. After having to give up her first two girls for so long during the war, she could not bear to relinquish her baby boy and was determined to keep him at home as long as she could.

Life in the United States was generally good. Like all families, the Schippers had a fair share of ups and downs, especially as immigrants, but Carla and Bernie found peace in America. They tried to put the pain of their past behind them, and no mention was made in the home about the Holocaust. "The minute we moved to the United States," Jedidyah said, "our past was basically erased. It was as if it didn't exist. It was always lurking but never confronted."

Carla said it was unintentional not to talk about the Holocaust. "We went through so much, but we never talked about it with the children," Carla said. She and Bernie were happy. "We were living a normal life. We are not the type of people to talk about it. We didn't see it as a necessity."

This reluctance to speak of the events of the awful past for so many years was common among survivors, particularly the ones I have known. The burden of upheaval, pain, and trauma beyond most humans' endurance was heavy – many survivors did not want it to define their lives or those of their children. They chose to suppress the past as well as they could and look to the future rather than reflect on or speak of their painful lives in the Holocaust. Carla's religious faith sustained her throughout her life despite the trauma.

The Schippers stayed and thrived in New York for several decades. They were leaders in the area in creating programs for young Jewish people with special needs, especially those with Down syndrome. They were proactive to ensure Jonathan flourished and lived a normal life. In 1993, when Jonathan was 36, he began living in Bais Ezra, a Jewish home for special needs people in New Rochelle, New York. He's lived there many years, developing a degree of independence. "He is very satisfied," said Carla.

Channa married and settled in Upstate New York. In 1984, she returned to the Netherlands for a ceremony honoring the Thoomeses, who had hidden her during the war. They were recognized by the Israeli government's Yad Vashem as Righteous Gentiles. Channa and her husband, Leon, now deceased, had two sons. Jedidyah became an Orthodox Jew and moved to Israel. She and her husband, Micah, have five children and 13 grandchildren. She remembers little of being hidden as an infant and toddler during the Holocaust, but she did return to the Netherlands in 1970 to visit the elderly Mulder couple. Ruthie, the first child of Carla and Bernie, is also an Orthodox Jew. She is strong and vibrant, a woman of great faith, and has remained in New York. She is a nurse, married to a man called "Yankee," and they have a son and two daughters.

With their children grown and scattered and Jonathan happily quite independent, Carla and Bernie decided to escape the cold weather of New York. In January 1995, they moved to Jacksonville, Florida. Soon after their southward trek, I met Carla and Bernie through other survivor friends they had quickly developed and invited them to speak to my Holocaust class. They readily accepted and spoke on several occasions during the next few years. They began to speak with other school groups around Jacksonville as well. Carla talked several times to my classes and exhibited both strength of character and warmth of personality. She carried with her the scars of a difficult life but enjoyed an engaging energy even in old age. I moved out of state in the summer of 1999 and lost contact with the Schippers. Bernie died in 2008 at 88. Carla lived several more years, and died October 3, 2013, at 96, a remarkably long life given the physical and emotional challenges she faced. Her life was not merely chronologically long but also one filled with much joy and hope.

Carla suffered horrendously during the years of the Nazi aggression, but she was able to rise above the horrors of hate that they spread. Her children, grandchildren, and great-grandchildren enjoyed the fruits of Carla's deep and abiding faith, courage, strength, and perseverance. Carla taught new generations of young people by sharing her story. Her story inspires all who know it, giving us encouragement that, despite the challenges of our own lives, we, too, can overcome. "Her survival [was] miraculous. ... She's a very positive person," her friend Rosalina Platzer said. "She's an affirmation of life."[1]

Juut and Philip de Groot (From: Stacey Goldring, On Wooden Wheels, *Xlibris Corporation)*

Carla Schipper, speaking publicly in April 2010, near the end of her long life. "Mandarin Holocaust survivor shares her story with high school students," Florida Times- Union, *April 29, 2010.*

3

RENE GOLDSTEIN JAKOB AND LESLIE JAKOB

KLUGE, ROMANIA

Rene and Leslie Jakob

Rene and Leslie Jakob were a passionate and animated couple in their seventies, committed to sharing their life stories of triumph over tragedy, when I met them in the fall of 1994. As I began to get to know them more deeply over the next several years through their testimonies to my classes as well as my personal conversations with them, I recognized in each of them a zest for life, a deep and abiding love for their family, a devoted loyalty to the nation that had adopted them, and an unwavering determination to share with ensuing generations their past – not as a sad commentary of pain but rather as testament to resiliency and hope. Leslie was more reserved, a man of relatively few words, sometimes reticent to share specific details of his past, possessing a rather tough façade seared with the pain of his past. His wife, Rene (pronounced REN-y), on the other hand, shared her story more openly and poignantly. Leslie was more matter of fact with his testimony, while Rene shared with quiet tenderness the pain of the Holocaust that would mark both of them for the rest of their lives.

The rather idyllic youth they shared in Eastern Europe turned into horrific tribulation during the Holocaust when Nazi Germany took over their nation at a time when the adolescent Rene and Leslie transitioned from teenagers to young adults. Their past marked them but didn't define them because they were living witnesses to the possibilities of overcoming incredible adversity. Through fortitude, along with a bit of keen ingenuity and an ample dose of courage, they not only survived unimaginable horrors but prevailed. They subsequently rebuilt their lives in the United States with the blessings of a large, loving family living in what they described as the American dream. Their history is a difficult one, like that of so many survivors of the Holocaust, filled with pain and grief, yet it is a testament to the human spirit. The words on these pages reveal their story.

Rene Goldstein Jakob was born on May 16, 1928, in Cluj, Transylvania (the Hungarian form was Kolozsvár; it is also sometimes spelled Kluj), in what was then Romania, to Stephanie and Elias (Ernest) Goldstein, who were Orthodox Jews. Rene had an older brother, Jonas, born in 1920, and a sister, Violet, born in 1924. Rene's Yiddish name was Refca, which is what her parents called her as she was growing up. She had two living grandparents, who had moved from Poland to Russia before settling in Romania. She was a member of a middle-class family; her father was a candle salesman and a veteran of the World War I. He had been wounded in the war and was in poor health for the rest of his life. He had survived two operations, but his poor health did not facilitate an active lifestyle and he became obese. Ultimately, he died at a relatively young age in 1940. Rene described her mother as a very beautiful, wonderful mother and housewife. Rene remembers her hometown of Cluj as a beautiful town with the Someş River running through it and the nearby rugged beauty of the Carpathian Mountains. In her childhood, she had both Jewish and Christian friends but never remembered a time when the Jews were not persecuted. In the 1930s, there were already Romanian fascists who authored pogroms that she said were to "pick on Jews." Rene recalled: "We couldn't put a candle by the window on the holiday of light because the fascists would break the windows." When they prepared a traditional meal of borscht, made from beets, "the fascists would say the Jews were killing Christian babies to drink the blood." Yet the already existent antisemitism dramatically increased in 1940 when Cluj was taken over by Hungary and escalated even more when the Germans came to town soon afterward.

The city of Cluj maintained a rather large Jewish population. Rene recalled decades later that Jews and non-Jews generally got along despite the antisemitism during her childhood. She enjoyed a happy life with family, friends, and school until the Nazi occupation began in the summer of 1940. She attended a Jewish school up until 1943, at which point it was shut down by Nazi decree; Jews were no longer able to attend school at all thereafter.

Jonas was drafted into the Hungarian Army later that same year. After a year or so, the Hungarian military "took away the Jews' guns, then took away their uniforms," she said. When Rene's father died near the end of 1940, the Hungarian military would not release Jonas until after his father's funeral in January 1941. He was able to come home briefly at that point but then had to return quickly to his unit in Ukraine. Shortly afterward, the family received a postcard from Jonas letting them know that his unit was being shipped out. Rene said it was the last time they heard from him. She later learned that he had joined the underground resistance, was caught, and was soon executed by the Nazis.

In 1943, after the Nazis invaded and took control of the area, they began instituting antisemitic programs. The Gestapo in Cluj began to clamp down and instituted various laws and policies of the Third Reich. One decree stated that the Jews would immediately be forced to wear armbands with the yellow Star of David.

The supply of food began to be severely rationed. Some Christian friends left milk and eggs on their doorsteps to help supplement the limited food rations. Soon, matters turned even worse, however, as the Nazis began deporting the Jews to newly formed ghettos. Rene's life would soon change dramatically. She was 15 years old and had been forced to grow up far too soon. Her idyllic childhood had come to an unfathomably horrific end.

On one particular Shabbat in the spring of 1944, what was left of the Goldstein family was sent to the ghetto. Rene's mother had just prepared a Shabbat meal when, suddenly, Hungarian Nazi soldiers came to the house, barged in, and rounded up the family along with the other Jews who lived in the apartment building. They lined up all the Jews and marched them to the other side of town to a newly formed ghetto, an area of Cluj that had formerly been a brick factory. The building where they were forced to gather was old and in disrepair, no longer in use, and had a leaky roof. The Goldsteins carried what they could – blankets and a small backpack with a few personal items – but almost everything of value was seized. The Hungarian military told them that all the Jews must pack whatever they could carry in a single suitcase and that "you will go to the ghetto, then from the ghetto, you gonna go to a work camp." The Goldsteins were able to smuggle a few of their personal items of value that they had been unable to carry – mainly their jewelry and money – to Christian friends with the hope they might one day return to retrieve them. Jews were told they would ultimately go to a labor camp to help with the war effort, and that after the war, they would be able to come back home. "They lied to us!" Rene exclaimed. Though it was "just a temporary way station," the Cluj Ghetto was home for several weeks, from early May until June 1944. Their next destination – this one far more sinister than even the cramped, filthy, inhumane ghetto – was already scheduled.

In June, Rene and her family were suddenly taken from the ghetto, with only a one-hour warning to pack a bag. They were then put in cattle cars at the train station – a hundred in a car –and taken to the notorious Auschwitz-Birkenau death camp. She was with her mother, her cousin, and her cousin's two children. Rene didn't know at the time what had happened to her brother, but she thought he was in forced labor somewhere. Her sister, who was blond and blue-eyed, had been given forged papers earlier by a kindly church official and fled to Budapest, where she posed as a Christian and worked as a maid. However, someone turned her in and she ultimately was murdered.

The journey to Auschwitz took two or three days, and the tightly crammed group was given a pail to relieve themselves. Rene sat on the hard floor of the railcar, with the sweaty bodies of dozens of others all around her, fighting for both air and rest as they slowly moved toward an unknown destination. Outside, it was warm and humid, the sultry air hanging densely in the countryside. Inside the tightly packed cattle cars, temperatures were even hotter. The nearly airless car was suffocating. They had no food or water and were too cramped to even move. Rene heard the constant cries of the very young and the old, wailing sobs that she would never forget. As the train pulled into Auschwitz, she saw the camp entrance's iron sign with the large, now infamous words overhead, *"Arbeit Macht Frei"* [Work Will Set You Free].

The train slowed to an eerie stop. It was nighttime and the weak and exhausted occupants were hurriedly forced from the train. The cool, damp air at first was a welcome relief, but the fresh air was quickly forgotten. As they exited the train, jumping from the opened doors to the hard ground several feet below, they were surrounded by Nazi guards and Jewish *kapos*, prisoners pressed into service as guards. Some Jewish prisoners had been given these jobs to support the German SS guards. The *kapos* had no choice but to do the work required. Rene said that the *kapos* "did the dirty work." Often, the *kapos*, fearing for their own lives, were crueler than the SS guards.

There were German Shepherd dogs all around, constantly barking and nipping at the heels of the scurrying prisoners, and guards shouting *"Macht schnell! Macht schnell* [Hurry! Fast! Hurry! Fast]!" in the cover of darkness, with bright lights blinding the prisoners. Confusion reigned. Rene remembered: "The Nazis started to pull us off the train and they were beating us with rubber hoses. They were dragging the old people and taking the babies from the mothers." The Jews were forced into lines for the selection process; the old, the very young, and the weak were quickly sent to the left, selected for immediate death in the gas chambers, while the healthy were selected for slave labor and sent to the right. If the mothers cried for the guards not to take their babies, the Germans would "push and shove and kick," Rene said. "Sometimes, they would jerk the babies from the mothers and throw them up in the air, and they would fall" to the ground and their deaths.

There, in the selection line, Rene made eye contact with Mengele himself, the "Angel of Death." Rene's mother was sent to the left, along with her cousin and her cousin's two young children. "This night was the last night that I saw my mother," she said mournfully five decades later.

Led single file into a building, 15-year-old Rene was forced to strip and told that she and the others in her group were going to take showers. "We were mostly young girls, and we were very embarrassed," she recounted. The Nazi guards "were walking around us, hitting us." All the hair on their heads and bodies was cut. They were given clothes – the striped camp uniforms prolific among concentration camp prisoners. Their bodies were then searched for valuables they may be hiding, in front of the male guards, which for a 15-year-old girl was traumatic. They were called "dirty Jews" and told they all needed baths. Rene said, with a reticent, sarcastic laugh – more of a lament than a snicker – "Well, we *were* dirty, since we were three days on the cattle wagon without food or water. We had to go to the bathroom in a bucket!"

When they went into the showers, they didn't know whether there would be water or gas coming out of the spigots; they had heard rumors of gas chambers. "We got water because we were the younger ones," she recalled. Upon exiting the showers, they were thrown clothes. "Whatever they threw [at] us we had to wear. To this day," she exclaimed, as if she could not believe she was unable to recall. "I don't remember if they gave us underwear. I truly don't remember!" When someone asked about other family members, they were told by the *kapos* that their loved ones "were the smoke [coming] from the chimneys."

The tiring and humiliating process of showers, shaving, issuance of clothes, and registering the prisoners took most of the night. Around sunrise, the prisoners were pushed out of the building and marched to their assigned barracks. Rene recalled that it felt funny losing my hair. She slowly ran her hand over her now-bare scalp, feeling the new sensation of baldness, when suddenly a female German guard forcefully and repeatedly hit her in the eye as punishment for feeling her own head. Many years later, living in the United States, her physician asked if she had ever been hit in the eye because of what she called "terrible headaches." The headaches would prove long-term consequences of the savage beating.

As quickly as the punching had begun, it stopped, and they continued their march to the barracks. Hers was a large barracks, but the rooms were small, perhaps nine feet by nine feet, Rene recollected. The beds were triple bunk beds, with no mattresses, only wood and chicken wire, with just a bit of filthy, lice-infested straw left by the now-dead previous occupant. There were 14 beds in the small room. There wasn't enough room for each one to get a bunk; Rene slept on the floor. That first day, prisoners were given a single small piece of hard, stale bread – to be shared among five people – as their only meal. Rene never forgot that meal.

"It was like a piece of sawdust; it was black," Rene said. "It was so bad. I didn't eat it. I laid it beside me; I was lying on the concrete floor. When I woke, my bread was gone. I had to learn it was dog eat dog; you couldn't lay anything down. It was like [we were] animals."

The next day, guards put two more triple bunks inside; now there were 16 triple-bunk beds for 48 women in a tiny room. "We couldn't even move," Rene recalled. "We had no blankets or anything. We just lay there all day, hungry, cold. There was [sic] no windows."

For some reason, Rene and the young women in her barracks weren't assigned official jobs. Sometimes, they were given random, menial, meaningless work such as moving rock piles from one end of an area to the other, then back to the first site, but "mostly we just lay on our beds." Often, one guard would blow a whistle, which was a signal to line up outside for *Appell*, or, roll call. When the prisoners heard the *Appell* whistle, they quickly jumped off the bunks and assembled outside in front of the barracks, lining up on gravel, with infinite small, hard pebbles. If one didn't move fast enough, or if the guards didn't like how they were lined up or were in a particularly hateful mood, they made the offending prisoner kneel on the pebbles for hours. "If they didn't like the way you kneeled, they would walk by and hit you," Rene recalled. "Our knees used to be full of blood." Once the women were in the *Appell* formation, German guards walked along, inspecting each one. "If they didn't like the way we looked or anything about us, they would say, 'Go to the side,' and they would take them to be gassed. We found out quickly what they were doing." A fellow prisoner later wrote of the Auschwitz *Appell*: "At almost each block, beside [those] standing in line, bodies of persons are lying. These are the victims of the night who have not lived to see the day. Even yesterday, they were standing numbers at the roll call and today they lie, lifeless and motionless. Life is not important at the roll call. Numbers are important. Numbers tally. How horribly they are looking, as if returned from the war. These are the marks of yesterday's work."

Only the strongest could survive – only those who continued to be useful to the Nazis. With Auschwitz's electrified barbed-wired fences, if a person touched them, the result was electrocution. It was a common event that prisoners, including young women in Rose's and Rene's building, ran to the fence – a suicide "because they couldn't take it [any]more." She saw this happen daily, often multiple times a day. "They would just be burned black," she said. Despite the horrors others saw in the suicides, many prisoners still did it – they felt hopeless amid the evils of hell they called Auschwitz-Birkenau.

The smell of burning human flesh constantly permeated Auschwitz. Rene recalled that "there seemed to be millions of people in the camp." In fact, in four-and-a-half years of operation, from 1940 until early 1945, approximately 1.3 million people were sent to Auschwitz-Birkenau. Of those, it is known that about 1.1 million were murdered – more than 960,000 of those killed were Jews. The gas chambers were in near-constant use for well more than two years of that period, with sometimes as many as 5,000 bodies daily removed from the gas chambers and immediately burned in the crematoria ovens. The stench was endlessly pungent, the smell of death always in the air. It accompanied the laborers at Auschwitz throughout their days. For the rest of her life, Rene said she was unable to eat steaks cooked on a grill because the smell made her sick. Disturbingly, this was a sentiment expressed by many Auschwitz survivors, particularly the ones I knew.

Rene turned 16 at Auschwitz, but the day passed without fanfare. Rather, the pivotal birthday was ignored in a place as close to hell on Earth as there has ever been. One day when the guards blew the whistle for *Appell*, the girls in Rene's barracks, Lager C as it was known, were lined up and separated. Rene's group was taken to another, larger building where each prisoner was tattooed. The process was slow, and they waited in line "all day and night." She was given the number A-13446, a number to be on Rene's forearm for the rest of her life. Rene was imprisoned at Auschwitz at the same time as Ella Rogozinski, Gina Freiden, and Richard Friedemann, also subjects in this book and all ended up in Jacksonville after the war, though none of the four knew each other, such was the magnitude of the camp's size.

The adjacent barracks of women, *Lager* B, housed Czechoslovakian Jews – families of mothers and their children. The day that Rene and her barracks mates got tattooed, Lager B Jews were lined up. The babies and young children were separated from their mothers. The children were being taken to the gas chambers and their mothers knew it. Rene still recalls the cries and screams of the mothers as their children were torn from their arms. A half-century later, she explained it was something "you don't want to ever hear." She paused then, misty-eyed. Continuing a few quiet moments later, she said, "Sometimes even today, I have nightmares about those screams. You know, I [have] never slept a night since Auschwitz. Even in the hospital, even under anesthetic, I never sleep. *Never!*"

Perhaps because she had no regular labor assignment while receiving the usual rations of a piece of bread and maybe watery soup, Rene said she didn't lose as much weight as many of the others. Still, she was malnourished, thin, and weak and had to do her best to appear healthy when Mengele would come into the barracks for periodic physical exams. She lived in fear that each quick exam could mean an immediate exit to the gas chamber.

Somehow Rene escaped the crematoria at Auschwitz. In September 1944, she was taken in another cattle car to a site just outside Hamburg, in northern Germany, about 285 kilometers west. Following two or three days and nights of difficult travel with no food or water, she came to Bergen-Belsen. There was bombing all around as they traveled west into Germany toward the camp. Several times the train stopped due to the bombing, but the prisoners were never let out of the cattle car, so they feared for their lives. Finally, the train rolled to a stop. The prisoners were forced off and marched through hills and forests. The German soldiers fired machine guns over their heads and then laughed hysterically. "It didn't matter if someone was caught with a bullet," she said. "That was their fun. We were Jews; we were worse than animals to them."

Finally, they arrived at Bergen-Belsen at the end of September. The weather had turned prematurely cold, particularly at night. They were housed in a tent, each with a single blanket and a bit of filthy straw as a makeshift mattress. They were not allowed to leave the tent unless told to do so. There was a latrine outside the tent, and they had to endure the cold outside to use it. There was a single spigot for water, but it was so cold outside that the water was often frozen. "We had no coat, no socks, no nothing," she said. "The wind would blow the snow, you know, a blizzard. I don't know how we survived."

On the first day there, Rene was given a small loaf of bread to be divided among five people. Afterward, she usually received a single slice of bread, occasionally with a smidgen of margarine. On rare occasions, she also got something resembling a sausage. She added that she didn't "know what kind it was, or if it was even from a human." They were rarely given any water. She did little at Bergen-Belsen the month she was imprisoned there except sit on her bunk in the tent. There were periodic inspections for which they were made to line up outside the tent. They were poked with a stick, presumably as a way of determining their health and strength.

Finally, at the end of October 1944, Rene was given a new uniform and forced onto yet another train. Once again, dozens of thin, filthy bodies were crammed into a cattle car, this time going to Duderstadt concentration camp, outside Hanover, Germany, about 50 kilometers away. There, Rene worked in a munitions factory outside the camp to make machine-gun casings as a slave laborer. Duderstadt was the least horrendous of her camp assignments; it had wood stoves in the barracks, running water, and showers. It even had a crude, makeshift dining cart that came by once daily for the Jews. They were given new striped uniforms and a blanket. They even had a thin mattress rather than straw on the bed. At first, the stove seemed to be a real luxury, but there was rarely any wood available to burn, so it was mostly useless – almost a tease in the cold barracks at night. Rene vowed to keep a low profile, hoping she would thereby extend her survival chances. Often, she recalled five decades later, she would close her eyes and just pretend she was not there.

She spent about six months at Duderstadt, working in the Krupp machine-gun factory, weekly rotating working days and nights in 12-hour shifts. She said some German soldiers were nice, feeling sorry for the prisoners, and would sneak in potatoes and salt. There were 12 women in a barracks. Rene continued to grow weaker by the day despite the relatively better conditions. After a long day of work, upon returning to the barracks in the evening, "they wouldn't let us rest. They used to blow the whistle and say, 'Line up.' They just wanted to harass us." They were lucky in one thing. They were able to work alongside German civilians in the factory. While the Jews were slave laborers, it was important for all workers to produce as much as possible – consequently, they were fed more than at Auschwitz or Bergen-Belsen so they could at least maintain a minimal degree of strength. At the factory, they received a daily bowl of hot soup and a piece of bread and, sometimes, even margarine and a piece of sausage.

The work was grueling and demanded strength, precision, and concentration. It was especially demanding for a paper-thin, malnourished 16-year-old girl weakened from her time in the ghetto, Auschwitz, and Bergen-Belsen. She worked on a huge machine, the size of a bed, and it took a fair amount of strength to operate. Her hands were raw, she said, "because the steel pieces were real big, and they were soaking in some kind of lye. I had to put my hands in the machine and push the machine, and the machine would automatically push the bullet out."

While making shells for machine guns, one day she had a bullet shell explode and enter her chest after she had accidentally put it in backward. The wound got infected, and she received no medical treatment; she had to treat it with her own urine. It remained in her chest for the rest of her life. If a prisoner claimed she was sick or hurt, she would be killed, so she kept quiet about her injury. After the accident, she was taken in to see a German SS officer and accused of sabotage. He didn't realize she was hurt, but he knew that she had caused a small explosion. Sabotage meant execution by hanging. Several guards and officers screamed at her that she had sabotaged her work and would be hanged. Rene's response was to laugh in their faces. She said, "I guess my arrogance saved me." She was desperate to stay alive, however, and see if she could endure it all until potential liberation.

In April 1945, she was relocated yet again, this time force-marched about 600 kilometers south to the notorious Dachau concentration camp, a grueling journey that took more than a week, walking mile after debilitating mile each day. During this painful trek, already malnourished, underweight, exhausted, and extremely weak, Rene and the other prisoners were given no food at all, forced to march nearly 80 kilometers daily, an extremely arduous feat for even the strongest, healthiest person, much less concentration camp prisoners near death. Though it was spring, German springs can be wet and rainy, and nighttime temperatures sometimes fell below freezing. The spring of 1945 was no exception, and the weather made the long march more difficult. Many of the prisoners died enroute; Rene was barely clinging to life when she reached Dachau. Her stay there was to be brief. Soon after arriving, Rene was transferred once again, this time east into Czechoslovakia to Theresienstadt.

Finally, on May 7, 1945, after a couple of weeks in this notorious ghetto transit camp, Rene was liberated by the Soviet military, which she described as yet "another cross to bear." The liberating Soviet soldiers were sometimes nearly as cruel as the Germans. After only a couple of days, however, the newly liberated prisoners were organized, given food, and told to go back home. Finally free, she recalled that she had "never cried in the concentration camps. … It was like being an animal." Still just 16 years old at liberation, one of the things she wanted most was, simply, underwear. A teenage girl deprived of so much, including the most basic things of life, Rene had not given up on simple pleasures. Years later, she couldn't remember when and how that wish was granted, though she finally did indeed receive new underwear. She also was able to make it back home to Cluj, but when she got there, she discovered that no one else in her family had survived. She was turning 17, still a child really, and now she was all alone. She recounted that she experienced great guilt to be the only surviving family member, an emotion common among Holocaust survivors. It was an intense sentiment; one she would carry with her for the rest of her long life.

Rene's future husband, Leslie Jakob, was born on September 8, 1922, also in Cluj, to Eugene and Bertha Jakob. Leslie attended the same school as Rene but, being six years older, he and Rene were acquaintances rather than friends growing up. His father, born in Cluj as well, had attended art school in Vienna, and after Hitler came to power, he told his children that he had met a young Hitler while living in Vienna. He attended the same art school that had rejected Hitler's admission and laid claim that their paths crossed there. Leslie had one brother, Zole, and two sisters, Boje and Lea, two and four years older than him, respectively. The family of six lived together in a modest, two-room house. They spoke both Yiddish and Hungarian at home and Romanian at school. Leslie's nickname was Laci, which became Leslie; his Hebrew name was Moshe. Eventually, both sisters were killed in the Holocaust; Zole, two years younger, survived the horrors.

Young men in Romania were usually conscripted into what was called premilitary upon reaching the of age 18. Leslie was called up but as a Jew wasn't allowed to join other young men in the military unit from Cluj. Instead, he was sent to dig ditches with other young Jewish men. Though trained as a mechanic, when the war began, he was forced to be a fireman and dig ditches for 24 hours at a time.

Ultimately, Leslie refused and continued his regular job as a mechanic. One night, returning home from work, a sergeant was waiting for him, arrested him, and put him in jail. The next day, a judge sentenced him to six months in jail for his refusal to perform the forced labor of digging ditches.

After the Hungarians had taken over Cluj in 1942, life for the Jews and the Jakob family, like Rene Goldstein and her family, began to take a significant turn for the worse. On October 4, 1943, before the Cluj Ghetto had been created, Leslie was taken to a Hungarian forced labor camp in Transylvania, where his assigned job was to dig up cable. From this camp, he was soon sent to another labor camp, this one in Karlsbad, Czechoslovakia, where he was forced to walk the entire distance – hundreds of kilometers. Upon arrival, he was given the job of digging bunkers for the army. After a while, he was sent to a labor camp in Poland, again being sent on a forced march for the long journey and given little food during the long and exhausting trek. At this camp, he was assigned to join a detail where he dug large pits known as "catchers" for army tanks. The catchers were enormous, 14 by 7 meters. After digging the catchers, the workers had to cut wood and fill the sides. The idea was that the Soviet tanks would come along and fall in.

Leslie described his experience in Poland as a very hard time. "They would get so much snow, six feet of snow. We didn't have any barracks; we took the bark from the trees and put it on the snow and slept in it. ... There was a guard that always came to me and slapped me. He didn't even know my name. He just came to me and slapped me. I couldn't take it anymore, so I slapped him back."

Leslie was immediately punished for his offense. His punishment was that they hung him by his arms. "The way they did it over there was to tie your hands up and pull you up from a tree. Their law says the point of the toe must touch the ground, but they pulled me up about ten inches from the ground." Though in considerable pain, Leslie knew he had to do something to take his mind off the excruciating agony, so he began to sing and laugh. "Finally, after a long time, a captain came along and made them take me down. But it was too late; my arms and muscles were all torn. I couldn't lift my hands. I knew that I couldn't work anymore and they would kill me."

Hanging was entertainment for the guards. He said they would "make everybody stand up and make a line. Every tenth person they would hang. They would gather everybody around a tree and have a hanging. This was all the entertainment they had: to kill people." There were eight in Leslie's group that had come "all the way together. We decided this was it. We had to escape to live. It was night. We did what we had to do and sneaked out of camp."

The band of eight men hid during the day and traveled under the cover of darkness at night. After days of covert travel, finding food wherever they could, including in farmers' fields and among wild plants they found in the woods, the group made it into Hungary the day after Christmas, December 26, 1943. "I will never forget that date," Leslie recalled. Their entrance into Hungary meant they had to cross the Tisza River.

As they quietly approached the prominent Hungarian waterway, deciding what to do and where to go next, German soldiers saw them and began shooting. With no other choice, they jumped into the river. Russian soldiers were on the other side of the river and observed the shooting. Four men in the group were shot, while four evaded the shootings and escaped across the river. Leslie was among the lucky ones who survived. The Tisza River's currents were quite rapid, so when Leslie and his three companions made it across, the Russians helped pull them out.

Once safely on the shore with the Russians, Leslie and the surviving trio wanted to continue their journey; they wanted to go home. The Russian soldiers, however, would not allow it. These soldiers were "Mongrels from Siberia" (actually, Mongols). Leslie said they were simple-minded and uneducated; most could neither read nor write. They treated Leslie and his three friends harshly, worse than the Germans did. "They put us in a basement and gave us a pail of water and dried bread. We were hungry, so anything was good. ... They said they were going to take us to Siberia. After the way they treated us here, I knew I didn't want to go to Siberia."

The soldiers had pillaged the Hungarian countryside as they made their way westward into the country, fighting the Germans. This group had seized two carriages that they filled with jewelry, gold, and diamonds. Each overflowing carriage was pulled by six oxen, all stolen from Hungarians. The soldiers took Leslie and the three other Jews, along with their carriages and loot, all the way to Czechoslovakia. They wanted them to be translators. Not wanting to travel any farther with this ruthless band of vagabond soldiers, one night they got their Russian captors good and drunk and were able to quietly escape after the soldiers passed out. Leslie and his companions went into hiding for the next three-and-a-half months, every night walking surreptitiously a couple of kilometers closer to home.

Leslie finally made it home to Cluj, but the city was extremely dangerous. The Russian military had defeated the Nazis there and now it was the occupying force. "You couldn't go out in the streets in the city," he said. "The Russians would strip you and the women were forced to bed." Leslie was hoping beyond hope that he would find some surviving family members in the old homestead. Yet, trying to be in safe hiding from the Russian soldiers, he waited two weeks before making his way back to find out. When he finally entered his family home, it was empty. Like his future wife, Rene, he discovered that no one else from his family had returned.

His brother had suffered a fate unlike Leslie's. He had been sent to a concentration camp where he met his death. Leslie never knew what happened to his sisters, but they, too, never returned. Leslie, despondent and angry, was nevertheless determined to survive by whatever means necessary.

Leslie could speak Russian, so the occupying Russian Army made him a "detective." He said he and another Jewish survivor were ordered to enter various hotels "and make sure prostitutes had 'a book.' They were supposed to have a book. We would check the girls; if they didn't have a book, we were supposed to take them to the police station. I didn't give a damn for that!"

Instead, he decided that his "detective" work would be to safeguard women against the Russians through his work in the underground Haganah movement. Handfuls of surviving young Jewish women had started to come home from concentration camps in late 1944 and early 1945 and the Russian soldiers would "stop the trains and rape the girls," he said. Leslie told himself, "'You know what? We're gonna stay by the train, and we're gonna watch them.' And that's what we did, we watched the trains. When the young girls used to come in, we didn't let them [Russian soldiers] do nothing to them."

Leslie had been in forced labor for 15 months, from October 1943 until December 1944. He spent a total of eight months in the underground resistance after escaping his slave labor, now defying the Russians instead of the Germans as a detective and protector under the Romanian police, whose chief was a Jew. Initially, upon returning to Cluj, Leslie's health "was lousy," he said. "I was skinny like my little finger, but I had a friend of mine who opened a restaurant and they built me up."

One day, shortly after the war's end, Leslie saw a young woman exiting a train. He recognized her from before the war. "Then," pausing for several seconds with his eyes closing, Leslie slowly said, "I saw Rene." No longer a child, Rene was now 17 and Leslie 23. They quickly fell deeply in love. They left Cluj with false papers, traveling to Austria to see if they could find their parents or any other surviving family. Leslie sharply recalled: "We didn't find nobody." With no family, they soon went to an Austrian DP camp in Bad Gastein, just outside Linz, where he and Rene were married on November 24, 1945. The Americans soon put them up in an Austrian cottage near the DP camp and offered them German prisoners as servants, but Rene and Leslie refused.

Their first daughter, Lea, was born in Austria in the DP camp in May 1947; the second, Anna, was born in Italy in 1948. They spent three years in an Italian DP camp, from 1947 to 1950, after thinking they would pass through and eventually emigrate to Israel. When they traveled from Austria to Italy, they crossed the high Alpine Brenner Pass on foot. It took them three days with their little six-week-old girl, Lea. However, upon crossing the border, they were arrested by Italian and English police. They were quickly released and taken to Milan. Since little Lea was quite sick, however, they were unable to continue to Israel and so they stayed in Italy.

"Italy was good," Leslie recalled decades later. "I was a truck driver, and I made beds. They had a machine nobody could work. I could work it. Italy was very good because they paid me. They gave us food and gave us electric; we didn't have to pay [for] that, so that was good."

When their baby finally recovered, Leslie still thought Israel was the best place to live. "I felt that this was the only place I could be safe," he said. "But you couldn't go to Israel unless you leave everything you got. I wanted to go, but for the second time, I didn't want to leave everything. They would take you to a ship in the night. My wife said, 'No, I don't want to go.'" Then they considered a move to Australia, but Rene wanted to go to America. It took three years, but they finally got permission to go to the United States.

Leslie and Rene had spent five years in four different DP camps. They came to the United States from Italy, under the auspices of the Displaced Persons' Act, departing September 1, 1950, and arriving at New York harbor on September 12 aboard the USS *General M. L. Hersey*. When they landed on Ellis Island, setting foot on American soil for the first time, they were full of joy, though they had only two dollars to their names. Soon they settled in Brooklyn, where Leslie was able to get a job as an auto mechanic. Later, he was an accomplished jewelry maker. They lived in Brooklyn for 12 years, from 1950 to 1962, before buying a small home in Long Island, where they lived in modest comfort for the next 27 years. They added five more children to the family: John in 1951, Ira in 1956, Elizabeth in 1957, and Toby in 1962. In 1989, after Leslie retired, they moved south from Long Island to Jacksonville to escape the harsh northern winters. Their children and grandchildren were soon living in Northeast Florida as well.

Rene said she survived because she wanted to see how it would all end. Despite the agonizing years of persecution and suffering, losing so many members of her family and friends, and enduring the perverse pain of the ghetto, Auschwitz-Birkenau, Bergen-Belsen, Dachau, Theresienstadt, and forced marches, she survived to be liberated and into freedom and immigration to the United States. She had a long and loving marriage with Leslie, seven children, multiple grandchildren, and now great-grandchildren, and a rich life filled with much joy, happiness, and success. Their multiple generations of progeny are today scattered, largely throughout Florida, and are vibrant contributors to their respective communities, enjoying the American dream, not only because of living in the land of opportunity but because Leslie and Rene Jakob passed on a legacy of resilience, courage, and moral character. The "end" was not what Hitler and the Nazis had in mind – the complete eradication of the European Jews – but rather one of the ultimate triumphs of the human spirit.

Daughter Ann(a) Jakob Sussman related that while she was growing up, she knew both parents were Holocaust survivors and had endured Nazi concentration camps but said they rarely talked about it. "Holidays were not a happy time," particularly Passover, she recalled, though there was not much talk from Leslie or Rene as to why. Ann was born in the DP camp in Tronti, Italy, in 1948 but has lived in the United States since the age of two and has no real memories of the DP camp. She is not religious, she says, but appreciates the religious and ethnic traditions of her Jewish heritage. Only two of the Jakob daughters married Jews; the others married out of the faith. Both of her parents were very religious, though her younger sister, Tina Jakob Hart, born in the United States in 1952, related that her parents' religious faith had been shaken to the core by their experiences in the Holocaust and their early years in the United States. Tina said that she and her six siblings were raised in a secular way during their formative early years. Soon after moving to the United States in 1950, living in New York City and filled with excited optimism that they would finally be able to outwardly express their Jewish faith, Rene and Leslie were turned away from a Rosh Hashana service at a synagogue door because they did not have a reservation and there was no room to seat them inside. Feeling rejected in a new home that had been so full of promise and hope, although the couple maintained their faith's traditions, this blatant rejection at the temple led them from religious adherence. Later in life, however, they returned to regular temple attendance, worshiping at Beth Shalom Conservative Temple in Jacksonville.

Ann visited her parents every week when they were older and talked for hours. Years before, when she was a little girl, Ann asked her mom about her tattoo and Rene told her that it was given to her when she was little because she couldn't remember her phone number. Like so many other Holocaust survivors, the Jakobs wanted to protect their children from the horrors they had experienced and start a new chapter of their lives filled with hope and optimism, free from the pain of European antisemitism and the horrors of the Holocaust. They refused to dwell on their past but, rather, looked to the future with their large family. Their lives in New York and Jacksonville were full and happy, yet the pain of their former lives could never be completely suppressed. Leslie had nightmares for the rest of his life yet refused to speak about them with his children or grandchildren. After he died in 1999 at the age of 77, Rene was unable to sleep because she was so filled with grief, losing the man who had been her partner her entire life after liberation. Only after lengthy, intense counseling could Rene once again sleep at night. Rene died ten years later, in 2009, at the age of 81. During the last years of her life, her relationships with her grandchildren grew much closer. She finally seemed at peace.

The children and grandchildren, as second- and third-generation survivors, continue to bear the scars of Leslie and Rene's torment.

While the long night of the souls of their matriarch and patriarch eased over time, it could never be forgotten or completely suppressed. In their seventies, Rene and Leslie began to speak to school groups, to educate the next generation so that something like the Holocaust could never occur again. Forever thankful for their lives in the United States, they charted a new course, always trying to look to the future rather than their painful past. The Jakobs were able to survive the grip of Nazi henchmen who wanted to eradicate them and all the Jews of Europe. Moreover, they nurtured children and grandchildren who have successfully thrived in the United States. Like so many other survivors, they created numerous small victories that gave their progeny hope for the future. Their lives lay claim to the testimony from the Torah: "When the Lord your G-d gives you rest from all the enemies around you in the land, He is giving you to possess as an inheritance, you shall blot out the name of Amalek from under heaven. Do not forget!"[1]

Rene and Leslie Jakob with their first daughter

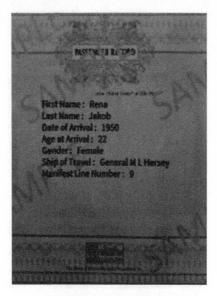

Rene Jakob passage to the US

Rene Jakob with family

Rene Jakob

Leslie Jakob

The Jakob-Hart family, including a daughter and two grandchildren, with the author (in the center), in Palm Coast, Florida, October 2020.

4

RICHARD FRIEDEMANN
KRAKÓW, POLAND

Richard Friedemann during the Holocaust.

Richard (Dick) Friedemann, born a Polish Jew just a little more than a decade before Nazi Germany took over Poland, lived his teenage years enduring an almost indescribable and unbelievable series of horrific experiences. He spent three years on the run, bouncing from one location to another, before being sent to a succession of concentration camps for the next four years. He defied death on several occasions, and through ingenuity, perseverance, extraordinary bravery, and perhaps a bit of providence, he was able to outwit the Nazis and emerge from the terrors of the Holocaust to live a long and rich life. Having improbably survived beyond his teens, remarkably he lived 92 years, most of them filled with joyful exuberance. I was privileged to call him a friend and hear him recount his courageous life on several occasions. While he spoke often in the final quarter-century of his long life about the camps, even his children knew nothing of their father's time during the Holocaust until the time he first spoke in my class in 1995 when he was 68. They did not know of the ghettos and the camps, his narrow escapes and act of heroism as a mere boy, or even their Jewish heritage. The narrative that follows here is an account of courage, wit, fate, and ultimately a life well lived, free of Nazi tyranny.

Born in Kraków, Poland, on December 17, 1927, the second child of Leon and Lilla Frischer Friedmann (the spelling of the last name was changed when Richard immigrated to the United States after World War II), he enjoyed a briefly idyllic childhood before the Nazis invaded Poland in September 1939. A little more than three months before Richard's 12th birthday, the invasion tore his family apart forever. In Richard's early childhood, the family lived a comfortable, upper-middle-class, affluent lifestyle. His parents were well educated, and his father, Leon, was a successful attorney who received his law degree from Jagiellonian University in Poland and practiced both at home and internationally. His mother was a homemaker. Richard and his brother, Zygmunt, who was seven years older, lived with their parents in a grand home near the center of Kraków. They enjoyed many of the luxuries of a prosperous Eastern European life. Lilla was a lover of the arts and high culture and passed this love on to her children. There were frequent trips to the art museum, and their home was filled with music and fine food.

The Friedmann house, an elegant ten-room flat, was spacious for an Eastern European apartment of the last century. The walls were covered with colorful frescoes, beautiful chandeliers hung from the ceilings, and the floors were graced with expensive Persian rugs.

The home was filled with precious antiques. Richard said he had pleasant memories of a loving family enjoying life and one another.

The Friedmanns were assimilated Jews who considered themselves Poles first and Jews second. They were proud Polish citizens and thought themselves no different from their non-Jewish neighbors, actively participating in Polish social life. The only holidays they observed were the High Holy Days, and they did not keep kosher. Richard and Zygmunt had mostly, but not all, Christian friends. There was a large extended family on the father's side and a smaller family on the mother's, but these extended relationships were not particularly close.

Richard attended grammar school at St. Wojciech, about a thirty-minute walk from his home in the center of town. Small in stature, he learned to defend himself against older and larger bullies but more often took up for his less aggressive classmates, coming to their defense against their oversized opponents. As a result, he picked up the nickname "Richard the Lion-Hearted." He recalled years later, "I had already in my childhood, identified with the underdog."

Richard's early experiences with antisemitism in Kraków were minimal. He had memories from his younger days of two right-wing nationalistic political parties in Poland, but they were far less violent than the Nazi Party in nearby Germany. There was always the air of antisemitism, but as an assimilated family, they did not overtly feel it daily. There was anxiety, even fear, of the German nationalistic, antisemitic Nazism immediately to their west, but, he said, they "were counting on the cultural aspects of the German people and the cultural aspects of Europe itself, and also we were counting very heavily ... on the might of the Polish [army] ... to defend Poland ... to the last drop of our blood" should an invasion occur.

On September 1, 1939, the idyllic existence suddenly changed when the German Wehrmacht invaded Poland. Life for young Richard and his family would no longer be placid and delightful, filled with school, learning, good food, cultural activities, and a gentle life with a loving family and myriad friends. When the bombs began to darken the skies of Kraków and the stench of death began to permeate the city, the Friedmann family realized their lives would never be the same. However, they didn't fully grasp the level of change to come. The Nazis now ruled, and Richard's childhood was abruptly over. His family was fractured and dispersed. Life was turned upside-down.

Within days of the German attack on Poland, the family learned of atrocities committed by the invading forces in the cities they had captured. Richard and his mother fled east by train, leaving from the Prokocim station in the Kraków suburbs, and traveling about 250 kilometers to Przemyśl. They thought they might find better protection from the Polish army. His father and brother Zygmunt were called up by the Polish army reserves. Leon was a captain in the reserves, and Zygmunt planned to go study at an American university, but as an army reservist, he had to change his plans.

Despite the relatively short distance, the journey for Richard and Lilla to Przemyśl ended prematurely in Niepołomice, just 65 kilometers outside Kraków. It took several days just to make it that far because the train was repeatedly attacked by the Luftwaffe. "Every once in a while, our train had to stop because the newly repaired tracks were very unstable," he said. Looking out the train window, he saw discarded luggage and articles of clothing littering the tracks. The debris was from civilians who had attempted to escape the bloodbath. The tracks were also covered with dead bodies of those who never had the chance to find safety.

"They were all [lying] dead in a grotesque manner," Richard recalled. At one point, after it was bombed nonstop for six hours, the train pulled to a stop at the Niepołomice station, unable to go any farther because of the destruction. Passengers fled the train and ran to a nearby forest for shelter. With bombs falling all around and gunfire sprayed at them, it was utter chaos. Sprinting toward cover, children were separated from their parents. Entire families were in disarray, screaming for one another, their voices unable to be heard due to the thunder of bombs and artillery fire everywhere. Thousands never made it to the relative safety of the forest, losing their lives in the Nazi onslaught.

Four thousand Polish civilians from that single train were killed or wounded. Richard and his mother were among the lucky few, safely reaching the forest 150 meters away. Once there, they lay concealed at the foot of a large pine tree, waiting for the carnage to end. The forest filled with smoke as survivors walked around dazed as if in a dream, Richard wrote years later. "I cried when I saw burnt people and dead people turned actually to jelly from the impact of the explosions." This was the first of what would be several narrow escapes from the scythe of death. It was the first of many he would never forget.

With no other transportation, when "only determination would propel us," Richard said, he and his mother walked the remaining 70 kilometers to Przemyśl. Alongside, many more fleeing refugees walked, ran, and crawled toward freedom. Periodically, bombs came spiraling down on and around them and the fugitives had to dive for cover. Dead horses and cows littered the fields right and left, "with wide-open eyes and purple tongues hanging out," Richard recalled. "This was such a hellish picture to look at." It was particularly so for an 11-year-old fleeing, with his future so unsure.

After several days, they finally reached a small village called Jaroslaw nestled on the western edge of the San River. When Richard and Lilla found out the German army would attack the town soon, after one night's restless sleep, they paid a local peasant farmer to let them hop on a wagon with others, pulled by a strong but skinny horse and a buggy and headed farther east for the village of Lemberg, closer to Lvov (now Lviv, Ukraine), where they hoped they would be safe from the merciless German forces.

Leon, not trusting any banks after they had all collapsed during the Depression, had invested much of his wealth in various foreign currencies and precious metals. On that particular treacherous journey, Richard carried a leather satchel filled with about 80 pounds of gold and all manner of foreign currencies – in total worth about $20,000 (equivalent to $440,000 today). As they headed toward Lvov, they were again besieged by German fire. Compelled to jump for their lives from the newly acquired buggy, they took cover in a ditch. Unfortunately, their satchel, the same one that held the essence of their very lives – that is, the financial necessities for them to perhaps survive and live their lives if and when this hell was finished – remained on the farmer's buggy. The peasant farmer realized his chance and left Richard and Lilla behind. They ran after the farmer and the buggy for a while, but their efforts were futile. They lost all their money, gold, and silver. A while later, a Polish soldier who appeared on a bicycle came to their aid. The sergeant rode after the farmer, caught him, and threatened to execute him on the spot. He recovered the leather satchel and returned it to Richard and Lilla, who then kept walking. Richard had learned his first adult lesson about whether to rely on someone. Would that person be honorable or nefarious? It would not be the last such lesson he would absorb in the next few years.

After several days of walking, mother and son finally came to a small village. Sarny, in eastern Poland, was situated along the Ukrainian border. Here, they were free from the threat of German bombings. They met few refugees in Sarny. There were skirmishes between the Soviet military and Polish resistance fighters, though, so Richard and his mother returned to Lvov. It took about 36 hours by hired wagon.

Lvov had been occupied by the Soviet military, which kept the German army at bay initially. Several weeks after they reached Lvov, Zygmunt appeared. The two brothers and their mother stayed there for six months. Zygmunt said he didn't know what had become of his father.

The Polish army had been defeated by the Nazis in a mere three weeks; soon after, the Soviets invaded Poland from the east.

Thinking their chances to be able to live through this newest development might be better under German rather than Russian occupation, the Friedmanns crossed to the German side, back to Kraków. Before leaving, they dug a deep hole behind the house where they had been staying. Secretly, they buried money and valuables, covering the stash with lumps of coal. They hoped the war would soon end and they would be able to recover their precious metals and cash. The Friedmanns felt like the Germans were more educated, more civilized, Richard said. It was, sadly, a mistaken impression. With Poland controlled by Nazis, the awful situation grew much worse.

Kraków was the largest city in southern Poland and, unlike many other of the larger Polish cities, it had so far been largely unblemished by warfare. The Nazis had taken over Kraków and made it the capital of Germany's General Government, meaning it was strategically important. Despite avoiding physical demolition, the city saw most aspects of Polish culture stripped throughout. The area was "Germanized" with totalitarian harshness, bolstered by antisemitic and anti-Polish policies and, ultimately, mass slaughter of its Jews. The old market square was renamed Adolf Hitler Platz; many street names were altered to honor the Third Reich. The city, while architecturally still beautiful, lost its charm – and it lost much more. The Friedmann family, like all Kraków Jews, was no longer welcome there.

Richard, Zygmunt, and Lilla were relieved to find Leon at their family home. The once robust man was a shell of his former self – noticeably thin, sad, and reserved, reluctant to speak of what he had experienced. Young Richard was glad to be home, though, and quickly met up with friends and returned to school. Just turning 12, he had experienced so much – more than any child should ever see – but he *was* a child and wanted to live his life like a normal one. It was not to be. One by one, many of Richard's teachers vanished; it was said they had been taken to a camp called Auschwitz. In the winter of 1940, Hitler issued an edict expelling all Jewish students from school.

Ultimately, a traitorous neighbor betrayed the family. The Gestapo, along with SS officers, pulled up in front of the Friedmann home in three limousines. The soldiers put Leon in one side of the house and Lilla in the other, leaving Richard alone; Zygmunt was not there. The officers shouted *"Verfluchte Schweine! Verfluchte Juden* ["Damn pigs! Damn Jews]!" The military harassed the Friedmanns for six hours, stealing most of their valuables and furniture, which they hauled away in five trucks. The next day, a German family moved in and the Friedmanns were forced out, allowed to carry only a few items as well as about 16 pounds of personal items.

They fled to a nearby village just outside Kraków, Podgórze, but soon went to the tiny village of Wawrzeńczyce. In this small town, they were hidden by a kindly Christian widow, Adela Pilch. There they lived for about three or four months. Unfortunately, the Nazis' Sonderkommando [Special Action Units] began investigating the area, aiming to round up Jews. Not wanting to endanger the Pilch family, the Friedmanns went back to Kraków. There they quietly remained for about a month, though the family split up –Lilla in one place, Richard and Leon in another. Zygmunt returned to the underground resistance.

One day, Lilla disappeared, failing to show up at the family's daily meeting place. Apparently, she was betrayed or perhaps captured in a routine street-clearing operation. After about a month, Richard and Leon received a visit from the Gestapo, who entered the home, held them at gunpoint, and stole everything of value left. Two days later, they were told that within 24 hours, the house was being taken by the Nazis and they must pack no more than 16 pounds of personal items and get out. At this point, with no home, jobs, money, or personal possessions, and learning that Kraków would become a Jewish ghetto, the remaining Friedmann family decided to go into hiding. They relocated to a small rural village where they lived with various peasant families for a year. However, the *Einsatzgruppen* [mobile killing units] were nearby, so they chose once more to return to Kraków for the relative safety of the ghetto.

It was now 1941, less than two years after the German invasion. The Friedmanns were not registered in the ghetto because they had been in hiding for such a long time. Quietly, they hid in various places in the ghetto for several days, trying to be as inconspicuous as possible. Zygmunt, by that time working with the Polish underground, attempted to get forged papers for the family so they could leave the ghetto. The family was now separated, as Zygmunt covertly moved around within the underground, and Richard and his father lived separately in hiding for a month in an abandoned sauerkraut factory. If only they could locate Lilla.

It was not meant to be. She had recently obtained some false identity papers identifying her as a Gentile Pole but was apparently denounced as a Jew and turned in. She disappeared and was never to be seen by her family again. Much later, they learned she had been murdered in a notorious prison in Kraków.

With the disappearance of Lilla and increasing threats to their own lives, they decided to come out of hiding and sneak back into the ghetto, unregistered, to at least have access to the limited provisions. They stayed there for several months. Rations, hygiene, and material comforts were abysmal in the Kraków Ghetto, but Richard and Leon were able to survive there until rounded up in the fall of 1942 and deported to the nearby Zwangsarbeit Lager I (Plaszow Forced Labor Camp I, known to many from *Schindler's List*). Zygmunt had also been deported to Plaszow shortly before Richard and his father, having been caught spying for the British. Zygmunt had been brutally tortured in captivity for several days, narrowly escaping execution, before shipment to Plaszow.

The conditions in Plaszow were much worse than even the ghetto. About 2,500 prisoners were relocated to rundown barracks, "without insulation, running water, and only a few windows," Richard said. Each barracks housed 300 to 400 people, with a single bathroom and little running water, and in the cold winter of 1942, it was only a few degrees warmer inside than outside. Their clothing soon got filthy, with scant protection from the cold, and their bodies became covered with lice. Their food consisted of a morning piece of stale bread and, on some days, later a bowl of watery soup. Every morning, prisoners were lined up for *Appell* at 5 a.m. before putting in a 12- to 16-hour workday. The camp was surrounded by barbed wire and electrified fences, typical of the many Nazi concentration camps scattered throughout Germany, Poland, Czechoslovakia, and Austria. There were towers at various intervals, each equipped with floodlights and manned with guards and machine guns. Escape was virtually impossible. Richard's job was on the railroad – backbreaking work of loading shovelfuls of coal for hour after painful hour. Leon cleaned streets all day long, but father and son at least were together in the evenings back in the barracks. Zygmunt's whereabouts, however, were still unknown.

In the spring of 1943, Richard and his father were transferred from Plaszow I to Plaszow II, force-marched from one camp to the next on roads constructed of desecrated Jewish grave markers from the Kraków Jewish cemetery. The prisoners were marched in two groups of 300 to 400 each. The group that Richard and Leon were in entered Plaszow II as the other group was being executed, never being permitted to come into the new camp. Thankful for their lives upon arriving at Plaszow II, they found that Zygmunt was there and enjoyed a grateful reunion. Zygmunt, however, was in poor physical shape after being beaten and tortured. Richard and Leon told Zygmunt that Lilla had not survived, quickly diminishing the joy of the reunion.

Richard and his father were crestfallen at the loss of Lilla. Richard said a prayer for his beloved mother:

You gave me life. Yet, I was not holding your hand when you ended yours. Were you in a dark cell, tortured? Were you cold and hungry without my help or my presence near you? You disappeared without a trace. Only the executioner knew how and where. I feel pain, but your pain was greater. I know what went through your mind. Sorrow for us who were left behind. Mother's sorrow, mother's grief. Your love never ended; and my love for you is endless. I cry in my prayers for justice, which failed to protect you. Rest peacefully in the arms of G-d, Mother.

Years later, Richard recalled that the camp commandant at Plaszow, the notorious Amon Goeth, was "extremely cruel, extravagant, and given to mood swings during which he would kill or drink incessantly. ... He was king and judge of life and death in the camp." Goeth would stand on the balcony of his villa overlooking the camp and aim his rifle at unsuspecting prisoners, taking great delight in shooting them from a distance should they falter or work too slowly. The prisoners lived in constant fear.

After about three months in Plaszow, Richard's father developed a festering wound on his right calf, thought at first to be gangrene. Fortunately, it soon healed. However, soon after their transfer to Plaszow II, Leon grew very ill and developed a high fever. After several days, he was admitted to the camp hospital with typhoid. He died there a week later. Richard noticed after seeing his father's body that there were unnatural bruises, including on his head and face. He suspected that his father may have been killed. The night after, Richard and Zygmunt found their father's lifeless body on a cart destined for a mass grave. They crawled under a barbed-wire fence, pulled his body from the cart, and buried their father in a hand-dug grave "where we were hoping he would lay peacefully," Richard said. Barehanded and in the darkness after midnight, with even the stars hidden, they hastily and covertly dug a six-foot grave to lay their father to rest. They did not want their father to be thrown into a mass grave and so determined that they would "steal our father's body and bury him ourselves." Just a boy, Richard wrote a prayer for his father after the burial:

It was a gray,
sunless day when you closed your eyes forever.
But please see why I couldn't help you.
Maybe I was a coward?
Saving my life at the expense of yours.
I knew you needed me there, and yet,

I would not come through these
Wooden walls that seemed to be made of steel.
Now I see I should have been there with you – life or death.
My grief screams in my heart because I was blind.
I saw you always strong,
Never giving in, not even to the death, never.

Grief will not change the truth.
You will not be with me again.
I could not help save your life
Though you have given me mine.
This pain will last forever. G-d knows.
Please G-d, give him life eternal.
Give him peace.

Only 13 years old, Richard was now an orphan, living a harrowing existence in what was but the first in a series of concentration camps.

Richard suffered a bout of typhus when the epidemic hit the camp, but he recovered and survived. During his eight-month stay at the camp, he was forced, in a twisted irony, to dig mass graves for liquidated Kraków Ghetto victims. For 72 hours nearly nonstop, Richard and 150 or so men at this task dug a 20-foot-wide and 15-foot-deep trench. As soon as they finished, the bodies arrived. Fifteen thousand Kraków Jews – children, elderly, those unable to work for the Nazi machine – were immediately interred there, their bodies still warm.

"The earth was angry," Richard said. "It was bubbling. I'm saying this poetically. It looked like the earth did not want to accept all these dead people. For days it was moving. It was not moving because these people were alive; it was moving because of the expansion and the blood was oozing out from it. A great big red river, not a river, a stream of blood coming out from this. But the earth did not want to accept it."

Richard was markedly impacted by what he witnessed. He was succumbing to the Nazis' goal of dehumanization; he became numb, desensitized, and began to repress his emotions. He said that later in life he became much more sensitive to death, though he would forever be emotionally scarred from his experiences at the camps as a teenager.

It was not so much that Richard had lost his compassion for others. At one point late in his tenure at Plaszow, he noticed that in the adjacent subcamp housing Christian Poles, the prisoners were in even worse physical condition than the Jews. They were starving to death, and so Richard devised and carried out plans to smuggle food rations to the camp to help keep the Christian prisoners alive. The life-saving acts put his life at great risk, but Richard showed courage and selflessness to help his fellow prisoners, Jewish or not. It wasn't the last time he would engage in such acts of selfless bravery.

After Plaszow, Richard and Zygmunt began what the younger brother called "a hellish journey" from one concentration camp to another. They shrewdly learned that life expectancy at each camp was fairly short, and so both volunteered to be transported to another labor camp, where they did all they could to stay only briefly. In the summer of 1943, they were sent to a Plaszow subcamp between Starachowice and Kielce called Hermann-Göring-Werke, where they helped manufacture train parts. The camp, as Richard later described it, "was not necessarily an extermination camp but, rather, [a] slow death camp where the prisoner would succumb due to an injury, labor exhaustion, hunger, or disease." Prisoners had to march five miles each way to work and put in long hours of hard labor. Like most camps, hygiene was terrible and there was little food or drink rations – even less than in Plaszow.

"Hunger was our daily reality," Richard said. "In reality, my guts were gnawing and craving food. My body was depleted from all the vitamins and body fat. The skin became grayish white from undernourishment. All the prisoners, when undressed, looked at themselves and saw an unfamiliar person with distended stomachs or sometimes a skeletal-like image. They worried about the future selections and how the SS would react to their near-skeletal conditions."

Unable to handle continuing their existence there, Zygmunt and Richard were leaders in a detailed escape plan from the camp along with a group of other prisoners. However, fearing that guards might have suspicions of their plans, they decided against daring an attempt.

In July 1943, the camp was liquidated and Richard and Zygmunt were forced into cattle cars for deportation to an unknown destination. There were about 150 in their car, stuffed in the cramped space on a sweltering summer day with no water and only a single bucket to use as a bathroom. "The stench eventually became impossible to stand," Richard said. "People were breathing through their mouths to prevent themselves from vomiting. Some people did vomit. ... There were women in our transport, and they were even more traumatized by the lack of privacy and hygiene."

After several long, slow days of travel, the train rolled to a stop near the Polish town of Oświęcim, just outside the gates of Auschwitz-Birkenau. After a couple of hours that seemed like an eternity, they slowly moved forward again, and then they were inside the camp. The train came to a screeching halt. Richard and Zygmunt were familiar with the rumors that Auschwitz was a notorious death camp. Richard remembered being told, "Oh, you're going to Auschwitz? Anyway, you're going to die there because there's only one way out, and it's through the chimney."

When the train got to Auschwitz early in the morning, the Jewish prisoners were weak, starving, dehydrated, heat-exhausted, and groggy. Climbing up to look out the window of the car, Richard said he "peered into the haze of the morning and saw a Gothic-like structure of two towers and a gate that reminded me of a triumphal gate, greeting soldiers from some special expedition or a national holiday parade. As the train moved forward and sped up a little, I read the ominous inscription placed on top of the gate *"Arbeit Macht Frei."* As the train rolled to a halt, suddenly Strauss waltzes and other chamber music came over camp loudspeakers. The doors to the cattle cars opened and prisoners began jumping out onto the camp's adjacent ramp. Guards immediately began shouting, *"Raus, Raus! Immer schnell, immer schnell weiter gehen! Raus aus dem Wagen!* ["Out, out! Always fast. Go forward. Get out of the railroad car!]!"

Richard described more about their arrival at Auschwitz: "So we jumped immediately when they opened the doors. And ... announcements are blasting loud to scare you. *'Alle Juden raus! Recht! Links* [All Jews out! Right! Left]!' They're yelling at you, and dogs are barking, machine guns aimed at you, and they're beating you. ... And they hit you in the head with anything they had – sticks, riding sticks, canes over the head, creating havoc, people tripping over each other. Women, children, they get lost, they get separated, they're screaming. Unbelievable sight."

Once they were off the train, standing on firm ground at the Auschwitz ramp, almost right away selections began. Most prisoners tried to stay with their families if they were with them and not be separated in the chaos. It was to no avail as men and women were segregated into separate lines, and children were taken from their parents. As with all Auschwitz selections, the very young and old and the weak and infirm were selected for immediate murder in the gas chambers. Those who appeared strong enough for forced labor were selected, for now, to go on to the adjacent slave-labor camp, Auschwitz II-Birkenau.

Selections were done with a brief, several-second visual scan, most often by Mengele, the chief camp physician who, in addition to making these life-and-death decisions, was also in charge of many horrendous, ghastly medical experiments, often on children. Mengele's significant intelligence and thorough education as a scientist and physician did nothing to steward his soul or soften his heart when it came to the Jews. His German education had not bestowed any degree of human virtue whatsoever. He had enjoyed superior academic training yet had not gained wisdom. His brain had been challenged, but his heart was devoid of the human flourishing that separates men from animals.

Richard recalled Mengele personally made selections the day he arrived. He saw Mengele as a tall, handsome man, well dressed, with gleaming, freshly polished leather boots, and a long, leather SS coat. Mengele wore stacked-heel boots to add to his natural height, but intimidation and control gave an illusion of height. Richard was only about five feet tall himself then, so this made the evil monster in boots appear even more sinister. Mengele "sported elegant white gloves," Richard said, and his mannerisms "exuded superiority."[1] He took off one of his white gloves and nonchalantly moved it to the left or right, making decisions as to whom would live or die. Decades later, Richard vividly recalled the scene when it was his turn to walk past Mengele to have his fate determined.

"He looked at the physical appearance of the men that he was selecting, and when he looked at me, I looked him right in the face and smiled," said Richard, who was 16 at the time. "I don't know why! But I did my chest a little bit [expanding his muscles]. 'Go ahead, do it! Screw you!' I was saying to him, and I was looking right at his face. And he selected me to live. My brother, too."

The selection scenario was surreal. Prisoners' lives were being determined amid the tumult of shouting guards, barking dogs tearing at innocent victims' flesh, and people being beaten and shot. One young child near Richard was bayoneted through the throat. New arrivals were confused and shocked. All the while, orchestras of Jewish inmates were playing classical and contemporary music, women were planting flowers in colorful gardens, and lovely blankets were hanging from overhead wires, all done to make some attempt at calming the incoming prisoners and creating a false security that everything was truly normal. The reality, of course, was that there was nothing normal whatsoever happening in Auschwitz-Birkenau.

After selections, Richard, Zygmunt, and the others were marched into showers where they got a quick, cold spritz, shaved, and were dusted with delousing powder. Men and women were separated to opposite sides in the hall, though in close visual proximity, and then they stripped naked – stripped of their dignity and humanity, pierced to their souls. They were given Auschwitz tattoos; Richard got B-4112 and Zygmunt B-4111, inked "so that you don't run away," exclaimed the prisoner detail in charge. "On the average, people last here two to three months, sometimes less, sometimes more. The only way out of here is through the chimney." Richard was given his blue-and-white striped uniform, with the same number from his forearm stenciled on the left side of his shirt. The whole process was one of herding the prisoners in assembly-line fashion like animals, a dehumanizing and degrading experience.

The brothers were sent to Birkenau subcamp, hence the B prefix to their tattoos. At his assigned barracks in *Abschnitt* [Unit] D, Richard saw the wide-open room filled with bunks six levels tall, nearly floor to ceiling, each scattered with a bit of lice-infested straw. The building housed about 300 prisoners. The barracks had no windows. Instead, it had a swinging-gate-like opening. Richard could hear the buzz of the nearby electrified fences. Each prisoner was given a single blanket, the custom at Auschwitz, but no sheets or pillow. Every morning began with an Appell formation for accountability before going out on their daily work detail. Should someone die during the night – a frequent occurrence – the body had to be accounted for as well, and fellow prisoners were forced to bring the lifeless form to the *Appell*. Roll call accountability was achieved through the calling out of each prisoner's tattooed number. The prisoners were nameless to the SS guards and Jewish *kapos*. Richard recalled: "I did not have time to pray. Did not have time to dream. Did not have time to hope. One gray day was just like the other."

Prisoners given authority over this new crop of Jewish prisoners, Richard quickly noticed, were assigned triangles [*Vinkel*] affixed to their uniform shirts. Red denoted political prisoners, green signified criminals, and homosexuals were assigned purple triangles. To preserve their own lives, many of the prisoners "in charge" were sadistic in their treatment of Jews. In no uncertain terms, they quickly let prisoners in *Abschnitt* D know who was in charge, distributing regular beatings, hurling insults and threats, and showing the prisoners they had the authority to kill them if they wanted.

Hygiene was awful. Prisoners could go to the bathroom only at appointed times; the crude facilities had a long, sitting plank about 50 centimeters wide, running the length of the latrine, with a long ditch underneath. One had to carefully balance, placing one's feet on the ground, half-sitting and half-standing. On occasion, prisoners were so weak they no longer had the strength to hold themselves up and fell into a sewage pit below. Some even drowned there. The smell was unbearably pungent and there was no toilet paper, adding to unsanitary conditions. Water was turned on only five minutes daily; often, prisoners had no time to rinse their bodies or wash their hands after using the toilet.

Meals included morning ersatz coffee, served tepid with no cups; prisoners cupped their hands to receive a couple ounces of filthy coffee, drinking from dirty hands. Lunch consisted of a ladle of soup, piping hot, with no bowls or spoons. The ladle of soup was poured into the hands of the prisoners receiving it, burning their hands in the process. Their choice was to stay hungry and be one step closer to death from starvation or eat a couple of ounces and burn their hands. Some prisoners would go to the end of the line, hoping that there would be soup left and that it would be a bit cooler by then. However, those at the end were beaten and forced to move to the front. Many were unable to contain the boiling soup in their hands and it spilled to the ground.

Regularly, prisoners would die overnight in the barracks. The surviving prisoners were required to check each morning for the recently deceased, placing the emaciated bodies on carts located outside the barracks so the number of dead could be recorded.

Failure to place the dead on the carts resulted in beatings of the rest of the barracks' prisoners. They also had to strip the dead of clothing, placing the clothes next to the cart, to be used by the next trainload of prisoners. For those who survived each night, there were periodic selections to eliminate the weak who were no longer useful for slave labor. At other times, selections were merely random, with every third or every fifth person chosen for the gas chamber. The first time there was a selection in Richard's barracks, the *kapo* announced: "Some of you will go through the chimney. Be happy!" They were told that they would all be selected within three to six months after arrival, if not sooner. Each day brought the dread that it could be their last on earth.

Some of the more religiously devout Jewish prisoners would quietly and secretly pray in the corner of the barracks for the dead as well as for the living. Many, including Richard, felt like G-d had abandoned them and that sooner or later they would die. Regardless, they all grieved for themselves as well as for those family members, friends, and neighbors who had already perished.

At one point during Richard's time there, he noticed a new group of Russian prisoners. By all appearances, they were starving and malnourished. "They were not only emaciated," Richard wrote later, "but they walked in a kind of methodical, robotic-like step, bent forward." Much as with a previous group of starving Poles, Richard was determined to help. One night, under the cover of darkness, he sneaked out of his barracks and crawled under the barbed wire surrounding a small building where food was stored. He was only a tad over five feet tall then and small enough to attempt the maneuver. He was able to break into the building and steal quite a bit of food, which he gave to the starving Russian prisoners. His unselfish act of bravery helped save their lives – and then his own.

A couple of weeks later – it was now October 1944 – Richard was selected in a morning *Appell* for execution in the gas chamber. As he was being marched toward his death sentence, the Russian prisoners he had helped were on a nearby work detail, recognized Richard, and realized what was happening. Several of them quickly caused a commotion and drew the attention of the guards away from the group for a few moments while a couple of the Soviet prisoners whispered for him to quickly walk by them. It was just enough time to let the quick-thinking Richard hide behind a cart, rip off his shirt, and exchange it for one from a nearby dead political prisoner while hiding his own under a bale of hay. He then emerged with the Russian prisoners on their work detail and his life was miraculously spared, at least for the moment.

Richard now had to decide how to not stand out among these prisoners in different uniforms and to reenter his barracks without being caught. For the rest of the day, he hid behind a barracks; when dusk fell, he climbed atop another barracks and lay down, hiding on the roof. After a while, silently from the rooftop, Richard noticed an adjacent chimney with smoke and ashes pouring out of it. He realized that he was hiding on the roof of one of the barracks and the ashes were from burning bodies.

Because of the shirt switch, for the rest of his time at Auschwitz, he wore a dead man's shirt marking him not as a Jewish prisoner with the yellow Star of David patch on his breast pocket but with a red triangle identifying him as a political prisoner, with a different number than the one tattooed on his forearm. The quick-thinking Russians had saved his life, and the new shirt increased his chances of continued survival for a while because the murder rate for political prisoners was somewhat lower than for the Jews.

Richard was interned at Auschwitz-Birkenau for 18 months. He and Zygmunt then were both "resettled" and told they were being moved to a German camp to help with the war effort. They essentially volunteered for the transfer, which was a great risk, because they didn't know if they were being sent directly to the gas chambers or truly being sent to work. However, they both knew their life expectancy was near its end if they stayed at Auschwitz. Richard and Zygmunt, along with 75 other volunteers, were loaded on the backs of trucks and driven west into Germany to an unknown destination and fate.

After a day's journey, the trucks rolled to a stop. Looking out the back of the vehicle, Richard saw a sign bearing the notorious words "*Konzentrationslager* Dachau." Dachau concentration camp was just northwest of Munich and about 600 kilometers southeast of Auschwitz. He and his comrades didn't know what to expect other than that it could be no worse than Auschwitz. Forced off the trucks and marched into the camp, they saw that the place looked barren, devoid of trees and grass. There was only white crushed gravel on the road and the white-and-blue striped uniforms of the prisoners, as in Auschwitz-Birkenau. Richard and the others were marched into a quarantine barracks. The building was dark and isolated from much of the rest of the camp. They waited for hours, well into the night. Richard wondered what their fate would be.

Richard spent only three days in Dachau's quarantine barracks when he was moved yet again, this time about 50 kilometers northeast. Backroads truck travel proved slow going. After several hours, they arrived at the Kaufering subcamp in Landsberg. It had dark, damp, earthen barracks with packed mud floors. Rations were even more meager than at Auschwitz and Dachau. Work was in a cave about three kilometers from the bleak barracks. The starving prisoners performed backbreaking manual labor in a quarry of sorts, carrying 50-pound bags of cement on their backs all day. Dozens of prisoners died each day from the exhausting work. One prisoner told Richard that life expectancy there ran about four to six weeks, no more.

After a few days, Richard's complete exhaustion and desperate hunger were worse than ever; he felt as if his demise was close at hand. He was desperate. One night, he stole bread from a good friend. The moral ambiguity that descended upon him that had prompted such an impetuous act haunted him for the rest of his life. On the one hand, he had risked his life several times to help prisoners starving even more than he was, yet he stole bread and endangered the survival of a beloved friend, Capus. Such ambiguity was, in some ways, part of the sinister Nazi scheme to dehumanize their victims, depriving these tormented souls of all righteousness and dignity. In the end, the Nazis' intentions, particularly in Richard's case, were thwarted.

After a month at Kaufering, still haunted by the demons that goaded him into deception, Richard devised a plan to steal food from the SS commissary. Under cover of night, he placed boards from his bunk over electric fencing, sneaked into the commissary, stole six loaves of fresh bread, and smuggled them into his barracks. He distributed the bread evenly among the prisoners while they were sleeping except for the friend from whom he had stolen – for Capus, he left a double portion. Most never knew to whom they owed their good fortune, and Richard never revealed his secret as their savior. For the next six weeks, Richard went repeatedly to the SS commissary to steal more bread and secretly distribute it. Finally, he confessed to Capus that he had stolen his bread, demonstrated sincere repentance and begged for forgiveness. Capus realized that it was Richard who was stealing bread and distributing it to others and forgave him. Despite his momentary lapse of judgment and compassion, Richard revealed the true decency of his character by repeatedly risking his own life to steal food for others. His courage provided physical sustenance to help save the lives of many, and his heroic acts gave equally important hope to his fellow prisoners.

One Sunday in early 1945, they were moved again, to nearby Augsburg and the Messerschmitt Werke, a forced-labor camp where he and the other prisoners helped build military planes for the Luftwaffe at a privately owned aircraft manufacturing corporation. The work camp held a conglomeration of Jews and other concentration camp slave laborers, prisoners of war from various European nations, and civilian workers – a grouping vastly different from Plaszow I and II, Auschwitz-Birkenau, Dachau, and Kaufering. Their quarters were huge aircraft hangars lined with bunks six levels high. A young prisoner, who had been there for six months, told the new folks they "don't beat you here, don't shoot you here, and there's no crematorium, but we are dying anyway from hunger, from work detail, and from dirt." He said young, strong men were often used on a bomb removal squad and might live two to three months.

Richard worked as a slave laborer at the factory for several months, making parts for the aircraft rather than working on the bomb removal squad. He and others at the Messerschmitt Werke were marched almost four kilometers each morning, then transported by train to the factory, repeating the journey in reverse in the evening back to their barracks. In between were 12-hour work shifts. His day began with reveille at four each morning. Richard and some other workers found ways to covertly sabotage their work from time to time, another small defiance of their Nazi captors. It was a pattern that Richard followed in each camp he had been in, which boosted his morale. He felt that with each act of resistance, in small ways, he was maintaining his humanity.

Life continued to be grueling and painful for Richard and his fellow prisoners. They were filthy, covered with lice, physically exhausted, extraordinarily hungry, and malnourished. Some prisoners had even resorted to eating rats. Finally, some hope began to emerge when they heard and then saw American planes flying over the camp. Perhaps victory for the Allies was going to be a reality and, with it, liberation for Richard and the others, if they could just survive a little longer.

Realizing the war was coming to an end and defeat imminent, the camp's now-fearful SS hierarchy and guards evacuated the place and forced prisoners, in units of 500, to march 50 kilometers or so back toward Dachau. It was April 1945. Each group was accompanied by 60 well-armed SS guards and about ten vicious dogs. The prisoners were weak, barely able to walk, with no idea where they were going. Another camp? To an execution? To the gas chambers? How far would their feeble bodies be forced to walk? Would they have the stamina to survive their march?

Weaker prisoners began to fall behind, and the dogs ripped into their flesh. Exhaustion forbade words spoken; all grew weaker with each step. Zygmunt began to wobble badly, unable to continue. Richard, weak and exhausted himself, picked up his older brother and carried him on his back. As the Allies encircled Nazi-held Europe, the crumbling Reich began trying to erase evidence of the camps and the insanity and inhumanity within whenever and wherever they could. Richard's group was herded into a long march into a western German forest. Having survived several brushes with near-execution, Richard and Zygmunt were forced on a death march from the subcamp adjacent to the Messerschmitt Werke in April 1945 in what they thought might be their certain demise. That was the design – to kill prisoners through sheer exertion. Those who survived the march were led into a clearing in the woods near Klimach, where they were to be murdered.

They arrived at a mass gravesite on May 7, 1945. While the Germans at the execution field waited for a kill order, American pilots flying reconnaissance flights overhead noticed something amiss in the forest below and communicated a request for a squadron of tanks to investigate. A US bomber squadron flying over the area spotted the execution field, popped some smoke, and alerted a nearby tank destroyer unit of the situation. When the formidable machines broke through, chaos erupted. The US Army unit (part of the Rainbow Division) rolled up on the site and saved concentration camp survivors from apparently certain executions. This was the day that Germany surrendered to the Allies.

The Dogface Soldiers – a nickname given to US Army infantrymen – urged the prisoners to run to safety. Instead, the 500 abused, tortured, humiliated, and starved Jewish and Soviet camp escapees charged the Germans en masse. At one point, Richard, still carrying his nearly dead, emaciated brother on his back, came face to face with a German officer. An American soldier, a sergeant, tossed him a machine gun, pointed it at the enemy officer, and told him to shoot the guy. Richard later recounted, "I said to myself, 'Ah, this is my chance. This is when I'm going to get rid of my whole anger and hatred.' I grabbed the gun. I see the German's eyes get glassy. I could see fear in his eyes." In a panicked voice the SS officer yelled for Richard not to shoot. Richard thirsted for revenge, his blood boiling with hate, wanting to kill the bastard who represented those who had killed his mother and father and so many more of his family and friends. He deserved to be shot, Richard insisted to himself, and now was his chance.

After a moment of reflection, as a plethora of emotions erupted inside him, he refused to take vengeance beyond running up to the German and hitting him across the face with the machine gun, knocking him to the ground. Richard then handed the machine gun back to the American soldier and said, "Thank you, but I'm not going to do what they did." "That was my decision. It was a moment of epiphany, so to speak. I became a human being again. I had risen above my hate." Later in life, Richard often pondered whether he should have taken revenge, but he stayed on the higher moral ground that he was not like the Nazis, no matter what this soldier may have deserved. "I used my conscience. ... I didn't stay. I spat on him. But I didn't shoot him."

Richard was finally free. As he wandered Bavarian forests and fields between Dachau and Landsberg, with no money, clothes, or possessions of any sort, he and several other survivors found an abandoned wagon. They loaded it with whatever useful things they found along the road, including semi-frozen, half-rotten potatoes. They dug the tubers from the ground and cooked them in a discarded pot. Richard and Zygmunt reunited and wound up in the small Bavarian village of Birkach. At this point, it was Zygmunt's turn to come down with typhus, but like Richard earlier, he recovered.

Richard was only 17 when he was liberated – he spent all his teen years until then in hiding in ghettos and concentration camps. Robbed of his adolescence, he had endured unspeakable vicissitudes including losing both his parents, burying his own father in a makeshift concentration camp grave, and being just one of six members of his extended family of 55 to survive. Now, he suddenly had to think about his future.

His first instinct was to nearly explode with anger. He had demonstrated exceptional restraint when he resisted a chance to shoot a Nazi guard, but he now tried to come to terms emotionally with his newly won freedom. Soon after liberation, he said, he found a German Luger revolver by the road, grabbed it, and went to "the first nice house and I said [to the owner], 'I am going to do to you what your brothers did to me in Kraków, Poland. I'm requisitioning this house and you are going to feed me the best food, and you're gonna clean me and you're gonna serve me, and I'm gonna live here as long as I want.'" He then placed his pistol at the homeowner's head and shouted, "You tell me 'No,' and I'll just as soon kill you because I got it in for you. You make one wrong move and your whole family's gonna die." It was for Richard, still a child but forced to be a man beyond his years, what he called "a small measure of revenge."

After two weeks in the Birkach farmhouse, Zygmunt's typhus returned. Richard took him to Augsburg – 38 kilometers away – to get him in a hospital. There was no hospital, though. He met nuns who cared for refugee patients in a convent. The German Catholic sisters agreed to take Zygmunt in; under their tender care, he was slowly restored to health.

Soon after liberation, Richard joined the Polish Guard with the ambition of returning to his beloved homeland. Regrettably, the Communist Party had already made significant advances and taken control of the Polish government. Richard joined his unit on a train supposedly bound for Poland, yet it became apparent at some point in the passage that the Soviet Union was the intended destination. Needing to react quickly and avert yet another imprisonment and perhaps even death, in an act of courage that had become part of the fabric of this teenager's life, he and several others jumped off the rapidly moving train. Those remaining aboard were likely executed once they reached the Soviet Union. Richard had yet again defied the odds and escaped death. He returned to the newly established American military base in Germany from whence he had come, comforted by temporary security and relief. From there, in 1947, Richard and Zygmunt were authorized to emigrate to the United States. Soon they were America-bound.

Not long after he arrived in the United States, Richard joined the US Army; he was a newly minted American immigrant proud to be free in his new home. Grateful, he wanted to repay this miracle by serving his adopted country, and he did so with pride. He served honorably for several years, including an assignment in Augsburg, just 50 kilometers from the former Dachau concentration camp.

In 1952, he returned to the United States and began his college education. He had been in ghettos and concentration camps in his middle and high school years and had a considerable academic deficit to overcome. Because of his keen intellect and his tenacity to succeed, he was able to thrive in the university environment. To help support himself while enrolled at the University of Rhode Island, he worked several assorted jobs. One summer, he was a cook in Old Orchard Beach, Maine. That is where he met the love of his life, his future wife, Katharine Oliver. He eagerly returned to the same job the next summer, in 1954, and proposed. Soon, Richard and Katharine were married. He continued his education, earning a bachelor's degree from Rhode Island in 1956, the same year they welcomed their first child, a daughter, Karen. Richard, with Katharine and Karen at his side, kept hitting the books, earning a master's degree in social work from Simmons College in 1958. A second child, son Mark, was born in 1960. The family moved from New England to Iowa, where Richard began his psychiatric social worker career.

As Richard Friedemann carved out his new life in the United States with his wife and two children and embarked on a distinguished career, he did his best to put the past behind him. Not wanting to burden his children, he spoke little about his past. He gave few details of his devastating experiences in the ghetto and camps and never even told them of his Jewishness. Richard had converted to Roman Catholicism shortly after the war and he and Katharine (called Kay) raised their children as Catholics. Richard had experienced a rather mystical and powerful interaction in concentration camps. While imprisoned at Auschwitz-Birkenau, he was for a time in an isolation cell. There, he heard a voice from the next cell, giving him words of encouragement and faith. The incident had a profound impact on Richard. Later, imprisoned in a similar cell at Dachau, he heard what seemed like the same voice, saying nearly identical words of encouragement, coming from the adjacent cell. Stunned and emotionally moved, Richard responded to the unknown voice, asking the identity of the mysterious person – and if he had also been at Auschwitz. It was a Catholic priest, Father Harte, who had indeed been the same voice speaking to him at Auschwitz. The experience was a catalyst for Richard to convert to Catholicism. There were other deeply felt reasons for Richard to convert and not reveal his ethnic and religious heritage to his children. "I'll admit that maybe this is the one sick part of me. And the reason I didn't do it [tell his children], I decided I'm getting into America for one particular reason, not to get food [but] to get freedom, and to never allow anybody [to] do to me what happened: deprive me of my parents ... deprive me of my wealth, deprive me of my freedom, and maybe warp me in a way that I don't even know I'm warped. Consequently, I swore to myself that I will not reveal my background to my children because, you see, when Germans captured Jews who were hiding, one of the things they did, they took their pants down. In Europe, in those days, the very mark of Judaic condition was your physiological sign. That's number one. Number two, they tortured some people even if they wouldn't be circumcised – if they had suspicion, they would torture you, and if they had any inkling if they were Jews, they were killed. I would not allow my children to be Jewish."

Richard had a great fear that history would repeat itself. He wanted to protect his family from discrimination due to their religion or culture. Despite an earlier conversion to Catholicism, he had no partiality to any specific religion; he was ecumenical and assimilated. For a period after the Holocaust, he lost all religious faith and even doubted G-d's existence, but, over time, he returned to a belief.

Richard lived a long and flourishing life in the United States. He was devoutly committed to his life's work as a psychiatric social worker, where he exhibited tenderhearted and compassionate sympathy, and, he said, helped "too many to count." He was a loving husband and father who deeply cherished his family, thankful that after losing most of his first family, he had one of his own to treasure. Always a storyteller, he made up tales for his children at bedtime like "Jonathan the Brave" and "Peppi the Pirate," though he shared none of the horrific truths of his teen years. As his parents had done for him, Richard exposed his family to art, music, culture, and travel. He took them on countless vacations throughout his adopted homeland, visiting nearly every state in America. He had grown up with a love of the arts; he was able to pass it along to his children. Not only was he zealous for fine art, but he also had a passion for traditional Polish folk music along with classic rock and roll. Wanting to do his small part in breaking down barriers of national, ethnic, and cultural blindness, he and Katharine invited into their home a plethora of foreign exchange students, showering them with hospitality and warmth, modeling this attitude to their own children. More than anything else, having lost his entire family except for his brother Zygmunt, Richard adored and cherished his family.

Richard stayed silent regarding his painful past to his children until 1996, when they were well into their thirties and he was approaching 70, half a century after his liberation and the end of the Holocaust. It was only then that he finally told his two children, Mark and Karen, the secrets he had hidden from them their entire lives, the "terrible history of his early life," and what the Nazis had stolen from him. And it was only then that he revealed to them that he was born a Jew.

Richard was not even 12 years old when the Nazis tore apart his family and his life. His parents, along with most of his extended family, were brutally murdered and he was left an orphan. Time and again, he narrowly escaped death himself as he witnessed the atrocities while surviving a death camp and five concentration camps. He lost his family, his country, his material possessions, and his identity. Finally, in 1996, he was prepared to overcome another significant obstacle in his life: sharing his past.

That year, Richard along with his son Mark, returned to his homeland in Kraków to reclaim one of the only remaining legacies of his childhood – his childhood home, the grand house where Leon and Lilla Friedmann had raised their boys, the home stolen from them by the Nazis during the Holocaust and, after the war, taken by the Polish communist government. Richard had begun quietly trying to regain his family home in the early 1960s, initiating a legal battle that would last for decades, one that he did not share with his children. Finally, after more than three decades of quiet legal efforts to win back his home in Poland, he succeeded. During the trip with Mark back to Poland to reclaim the property, Richard revealed the terrible history of his early life. In addition to his own history, Richard also introduced Mark to several old and new Polish friends, along with Polish culture itself. This was also the first year he spoke to my Holocaust Studies class in Jacksonville. He was on a quest to remain silent no more but to share with the next generation the tragedy of the Holocaust while also humbly revealing stories of courage, resilience, and hope amid adversity.

Richard and his wife had moved from Iowa to Florida in 1984, living in the Jacksonville area until 2016. During his three decades in Jacksonville, he was a member of the Polish-American Club and cherished his time socializing with his fellow Poles. He truly loved his adopted American homeland but continued to be a patriot of his nation of birth, Poland. At the age of 89, in 2016, he moved to Tallahassee to live with Mark, as his beloved Kay had developed dementia and was becoming too challenging to care for her by himself. Richard and his children returned to Poland one last time in 2018 for the publication of his autobiography in Polish titled *One of Many.* He continued the hard work of restoring the family home.

Richard spoke to my classes four times between 1996 and 1999. The first time he spoke, as he described in detail his life during the Holocaust from ages 11 to 17, there was a mysterious brown-paper bag on the floor next to him. At its conclusion, he silently opened the bag, pulling out the striped camp uniform he wore the day he was liberated from Dachau. Saying nothing, he put the concentration camp shirt on over his dress shirt. Students in the packed classroom grew eerily silent, many with tears quietly streaming down their cheeks. Richard's eyes, too, glazed over, his tears barely visible, as he stared straight ahead, unable or unwilling to make eye contact with anyone. A single tear rolled down his face as he recalled life in hiding in the ghetto, Plaszow I and II, Auschwitz-Birkenau, Dachau, slave labor factories, and death marches, the family he lost, and his adolescent years – unlike those of the teens peering at him – brutally taken from him by the Nazis.

After his first visit and testimony, however, whenever he came to speak to my students, he spoke not of his personal testimony; rather, he gave a third-person narrative of Holocaust history. Never again did he bring his camp uniform with him. It was too painful. Yet he did emphasize, over and over, that the family he was able to have in the United States was a wonderful testimony to redemption and that he was privileged to live and raise a family in the "greatest country in the world!" They tried, but the Nazis could not erase Richard Friedemann's life and progeny. While over 50 family members were murdered at the hands of the Nazis, Richard – along with his brother Zygmunt – survived to live long and vibrant lives and start their families anew.

Richard Friedemann passed away on August 20, 2019, at age 91 – 74 years after his liberation; his beloved wife, Kay, died two years later in July 2021. He remained in good health until shortly before he died, and in his final years, he was committed to sharing his story with schoolchildren and other groups. He was interviewed by the media several times and made more trips back to Poland. The Nazis robbed him of his family and his teen years, and he endured what no one, much less a teenager, should ever have to endure. Yet they could not take from him his great intellect, vitality, sense of humor, exuberant love of life, and love of the family he was able to enjoy in his new home, the United States. Richard was focused on family until the day he died. The Nazis could not take away his joy or his soul. For so many years, he hid the pain of his past from his family to protect them, never wanting them to worry. While they learned much about him in his life's final decades, some things he never shared. They discovered them only after he passed. His son, Mark, wrote upon his death: "He is my father, the greatest man I ever knew. My love for you continues on, boundless."[2]

Richard and Zygmunt Friedemann before the Nazis invaded Poland

Richard Friedemann's Identity Card

Richard and Katharine Friedemann on their wedding day

Richard Friedemann's concentration camp uniform, with its red triangle sewn on – indicating that he was a political prisoner, like the Russians in the camp. Technically, he wasn't, – but that little piece of cloth probably saved his life several times over.

*Richard Friedemann, as he looked while serving in the US Army
soon after coming to America*

Richard Friedemann as an American soldier in the Korean War

The iron sign above the gates to Auschwitz-Birkenau Camp, which translates to "Work Will Set You Free." Photo taken by the author, July 1995

5

ROSE MIBAB GOLDBERG
WŁOCŁAWEK (LUDMIR), POLAND

Rose Mibab Goldberg, 1990s, Jacksonville, FL.

I met Rose Goldberg in about 1996 when she was in her early seventies. She was a soft-spoken, dignified, and kind woman who had never spoken publicly to a large group about her experiences in the Holocaust. She was reticent to accept my invitation to speak but eventually agreed only if she could come with her good friend, Leona Krohn, also a Polish Holocaust survivor living in

Jacksonville. Leona and her daughter, Irene Jaffa, cajoled Rose to come with them to my class and share her powerful story.

She did so quietly and humbly, declining to focus on her acts of bravery and heroism yet sharing the still-painful details of hiding from the Nazis. Rose spoke just once to my class and, to my understanding, it was one of the very few public testimonies – if not the only one. She was petite, just under five feet tall; her size and modest tone, though, belied her strength of character and resilience. I remember her as a remarkable woman who exhibited unbelievable courage and moral strength during the Holocaust when the Nazis tried to take her life and that of her family. She lived a life of quiet, self-effacing moral courage for another 75 years after that, both physically strong and morally righteous.

Rose "Roza" Mibab Goldberg was born on December 5, 1923, to Chaya Katov Mibab and Chaim Mibab in Włodzimierz-Wołyński, Poland, known in Yiddish as Ludmir. After World War II, the eastern Polish city became part of Ukraine.

When the German military quickly defeated Poland in September 1939, it immediately began pogroms against the Jewish population, spreading the evil of the Holocaust. Rose was one of just 100 or so from her hometown of Ludmir to survive – more than 20,000 Ludmir Jews were murdered by the Nazis during more than five years of occupation. As a teenager and young adult, Rose saw several members of her own family murdered; bravely, she saved other relatives by helping them find hiding places, eventually living underground for months on end in a series of what were essentially holes in the ground. She described them as comparable to a septic tank. The quality of air was certainly an issue: Rose and her family had to share a pipe to get outside air.

Ludmir had enjoyed a long history of having a significant and vibrant Jewish population before the war. By 1937, 11,554 Jews were living in Ludmir, or about 45 percent of the city's population of nearly 25,000. Within three years, with the start of World War II,

Jewish refugees arriving in the area swelled their ranks to about 30,000.

The Jewish impact, however, had been felt for nearly 1,000 years. The town had a vacillating history as part of various Polish and Ukrainian kingdoms, Poland proper, Ukraine proper, the Austrian-Hungarian Empire, German occupation, and the Soviet Union. Nestled along the banks of the Luha River, it is one of the oldest towns in the region of Volhynia. Jews established a viable presence almost from the beginning, though periodically in the late Middle Ages they were expelled, only to return when more lenient, enlightened rulers favored them. By the first decades of the 20th century, the Jews had long held a significant minority population, ranging from one-third to one-half of the town's total. Jews were active in many trades and occupations and contributed much to their religious community – by the 1920s and '30s, there were about 20 synagogues. Ludmir's Jewish community also had a long tradition of education, formed over many centuries, and closely linked to their devout spirituality.

It was in this period that Rose was born, the fourth of seven children, all of whom had a warm, loving childhood, in a close-knit family, centered on Jewish religion and tradition. She was raised as an Orthodox Jew. She recalled an idyllic home filled with love and food – altogether a blissful life. Rose's brother, Moishe, nine years older, was born in 1914; brother Bentzi in 1917; sister Ruchel, a year older than Rose, in 1922; brother Herschel in 1928; brother Reuven in 1932; and the youngest, Peretz (Perry), a decade younger, in 1932.

As an adult, Rose reminisced about the pleasant aromas encircling her mother, Chaya, in her kitchen. She seemed to continually bake challah and traditional treats such as mandel bread, Danish, and babka. As a young girl, Rose loved playing games with chestnuts, making ragdolls, and bringing food to her beloved grandmother before Shabbos. The Mibab family lived a comfortable middle-class lifestyle. Rose's father owned two small millinery factories, and Rose loved helping there. Chaim, a hard-working, dedicated business owner, often came home late at night after a long day at work. Rose remembered her mother as a beautiful woman who dressed elegantly and generously helped her husband at work. The family business was a central part of family life. Chaya had a soft spot in her heart for aiding orphans; one way she did so was to help them find marriage partners. She often raised funds for weddings they could ill afford on their own.

Life would change dramatically for Rose and the large Mibab family when, on September 1, 1939, the Nazis invaded Poland and within days attacked Ludmir. The city was devastated by the bombing, which destroyed numerous homes and businesses and killed many residents. Two years of insecurity followed, as did a gradual institution of antisemitic laws and policies; the large Jewish population of Ludmir and surrounding areas wondered about their future. Rose, just a teenager, realized life was tenuous; a war was being fought all over Europe and Jews were targeted as an unwelcome race in the expanding Nazi regime. The Nazis officially began the occupation of Ludmir on June 23, 1941; upon this now-permanent status, a new brutal order descended on the city. Any violation of the German decrees was punishable by death. The Holocaust had begun in full force and a terrible darkness came over Ludmir and its environs, bringing destruction, forced labor, imprisonment, and death.

Upon occupying the town, Nazis formed a police force of local Poles and Ukrainians. Jews were not allowed on it – they were the main target of its pursuits. The persecution of Ludmir's Jews was in full force. There were only about a dozen German Gestapo officers in Ludmir, but due to the ruthless assistance of the newly created police force, those few were enough to control the 20,000 or more Jews still in the city. About 100 Ukrainian policemen enthusiastically volunteered to do much of the Gestapo's dirty assignments. Before the war, most Ukrainians were poor, minority outsiders; with the occupation, they had ample food, comforts, and assigned weapons, which they used freely to beat and torture Jews at every opportunity.

In the fall of 1941, two years after the initial invasion, Nazis forced the Jews of Ludmir into a ghetto. Like so many other cities in Eastern Europe taken over by the Third Reich, the ghetto was created specifically for imprisoning Jews in a holding station of sorts until their fates were determined. The ghettos allowed the Nazis to isolate, control, and humiliate the Jewish people of Eastern Europe. The Ludmir Ghetto area was carved out of the commercial district, enclosed by barbed wire, and bordered by the Luha River. The Mibab family was fortunate – one of their millinery businesses was inside the newly created ghetto, so they had their own quarters, so to speak. Despite staying in the shop, the family's living conditions were extraordinarily crowded and dismal. Sixteen people slept on straw mattresses in a single room.

Rose, by then nearly 18, was still healthy and strong, so she was forced into labor, working long hours every day digging up potatoes in the frozen fields, carrying human waste outside the ghetto, and cleaning the homes of the local Nazi administration. Her "payment" for a full day's work was a cup of watery soup. On several occasions, soldiers put a gun to her head and threatened to kill her, yet each time she was able to escape the death threats, frantically running away to safety.

By April 1942, all Jews in the vicinity had been successfully forced to move inside the ghetto. It was then locked from the outside on May 1. The ghetto was surrounded by a barbed wire enclosure ten feet tall [three meters] and the perimeter was constantly guarded by police. Jews from surrounding villages, along with Jewish refugees from western Poland seeking safety in the Soviet-occupied zone, were also rounded up and imprisoned there. The ghetto became home to around 22,000 Jews.

In May, the ghetto was split into two sections: one for those who could labor for the German cause, the other – children, elderly, the sick, the weak – for those whose fate was the gas chambers in death camps. The Nazis were establishing efficiency in the process of the Final Solution – the annihilation of all Jews in Nazi-occupied

Europe, a number close to nine million at the start of the war. The lives of those in the Ludmir Ghetto were appalling. The dense concentration of people in a small area made for crowded conditions; they suffered starvation and winter's freezing cold.

When Rose was growing up, before the Nazi occupation and the creation of the ghetto, one of the Mibab shops had been located close to the family business of Carl "Kisel" Goldberg, who was 11 years older than her. By the time of the Nazi invasion, Carl was married with a toddler daughter. The teenage Rose often cared for his daughter and other small children in town. During the invasion of Poland, Luftwaffe bombs killed Carl's wife and young daughter. For days, he rummaged through the rubble of the destroyed building, unsuccessfully searching for their remains. By the time the ghetto formed two years later, Carl was sad and alone. He sought to rekindle a friendship with the Mibabs. Not only had he lost his wife and young child, but his mother had also died and his only sister had fled to Palestine. Two of his ghetto responsibilities were to care for the German soldiers' horses and translate – he spoke seven languages fluently. Sometimes, Carl stopped by the Mibabs with extra rations of bread he procured due to these jobs. The relationships between the family and the lonely young man were rekindled.

One day, weak from lack of food, Carl fell ill. By then, Rose had grown into a young lady of 17, kind and beautiful. She began tending to the 28-year-old Carl, taking him soup that her mother made, nursing him back to health, and spending time with him. Though Rose had many young men closer to her age whom she could have chosen as a suitor, Rose realized she was in love with Carl. "He was the only man who could keep me awake." "Find someone closer to your age!" her father scolded. Rose, though, was in love. And she thought, "What's the difference? We won't survive anyway."

In September 1942, the Germans initiated the first of three *aktions* in the Ludmir Ghetto. They were planned operations of systematic killings of Jews or transporting Jews to death camps. The Nazis were intent on murdering millions of ethnic Poles along with the systematic extermination of Polish Jews. The Germans justified these genocides based on the Third Reich's racial theory, which regarded Poles and other Slavic peoples as racially inferior [*Untermenschen*] and regarded Jews as racially as the nadir of its so-called racial order, that is, subhuman. These theories depicted the Jewish people as a constant threat to the "Aryan" way of life. By 1942, Nazi Germany was implementing its murderous plans. Ultimately, close to three million Polish Jews, along with more than two million non-Jewish ethnic Poles, were murdered in just a few years' time.

In the Ludmir Ghetto, Rose recalled, 18,000 Jews were killed in the first *aktion*. Rose, spared for the moment, was put to work sorting the clothes of the dead. Soon, another mass roundup and killing spree occurred – this time, 2,000 more Jews died, including Rose's brother Bentzi and sister Ruchel. Rose, Carl, and Rose's younger brother, Reuven, narrowly escaped death by hiding themselves in an attic. Carl, afraid his father and three brothers had been killed, was distraught, particularly since he had already lost his wife and child at the ruinous hands of the Nazis. Rose, in an act of bravery to comfort the man she loved, risked her life running to find Carl's family. Sadly, she discovered Carl's nightmare was indeed true. They were dead.

In July 1942, the Nazis created a 12-man Jewish city council, or *Judenrat*, in Ludmir to put into practice a few ludicrous decrees. Being selected to be on the council, often by force, was an intentionally sadistic assignment – another way the Germans tried to dehumanize the Jews. In September 1942, when the first *aktion* was being carried out, a member of the *Judenrat*, along with his wife and 13-year-old son, committed suicide together when the German occupiers demanded that he assemble 7,000 Jews for deportation and their ultimate murder. Unable and unwilling to decide who should live and who should die, he refused to be responsible for sending fellow Jews to certain death. Later that month, most Judenrat members were shot and killed by the Gestapo. The council was then led by a single surviving member after a new council was created.

In the early winter of 1943, in the second *aktion*, Rose's oldest brother, Moishe, was shot and killed, leaving behind his young wife, Yenta, and their baby, Esther. By year's end, in December 1943, the Nazis declared Ludmir must be *Judenrein* – free from all Jewish life. By then, it was impossible to hide the fact that huge numbers of Jews were being killed; in fact, it was hard to see any Jews in the area. People began to create hiding spots, hoping to save their children and, if possible, themselves.

Rose's father earlier had the foresight to make a hiding place in the ghetto. He dug a large hole, making its entrance resemble a septic tank. He built several more hiding places outside the ghetto walls, too, and paid some former work associates, all Polish Gentiles, to help hide his family. These secret spots were made up of a series of tunnels and pits, "living graves" in the ground under buildings, barns, and structures within and outside ghetto walls. Regrettably, it was not enough to save his own life – he was killed, along with Rose's 14-year-old brother Herschel, in the Judenrein raid, as he prayed with a group of men in a concealed, makeshift synagogue that the Nazis bombed.

When the Gestapo came to search the Mibab family's small room in which they had been living, they found Rose's sister-in-law, Yenta, and shot her. While her life was brutally cut short, her murder spared her the horrors of a concentration camp. Rose, hiding under a straw mattress, was not found. The soldiers left and she started to run undetected to the ghetto hideout, the "living grave" septic tank hole in the ground. However, on the way there, she discovered her 18-month-old niece, Esther, alive in the corner of a shack, confused and frightened. Rose's sister-in-law had left her there, praying that a kindly Pole would find her and keep her safe. Rose knew that if she didn't take Esther with her, the little girl would certainly be killed. She didn't hesitate – she grabbed the child and ran to the hideout.

When Rose arrived there were already quite a few people inside. Her uncle refused to let them in because he and the others insisted that the toddler would cry, revealing their safe place and getting them all killed. Rose quickly snapped back, "If you do not let me in, we will *all* get killed!" He reluctantly let them in, but only after Rose promised to vacate the hole, with Esther, the next day. Her younger brother, ten-year-old Reuven, and three-year-old cousin, Chaike, also succeeded in getting to the sanctuary within a few days. Her mother and eight-year-old brother, Peretz, however, were picked up by the Nazis. Somehow, Peretz was able to escape; fortuitously, he pulled his mother into a cobbler's shack on the side of the road, where they hid, narrowly eluding deportation to a death camp.

At midnight the next night, Rose, accompanied by Esther, Chaike, younger cousin Sima, and Reuven, left the secret haven as promised and knocked on the door of a Polish woman, Wanda, who had been one of her father's employees. Wanda's father was a Polish police officer, so letting them stay with her would be extraordinarily risky. Fearlessly, she allowed them to temporarily hide in her potato cellar. Sitting on mounds of cold, damp potatoes with her mother and Peretz, who had found them there, they spent the day and the next night down in the cellar. Though Chaya had survived, she was devastated by the loss of her husband and four of her seven children and had little emotional strength left. Rose, at 17 the oldest of three surviving children, was forced into the position of family leader, seeking out places where they could stay – ones that let children in, out of the cruel Nazis' sight. They found temporary shelter underground beneath a latrine but then went back to Wanda's potato cellar. Wanda was trying to find another hiding spot for them and was frightened to let them stay any longer, so Rose traveled alone to the next safe place. It was on Mietek Schimitzky's land; he was a Polish farmer. She needed to be certain he was still willing to allow them on his property. Earlier, Rose's father had paid Mietek so he could dig another "living grave" on the Christian man's land. Rose walked six or seven miles through waist-deep snow, wearing nothing but boots, a nightgown, and a light jacket, to Mr. Schimitzky's farm. She recalled much later that she did not know how she found his home in the dark and deep snow, but by providence, she found the right farm. When she arrived at the farmhouse in the village of Usefin, Rose pleaded with Schimitzky and ultimately gave him everything she possessed to try to persuade him to let them stay.

As soon as she and the band of children were let inside, she lay down on the bread oven to warm her frozen body. As she sobbed, she convinced him to fulfill his promise despite his sincere fear – who could blame him? – and his family's protests. To minimize the risk, Schimitzky made Rose promise that she would bring only one child each night, so over the next six nights Rose walked the six or seven miles each way, back and forth through the deep snow, to this new hiding place, ferrying the youngsters one at a time. Still really a child herself, she courageously saved surviving family members one by one. A few days later, Carl, who had escaped the ghetto and remembered the hiding site from Chaim's earlier plans, made his way to the farm and hid with Rose and the remaining Mibab family.

The new spot was a hole in the ground beneath a barn that housed the farm's cows and horses. There, deep in a dirt floor, below animals living more freely and eating more food than did the surviving Mibabs, they lived month after month. The oxygen supply was scarce; they could hardly breathe. They couldn't strike a match to light a candle to be able to see. They had a bucket for a toilet, which they couldn't empty until after sunset. They opened the entrance for a little air and, when it was safe, emptied the bucket. When spring came, they were able to get a small pipe that went to the surface so a little air could get into the small, cramped hole in the ground. Sometimes at night, they could crack open a tiny door for a bit of fresher air.

The Mibab family was fortunate to have a farmer like Mietek Schimitzky to provide a safe haven, primitive as it was. Much of the non-Jewish population of Poland did little to help the Jews. Antisemitism had long run deep in Poland, and most Poles looked the other way when the occupying Germans began pogroms against the Jews. However, despite the long history of antisemitic attitudes, the German occupation, and a mortal risk to their lives, a significant number of Ukrainians and Poles did hide Jews who were otherwise doomed to die. These men and women, like the Schimitzky family, were heroes, much like the Polish partisans who fought with weapons in hand, because they were risking not only their own lives but those of their children and families.

One day, after weeks holed up in the barn sanctuary and many months of living cheek to jowl, Rose was unable to take it any longer. She felt so claustrophobic that, at the risk of death, she crawled out of the hiding place in the middle of the day. Not long afterward, a couple of Nazi soldiers happened upon the barn, and the Mibabs hiding below heard their voices and a gunshot. They were sure Rose had been caught and shot. Fortunately, however, Rose had also heard the voices of the German soldiers and managed to find a quick hiding place. As it turned out, the gunshots were to kill one of the farmer's pigs. Soon, the soldiers left, pig in hand, and Rose crawled back to the safety of the secret hole. Her family was ecstatically relieved.

They lived there for almost a year. The farmer and his family left them a bit of food when they could, but often Rose went out in the middle of the night, foraging for food for them all. Days and nights passed slowly, and the year seemed like an eternity. Already hungry, malnourished, and weak when they came to the hiding place, after months in the ghetto and previous hideouts, staying in the hole made them weaker. With little food and little balance in their diet, plus no exercise, limited fresh air, and confinement in a tight underground space in dampness and darkness without sunlight exposure, they had no sense of normalcy. Their bodies grew frailer; their mental health suffered. As the seemingly infinite days passed one after the other, they had no idea when or how their stationary journey might end.

After nearly a year, the family suffered a severe loss. The German military and the Polish resistance began fighting one another in the vicinity and burned down Mr. Schimitzky's barn and farmhouse. The Mibabs and Carl had no choice but to leave; they wandered in nearby forests. They slept on the cold, damp ground and ate little but raw potatoes scrounged from nearby farms at night. Carl chose to leave the Mibabs and worked with Polish partisans so he could get them enough food to survive, which he would sneak to them wherever they were hiding in the forest that day. Ultimately, Carl and the family were separated because his work with the partisans took him farther away. Rose resorted to wandering the forest alone at night to search for food for her family.

The bloody war had persisted for more than five long years. As 1944 slowly began to close, Russian military forces began approaching from the east, slowly but determinedly defeating the German Wehrmacht and liberating the oppressed people, town by town, drawing ever closer to Poland. Rose, nearly 18, along with her mother and the children – two little brothers, a young cousin, and her toddler niece – set out to travel eastward through the forest in the direction of the invading Russians. It was a perilous journey for this traveling caravan, moving on foot through dense and dangerous forest. Hiding from the fleeing German military and cautiously hopeful to find safety with Soviet troops, they made their way. By December, the Mibabs reached the village of Rogisht, occupied by the Russians. Everyone in the group was weak, malnourished, and in poor health. Rose, with a lack of nutrition and months of exposure to the elements, suffered from rotting skin. A Jewish pharmacist-survivor in Rogisht learned of Rose's malady and made a special cream to help heal her skin. Quickly enamored of Rose, recognizing her beauty, courage, and kindness, he asked for her hand in marriage. But despite his affection, she refused. She had promised Carl that if they both survived, she would marry him. Having lost contact, she had no idea where he was or if he was even still alive. Still, she hoped, she dreamed, she prayed. Other suitors in the small village followed, but Rose continued to hold out for the one true love of her life, Carl Goldberg.

At long last, she heard from several people traveling through Rogisht that they had seen Carl alive. Carl, too, learned that Rose was alive, but he had to desert the partisan resistance group to reunite with his love – an act punishable by death. He found Rose but immediately had to go into hiding until it was safe. Though they were alive and had so far survived the long ordeal, they had little to eat. Rose searched through garbage cans to find food for her family and herself. Life was still tenuous and the future far from certain despite their relative safety.

After several weeks, Rose and Carl returned to Ludmir, now occupied by the Russian Army. A Polish family had moved into their home, but when Rose and her family returned, the Poles moved out. The Mibabs moved in, and Carl joined them. They were happy to be back in Ludmir, free from Nazi tyranny and safe in their own home, but it was not the same. The life and vitality, and many family members, were missing, and it was a shell of what it had once been, a house but not a home. Only about 100 had survived in all of city, according to Rose. Some records indicate maybe as many as 140 survived and returned to Ludmir, but regardless of the exact number, it was only a fraction – less than one-half of one percent. Seven of these survivors, roughly seven percent of the town's total surviving population, were of the Mibab family. Most Jews of postwar Ludmir who were fortunate enough to survive the slaughter of the Holocaust later emigrated westward to Poland since Ludmir was now part of Ukraine, and from there to Israel, the United States, and elsewhere. In the 1980s, about 70 Jews lived in Ludmir; by 1999, there were no more than 30.

Rose and Carl married in January 1945 at the Mibabs' Ludmir home, with 250 Russian soldiers crowded around. The war's end was several months away, but Nazi armies had been defeated in Poland and they felt the time was right to take their marriage vows.

There was no rabbi to perform the rite, so a religious Jew made a *ketubah* [a marriage license] and conducted the ceremony. Rose, with no money and virtually no possessions, borrowed a dress from a friend. And so they spoke their lifelong marriage commitments to each other.

Rose, Carl, her mother, younger siblings, and niece did not remain in Ludmir long. They just couldn't fathom staying there any longer, so in July 1945, with the war over two months earlier, they left the house and moved outside Berlin, smuggled out of Soviet-controlled Ukraine as human cargo hidden in the back of a Russian Jewish soldier's truck. The family of seven lived in a single room in a military barracks in Eschwege, Germany, not far from Berlin, in a DP camp. From 1945 until 1952, more than 250,000 Jews lived in DP camps throughout Germany, Austria, and Northern Italy, administered by authorities from the victorious Allies and the United Nations Relief and Rehabilitation Administration. The quarters were a bit spartan, but survivors were treated well and felt like humans, free and unfettered.

Rose, pregnant with their first child, smuggled in flour, yeast, and sugar, and her mother used the contraband ingredients to bake rolls, which they sold for a little money to help them survive. Rose and Carl enjoyed a second wedding ceremony, with a rabbi performing the formalities this time. Almost miraculously, after the long ordeal Rose had been through, she gave birth to a baby girl, Eva, in 1946. She and Carl were overjoyed. With a family of their own, they could look to the future and put their past behind them.

Rose and Carl worked hard and were able to save enough money to help pay for Chaya, Reuven, Peretz, Esther, and Chaike to move to Palestine, but after paying for their transit, they had no money left for the two of them or little Eva to go as well. They planned to continue working and saving so they might join them as soon as they could afford it. It did not take long, however, for Rose and Carl to change their plans. Letters from Chaya told of a harsh life in Palestine, living in refugee tents, having little food, and being uncertain about what the future held. Chaya's letters convinced Rose and Carl that the United States would be a better option, and so in 1949, they, with nearly three-year-old Eva, came to the United States aboard the USS *General Ballou*, which sailed from the port of Bremerhaven, Germany, on September 26, 1949. After a nine-day journey across the Atlantic, the transport ship sailed into New York harbor. Rose, Carl, and little Eva soon headed south to Jacksonville thanks to the sponsorship of the Hebrew Immigrant Society.

The Goldberg family settled in the Southern city with no English, little money, and no family or friends. The transition was difficult, but after surviving the torment of the Holocaust, living in hiding, and always being on the run – even after liberation – they finally had a chance to establish a new home with prospects for a bright future. They had faced the past with great courage, which allowed them to survive. In that moment, they faced their future with the same courage – this time in the land of opportunity.

Soon after settling in Jacksonville, the Goldbergs had two more children, both daughters as well, Anita and Susie. When the children were young, Rose and Carl spoke little of their past; it was not until Anita was about eight years old that she learned of her parents' Holocaust experience. Rose and Carl's daughters grew up and had seven children among them; by her death in 2020 there were five great-grandchildren, with more born after her death.

The Goldbergs worked hard to live the American dream, earn a comfortable living, and raise their family with opportunity and freedom in their new-found homeland. They were able to buy their own home in Jacksonville; in it, they created a new family, filled with love and light. Rose could have lived a life of bitterness and hate because of all the incredible hardships she endured and the family members she lost, but she chose instead to fill her world and all those she encountered with hope and love. She and Carl actively participated in the Jacksonville Jewish community, and Rose zealously and lovingly ran the Jacksonville Hadassah thrift shop for many years. In addition to devotedly raising a family, she never met a person whom she treated as a stranger, and her home was regularly filled with endless friends and family across the generations, exemplifying a gracious spirit of warmth, generosity, and hospitality.

Rose Goldberg survived the cruelest, most brutal atrocity in modern history, afterward living a long life with the sad reminders of losing her father, several siblings, extended family, friends, and neighbors to the Nazis' evil ways. She lost her home, too, and was forced to hide from certain murder. She prevailed in the face of cruel, unimaginable hardships. Yet, after liberation and her marriage to Carl, she bloomed full of life again, thriving in a new American homeland for many decades spilling over with love for others. Her kind, gentle, and generous spirit left a tribute to the power of love, of a life not consumed with bitterness and hatred but brimming with faith in humanity. She instilled in her children, grandchildren, and great-grandchildren a legacy that all of us are called to respect, as well as an admonishment to love one another and to fill up our lives with joy.

When she passed away on March 1, 2020, at the age of ninety-six – miraculous considering the physical and emotional hardships she had endured in younger years – Rose bequeathed a heritage that could not be snuffed out by the evil tyranny that was the Holocaust. While the painful memories of that horrible time never left her, they did not consume her; love for her family and friends were her gifts to those of us fortunate to have known her. She retained a charming sense of humor and deep faith in G-d until her final days. Her last words to one of her granddaughters, Erin Davis, just weeks before her passing, were a Yiddish saying: *"Da mensch trakht, un Gott lahkt,"* or "Man plans, and G-d laughs." The Nazis were unable to vanquish her zeal for life, sense of humor, love for others, and faith that all of life is in G-d's hands.

Rose and Carl's legacy includes her three children: Eva, Anita, and Susie; eight grandchildren: Wendy, Andy, Emily, Jonathan, Andrea, Jeffrey, Erin, and Drew; and, so far, seven great-grandchildren:

Avery, Ethan, Jeremy, Gabi, Stella, Daisy, and Jerry. The Goldberg progeny are scattered from Jacksonville to Atlanta; Charleston, South Carolina; Washington, D.C.; and beyond, and they have been afforded the opportunity to live the American dream replete with professional and financial success – and the chance to have lives that imbue vibrancy and hope, contributing to their respective communities in substantive ways.

The Goldberg legacy remains one of courage, perseverance, and hope. In her later years, Rose was described by a Charleston acquaintance, Dr. Lilly Fuller, as "a warm and intelligent lady, proud of her family" while never forgetting her past. What's more, she "showed miraculous strength as she cycled through darkness and light, loss and creation in her inspirational existence."

A Charleston restaurant, owned by Rose's daughter Anita Goldberg Zucker and named in her mother's honor, is described by Anita as reflecting Rose's "endless love for baking and cooking [that] fed countless guests in her home," and that "she lived with an overflowing and most extraordinary kind of love." Anita also credited her mother for being "her greatest teacher," and that she had "an amazing strength and a dedication that binds us to this day." She added: "She's really quite amazing and I can't say enough about her. The one thing I can tell you is her faith never wavered. ... She taught me so much about the values necessary to achieve success." Her inspiration flows into the lives of multiple family generations and in those fortunate enough to have known her and be a part of that splendid light.[1]

A family photo with Chaika, Carl, and Rose ion the back row, and two unknown girls along with, Esther, Chaya, and Perry Milan in the front row. Copyright: "The Holocaust Quilt," Charleston Daily 3.8.22

Rose Goldberg visits cousins in Zawiercie, Poland, on the eve of World War II. Copyright: "The Holocaust Quilt," Charleston Daily 3.8.22

Rose with family members

*Presidential Medal of Freedom winner and Nobel Peace Prize winner
Elie Wiesel, with Rose Goldberg and her daughter, Anita Goldberg
Zucker. Copyright: "The Holocaust Quilt," Charleston Daily 3.8.22*

6

GINA SCULZ FREIDEN
WŁOCŁAWEK (LUDMIR), POLAND

Gina Freiden, 1990s, Jacksonville, FL.

Gina Freiden was born in Włocławek, Poland, a town along the Vistula River, on December 18, 1917, and died 83 years later in Jacksonville in 2000. Gina's story took her from Włocławek to Auschwitz-Birkenau, where she narrowly – miraculously – escaped death in the gas chamber, to other horrendous, near-death experiences Eventually, she went to Groß-Rosen, Dachau, and finally Bergen-Belsen. She was finally liberated and made her way to Florida. Gina was passionate and animated in sharing her testimony with school groups, her voice rising notably as she relived the terrible pain she suffered. Gina charged the next generations to learn from the sins of her tormentors, yet she quietly told of her triumph over evil, the ability to overcome wickedness and tragedy. She was a kind and benevolent woman in her golden years when I knew her, and while the pain of her past never left her, she did not allow it to destroy her. Her story is full of intrigue, including close encounters with death and frequent confrontations with horror, yet it is equally one of survival through strength of character and, perhaps, providence.

Gina Freiden was born Gitla Szulc, the daughter of an entrepreneur and philanthropist. Her father, Saul, owned a wholesale tobacco store and two retail stores. From an early age, she worked at the family's shop. She enjoyed the privileges of living in a pleasant home with her father and her mother, Elka, in an upper-middle-class, loving family. Gina was the oldest of three children – her brothers were Nathan and David. Their home was a six-room apartment above one of their stores. She enjoyed spending time with her grandparents, three uncles on her mother's side, three brothers and six sisters on her father's side, and their spouses. All told, her relatives numbered about 120, an extended, large, close-knit family that spent much time together as Gina grew up.

Gina described her father as very generous. He always seemed to be helping others. Both her parents were observant Jews of Ashkenazi origin, and their faith was evident throughout their household. The family spoke both Yiddish and Polish at home, and Gina studied Hebrew at religious school. Their hometown of Włocławek had slightly more than 27,000 people in 1934, of whom 10,406, or just over 38 percent, were Jewish. Jews comprised a significant minority of the population and had long been a vibrant part of the cultural and economic life of the town. They earned their living mainly from commerce and artisanship. Indeed, several Jewish families, like Saul Szulc's family, owned businesses and factories. Jews were also involved politically in Włocławek, including having a community council with 12 members; additionally, various Zionist parties and youth movements held activities. The Jewish community had welfare institutions and a hospital. Jewish schools included a high school, several elementary schools, and a Yeshivot for the study of sacred texts, as well as public libraries. The Szulc family was very much a part of the thriving Jewish community during Gina's youth in the 1920s and '30s. Following the German invasion in September 1939 and the subsequent German occupation, the town was renamed Leslau, and was administered as part of the Reichsgau Posen, eventually called the Reichsgau Wartheland.

The Szulc family had come from Germany and western Poland many generations earlier and had a longstanding, respected presence. Gina's parents were also active in the local Zionist organization. Gina (also called Guta) and her brothers were members of the local Betar group (a Polish Zionist youth group). In fact, her brother Nathan was reportedly one of the most enthusiastic members of the group. The Szulc home was described by Chaim Lazar, a friend of the family and a part of the Betar group, as "resembling a youth center more than a place where a family lived." The Betar group often met there. Gina and her brothers had planted deep in their hearts – by their parents and teachers – a love for their people and their homeland, as well as a vision for a recreated Jewish state.

After finishing public education, Gina went to work in her father's store. She disliked it and wanted to go back to school and continue her formal education. Gina recalled that she cried and cried to return to school; finally, her mother relented. Gina entered business college as she was declared ineligible for university because she was Jewish. Later that year, Gina graduated and moved to her parents' new home in Łódź. After many generations in Włocławek, the family decided to move in 1935 when they, like thousands of other local Jews, could not find employment and sought new sources of livelihood in a new city. Gina remembered Łódź as having a significant Jewish population – around 30 percent Jewish, 30 percent German, and 40 percent Polish. Young Nathan was not able to continue his education after the move to Łódź; instead, he was compelled to work in a textile factory to help the once proud and prosperous family support itself. Nathan and David remained active in Betar in their new city.

Life changed radically for Gina and the Sculz family beginning in September 1939 when the German army invaded Poland. At first, many in Włocławek and Łódź initially thought of the soldiers as the same Germans of World War I and threw flowers at them. However, at age 22, just three days after the German occupation of Poland, she, her family, and all other Jews were taken to the Łódź Ghetto, which had been carved out of the city. It was tightly patrolled and secured with barbed wire fencing to prevent the Jews from leaving.

"There was dying every day," Gina said. "Everybody was hungry, and everybody was afraid. When someone in the family died, they [other families] wouldn't report it because they would get less bread." Initially, two or three families lived in each home; later, up to six families were in each small apartment home. There were strict rules, including a 5 p.m. curfew.

The Jews who, unlike Gina and her family, had remained in Włocławek quickly began to be deported to various ghettos and concentration camps. By late February 1940, only about 4,000 Jews remained in Włocławek; by November, a ghetto had been created there. By the fall of 1941, the remaining Jews, at that point just 920 – mostly women, children, and the elderly – were deported to the Łódź Ghetto, where the Sculz family was living.

An entry in the *Chronicle of the Łódź Ghetto 1941–1944* recalled the arrival of these Jews from Włocławek:

> On September 26 the first transport arrived, as announced, bearing new residents for the ghetto. More than 900 people, almost exclusively women and children, all of whom had been expelled from Wloclawek, arrived by rail at the Radogoszcz sidetrack (in Maryann). ... On 6 November 1941, the ghetto was completely sealed off. The Jewish residents risked their lives in attempts to obtain food from their Polish [neighbors]. Those caught smuggling

food were summarily shot. Expert tailors and shoemakers worked for German companies outside of the ghetto. The main cultural activities in the ghetto were concentrated in a building near the cemetery that had previously served to purify the dead prior to burial; the building also housed a public soup kitchen and functioned as a site for political meetings. In the spring of 1942, the Germans began to liquidate the ghetto. On 24 April 1942, about 400 men were sent to [labor] camps in Kobylepole and other places in the Poznan District, where many perished under the brutal conditions. The ghetto was finally liquidated on 27 April 1942, when women, children and the elderly were loaded onto trucks and transported to the Chelmno death camp, where they were murdered in the deadly gas-vans.

Gina had lived comfortably in Łódź, working as a bookkeeper in a British-owned synthetic rubber factory. While working there, she met a man named Isaac Silber. Isaac was a chemical engineer involved with petroleum and chemical products used in the production of various goods from tires to rubber gloves to sponges. After courting for many years, Gina and Isaac married in 1942, after two years in the ghetto, when Gina was 25. Their wedding ceremony was part of a larger ceremony in an old movie theater with dozens of other couples. Gina said they married to save him from deportation to Auschwitz, which was commonplace at the time as single people typically went to the camps first. Their only wedding gift was an extra ration of bread.

One by one, her family members began to perish. Her grandfather, who had earlier lost his first wife and remarried at age eighty, died from starvation in the Warsaw Ghetto. Several uncles, aunts, and cousins also perished in the Warsaw and Łódź ghettos. Gina and her immediate family were evicted from their nice, large apartment and forced to live with five other families in a tiny apartment in the Łódź Ghetto. Gina referred to the ghetto as the slums of the city. She said they were forced to go there with whatever possessions they could carry "on their shoulders. Five, six families in one little apartment." By 1940, the Łódź Ghetto was home to more than 160,000 Jews. By 1942 and 1943, their existence had become a grim struggle. About 7,000 Jews from the Łódź Ghetto were lost during 1943 to deportations, disease, and starvation. Food was rationed and the Sculz family ate little; their strength steadily declined from malnutrition. Gina worked in the ghetto, first making shovel holders from scraps of leather, and later as director of an orphanage with 500 children – ranging in age from two days to 18 years – but by 1942, the orphanage had been liquidated, the children taken to death camps. Gina described the liquidation of the children: "And the Germans come in with trucks, put the children in sacks – two, three in one, and filled up a whole truck with live children in the sacks. Two of those kids, one tried to hide; one hided [sic] under the door, the other under the bed. When the SS man saw this, he slammed the door and the brain come out. The other [kid], he took it out and took his legs and slammed the child's head over the tire and killed the kid this way."

One day, while still in the Łódź Ghetto, just two minutes after the five o'clock curfew, Gina's mother was rushing home after attending her own mother's funeral. A Gestapo guard saw her and shot and killed her on a bridge, just minutes from home. Gina and her family, who were in the ghetto ahead of the curfew, were not even allowed to see her body.

Approximately 120 of Gina's relatives soon would be deported to concentration camps and death camps if they had not already died in the ghettos. Steadily, the Jews of the Łódź Ghetto went primarily to Auschwitz. By February 1944, the count of 160,000 occupants had shrunk to 79,777, the largest surviving Jewish population in occupied Poland at the time. A diary entry by an unknown resident described a roundup:

Today was marked by the roundup conducted by the Special Department. It began in the early morning hours and lasted until 12:15. Special Department patrols roamed the streets; passersby were stopped and asked to show their working papers. Since there had been no [prior] announcement of this action, many people out for brief errands did not, of course, have their working papers with them. Women out shopping or hurrying to get some soup for a sick husband or some medicine for a sick child, were stopped by the young men of the Special Department. They were rounded up like dogcatchers after strays. ... Many of these people even had their working papers with them and others had theirs rushed to them by relatives or friends. But to no avail ...

Five days later, the writer recorded: "In early afternoon, a 20-car train was assembled at the Radogoszcz track. The train was loaded in late afternoon. ... The scenes that were played out ... almost defy description." The writer concluded with: "Although most of the people involved were hopelessly sick, the despair of their families knew no limit."

Gina's youngest brother, Nathan, 22 years old, was the first in the family to go to a concentration camp. He had escaped the Łódź Ghetto and went to the Warsaw Ghetto with friends to join the revolt – the Warsaw Ghetto uprising – against the Nazis. Nathan was sent from the Warsaw Ghetto to Auschwitz-Birkenau, where he perished in the gas chambers, like so many other relatives.

Gina, her husband Isaac, the rest of her many family members, along with thousands more from the Łódź Ghetto, soon followed. They were crammed into cattle cars, as many as 200 in a car, with no food or water and, as in the thousands of cattle cars that had gone before them, a single bucket as their bathroom. Gina had seen violence and death in various ways during her two years in the ghetto, but those methods were merely the tip of the iceberg. After a two-day journey in the middle of the night, the train reached the Polish town of Oświęcim and the notorious death camp of Auschwitz-Birkenau, the train coming to a screeching halt. Gina, decades later, recalled their arrival as if it were just days before: "And when they released us [from the trains], they took the men left and the women right. They put him [Isaac] to the left, me to the right. He want to give me a piece of bread ... and the SS man saw this; he give me a piece of bread, and he knocked him [Isaac] over the head with a rifle and I didn't saw [sic] him any more to this day."

Isaac, her husband of only 18 months, was sent directly to the gas chamber. He was only 32.

As Gina and the others in her group were slowly processed inside the camp, she immediately noticed the large sign hanging over the entrance gate, which read: *"Arbeit Macht Frei."* She and her fellow female prisoners were shaved everywhere on their bodies, given a quick, cold shower, and issued a uniform. While being shaved, she managed to take off a diamond ring and conceal it in her mouth. Soon, that jewelry would come in handy.

Gina's first job at Auschwitz was on a crew digging ditches, but it was not long before she was given a new job as a woodcarver, with many of her projects involving making canes and walking sticks for the SS men who ran the camp. Her time in Auschwitz was relatively brief, just three months, but Gina said it felt like 30 years. She recalled extremely long days and piercing, bitterly cold weather. Food was scarce; meals were watery soups served in cans – one can for every ten people to share. On occasion, if they were lucky, a piece of cabbage or potato would land in the soup, yet no one wanted to be the one of ten to take the small piece of vegetable, so it would often be returned to the can uneaten.

At times, the efficiency of the German Nazis meant surprises were few; at other times, life in the camp was haphazard, with unexpected events. The Nazi death machine was designed to create confusion and chaos, preventing prisoners from knowing what to expect. Devastatingly, not long after she arrived at Auschwitz and was selected to live, Gina was inexplicably selected for the gas chamber. The diamond ring she had concealed earlier now had a purpose. She was able to use it to bribe a guard at the gas chamber. If she were smart, the guard told her, she would be able to stay alive with his help. She promptly gave him the ring and he allowed her to escape the selection by taking her up into a nearby building, leading her into the attic, where she sneaked out through a small opening in the wall and down through a pipe.

Once outside, her heart racing, the sweat pouring down her brow, praying she had escaped successfully, she suddenly heard three shots. They were intended for her. She was hit twice in her side and once in her right hand. She lay on the ground behind some rocks for three days, feigning death and remaining as quiet and still as she possibly could. Finally, she was able to crawl back into her barracks. An old friend from Łódź, a physician living in the barracks with her, pulled the bullets out of Gina with her bare hands and without anesthesia. Miraculously, Gina recovered.

While providence and courage had allowed her to survive this ordeal, Gina realized that escape from Auschwitz was nearly impossible. The camp was heavily guarded and surrounded by electric, barbed wire fences and hidden mines near the fences.

In addition to the periodic gas chamber selections, other methods of brutality and death were constantly all around them. Another of Gina's early jobs was to take out the large cans used as toilets in the barracks and empty them into the latrines. One day, when she and another woman working with her went outside, the bucket fell, its noxious contents spilling everywhere. The young woman with her, fearful of what the Germans might do because of her error, threw herself on the wires, electrocuting herself. The large pail was too heavy for Gina to carry by herself, so she abandoned it and returned to the barracks empty-handed. She was punished by being forced to kneel on the concrete barracks floor for several hours, her knees painful and bloodied by the time she was allowed up. She was later disciplined for various other infractions, such as when a group of Russian prisoners stole a large pot of soup that she was taking to the infirmary. Bit by bit, the painful endurance contest of Auschwitz wore away at Gina's physical, emotional, and spiritual state.

Auschwitz-Birkenau housed both a death camp (Auschwitz II/Birkenau) and an adjacent labor camp (Auschwitz I). The SS monsters at the death camp were responsible for gassing approximately 1.1 million people in four-and-a-half years, with some estimates as high as 1.5 million, nearly a million of whom were Jews. In addition, about 70,000 to 80,000 non-Jewish Poles were murdered there, along with 19,000 to 20,000 Roma and Sinti people (Gypsies) and a smaller number of Soviet prisoners of war. The gas chambers were used nearly 24 hours a day, seven days a week, often with more than 5,000 and as many as 10,000 gassings daily. The weak, the sick, the very young, and the old were immediately selected for extermination. Those selected for slave labor often met the same fate later, as they got weaker with the passing of each day of hard labor, minimal food, and harsh conditions.

While Gina defied fate and escaped the gas chambers and crematoria of Auschwitz, she nonetheless endured the horrors of daily life in the labor camp. Every morning she was up at 5 a.m. for *Appell*, often standing for extended periods in the freezing cold and snow while the guards, sometimes angry or hung over, sorted the living from those who had died during the night. This daily ordeal was followed by a ten-mile walk through the woods to work. The prisoners did not return to the barracks until seven in the evening. As they were marched to and from the work site, the prisoners were forced to sing as if they were happy. Failure to do so often meant being shot on the spot.

Extremely poor nutrition, long and harsh hours of work, lack of rest, prolonged exposure to the elements, and crowded and dehumanizing living conditions meant illness was always just around the corner. Illness at Auschwitz nearly always meant the gas chambers since prisoners would no longer be fit for work. It was rare for prisoners, particularly Jews, to be given medical treatment of any sort, and dental care was nonexistent. At one point during her imprisonment at Auschwitz, Gina developed a severe toothache. To relieve her pain the best she could, Gina warmed a red brick on the barracks' fire stove and held it to her cheek. Then she tore off a piece of worn cloth from her blanket and wrapped it around her face to keep the warm brick in place. An SS guard who chided Gina and abused her with daily slaps and beatings saw the wrapping. She ripped it away from Gina's face and slapped her so forcefully that, for the rest of Gina's life, her left cheek sagged lower than her right.

The same SS guard, whom Gina recalled was named Erika, was later involved in another incident with her. Gina had managed to hide two gold rings in addition to the diamond ring she had used to bribe the guard at the gas chamber. One of those two rings was the wedding band Isaac had given her, which she sold to a Polish prisoner for a bowl of soup and a piece of bread. The other was her mother's wedding band. The SS woman discovered Gina wearing the remaining ring, came to the barracks, and sarcastically called for her, saying: *"Schmugstuck! Schmugstuck* [My precious jewel! Precious jewel]!" – a German term of endearment. She demanded the ring. Gina began to cry and responded, "This is from my departed mother; please let me have it!" The guard continued to demand it. Gina then said the ring was too tight and could not come off. The guard responded that she would just take the ring with the finger attached. Gina relented, placed her finger in her mouth to wet it, and removed the last tangible piece of her mother's memory, handing it to the foul female SS guard.

Gina held a variety of jobs during her seven long months at the death camp, but she quickly settled into the job of woodcarver. This not only became her responsibility but was somewhat cathartic in a sense. Perhaps inexplicably, Gina carved gifts made from wood scraps for the SS guard Erika. After being forced to give up her mother's wedding ring, Gina went to her bunk and brought a checkerboard she'd made from of a piece of cardboard and checkers she had carved by hand. Delighted, and certainly bewildered, the SS woman took Gina's hand, raised it high above her head for all the prisoners in the barracks to see, and shouted, *"Kunzenschnitzer! Kunzenschnitzer!* [The carving artist! The carving artist]!" The guard never mistreated Gina again. Not long afterward, when the guard received a package from home, she shared some salami and bread with Gina. Even decades later, Gina bore no hostility toward the guard, simply stating, "She did her duty." Gina was able to rise above the hatred and cruelty, refusing to succumb to the Nazis' goal of dehumanization, and found it in herself to be selfless and kind. These were the traits that allowed her to survive the barbarous years in the ghettos and camps and, in later years, to live a life of love and kindness, rather than one consumed with hate and bitterness.

Ultimately, Gina managed to escape from the gas chamber line in Auschwitz on three different occasions. Countless times in the labor camps she managed to maintain the will to live and focus on the future, hoping to one day be free again. In fact, the will to be free was the only thing that the camps were unable to take from her; in all other matters of health, emotions, identity, and dignity, Nazis had stolen her humanity.

From Auschwitz, with the approaching Soviet Army nearby, Gina was force-marched 155 miles [250 kilometers] west to Groß-Rosen in Upper Silesia. In Groß-Rosen, a guard told Gina that she looked like his daughter and gave her bread and salami. The next day, he invited her back to the kitchen for more bread, but, she said, he "wanted to mess around with me." She refused but said some women would allow themselves to succumb to such advances out of desperation for food and survival.

Her stay in Groß-Rosen was short – she was evacuated again and marched south to Dachau, near Munich. After a brief stop there, she went to Bergen-Belsen, further from advancing Soviet troops. She was there for two to three months. Conditions at Bergen-Belsen were deplorable; Gina referred to it as the "Typhus Camp." The prisoners were given no food for days, lice were prolific, and typhus and other diseases ran rampant. It was at Bergen-Belsen that Anne Frank and her mother, Edith, perished – Edith from starvation and Anne probably from typhus just days before the camp was liberated by British forces. Gina said she and other prisoners dug graves for Anne and the other children and teens who had died of typhus and buried them there within the camp. After the war and liberation, in 1946, Gina returned to place a wreath on a newly erected tombstone memorializing the departed youth.

When the war finally ended in the spring of 1945 and the British army liberated Bergen-Belsen, Gina Freiden weighed only 70 pounds. She was unshackled from Nazi tyranny but barely alive. A French doctor found her lying on the ground in the camp. There on the ground, Gina cried because she was at last free, but too weak to stand up in joy. Though she had little chance of survival, she was transported to St. Bonifatius Hospital – run by Roman Catholic nuns – in Lingen (Ems), Germany. She had dysentery. Her condition was so critical that one day, while under hospice care and medical staff thinking she would not last through the night, a priest was called so she could confess her sins. She told the nurse, however, that she was Jewish and that her dying wish was to be buried in a Jewish cemetery. A bit startled, the nuns responded by fetching a British army rabbi to speak with Gina.

The rabbi also asked about her last wishes. She responded by asking for just three things: lemon, coffee, and sacramental wine. The lemon, she recalled years later, was to "refresh [her] a little bit." The coffee, she thought, could be used as a form of medicine to dissipate her constant diarrhea. The wine might be useful to help kill germs and heal her wounds. Soon, another rabbi brought lemonade (instead of a lemon) along with coffee beans and an entire bottle of wine. Gina promptly drank the lemonade, which brought her much-needed pleasure, then used the coffee beans to make a tiny bit of fresh coffee – she had but three beans – and then kept the bottle of wine at her bedside table. The British rabbi also told her that during Shabbat prayers the coming Friday, during the blessing of the wine, he would remember her.

She had a raging, nonstop fever, so she drank water nearly constantly. That first night, though, with the aid of her nurse, then afterward on her own, she slowly drank the wine – about one-fifth of the bottle. Gina soon fell fast asleep. The doctor and nurses knew she was still alive, she later said, because her heart was still beating, but according to Gina, "They could not bury me, neither [sic] wake me up." After 36 hours of deep sleep, she woke up famished and immediately asked for food. Her first meal, if one could call it that, was merely a slice of bread and a lump of sugar. Soon however, she began to eat more substantially – something she had been denied for years. Over the next nine months spent in the hospital, she gradually regained weight until she gained 100 pounds and reached 170. Gina was blind for her first three months in the hospital, and it was nearly the full nine months before she could walk again. But her will to live and her emotional and spiritual strength allowed her to survive.

After her recovery, she was sent back to Bergen-Belsen, which was now a DP camp. She waited four years for permission to emigrate to one of three countries she had chosen as an ultimate destination: Australia, Palestine, or the United States. In the DP camp, Gina fell in love and before long remarried. Her new husband was another survivor, Phillip Freiden. Gina was soon pregnant, but in 1949, the child was stillborn. Phillip was so furious at the German physician who treated her, an ex-SS officer, that Gina feared her husband might kill him. At the DP camp, she worked for the British government, aiding in the resettlement and assistance effort for the thousands upon thousands of displaced Jewish refugees. For her diligent and exemplary efforts, she received a letter of commendation from the British military.

Ultimately, the long-awaited paperwork was approved, and they emigrated to the United States, sailing aboard the USAT *General Ballou*, which had been a naval transport ship during the war (and was the same transport vessel on which fellow survivors from a previous chapter, Rose, Carl, and Eva Goldberg, had sailed just a month earlier). The voyage across the Atlantic Ocean took 11 days, and they arrived in New York City on October 18, 1949. She and Phillip began to rebuild their lives. On Ellis Island, Gina chose a birthdate and a new name, a name that would add up to the word

ח׳ (pronounced chai), meaning "life." (Hebrew letters are used as numbers as well. The letters of chai add up to 18). Now that she was remarried, her new surname became Freiden, short for Freidenreich. In German, *frei* means "free," and she had finally become just that. Her new "birthday," while officially still December 18, symbolically would be also on the 18th day of October – a date of new birth in her new homeland.

For three months, Gina and Phillip lived in New York, waiting to leave for Dayton, Ohio, where Phillip was to be employed in the auto industry. Due to a prolonged strike in auto manufacturing, however, they were unable to leave for Dayton to start work. Their extended stay in New York was not without its problems; they were in a tiny, cramped, dingy hotel room. On one occasion, a key to their room was given to another couple. With the uncertain prospects in Dayton, the Freidens returned to the Jewish relief agency to ask about other potential locations where they might relocate. Jacksonville was recommended as a good spot, with a growing population and attractive job market, so the Freidens headed south to set up a new life there. Having spent considerable time in the large industrial city of Łódź, and several months in New York City, Gina was rather surprised to find Jacksonville was a small, somewhat bucolic city at the time. With a population of only 200,000 spread out over a large geographic area, surrounded by rural communities and having the slow-paced life of a small Southern city, it was rather a cultural shock. Phillip promised Gina that if she didn't like Jacksonville, they would return the next day to New York. They never moved back to New York and, in 1992, Gina exclaimed, "I got stuck here for 43 years!" Ultimately, Gina lived the rest of her life in Jacksonville, more than half a century. It was a home she quickly grew to love. In Jacksonville, she and Phillip were finally able to build a new life together.

In 1950, a year after arriving in the United States, Gina Freiden gave birth to her first child, a son, Saul. Two years later, in 1952, a daughter, Elisa, was born. Gina and Phillip opened a grocery store in Jacksonville, and Gina continued to run the store after Phillip's early death at age 48 in 1963. With the adjustment to her new life in her adopted homeland of the United States – learning a new language, immersion in a starkly different culture, running a business in a new environment, and raising a family – she tended to not dwell on her past and put the painful experiences of the Holocaust and the loss of family behind her. When her children would ask, "Mama, why [does] everybody have a grandma, a grandpa, cousins, and we have nobody?" Gina would gently respond, "If you grow up a little to be older, Mama will tell you."

She never shared her experiences in the concentration camps with her children when they were growing up, not so much because of the pain of the memories but rather because "I no want [sic] to put hatred in them, because I have a lot of hatred" and "I didn't want them to be filled with hate." She did not share with her children until they were adults that her brother, Nathan, was gassed at Auschwitz. She refused to tell them about the thousands of people who were consumed each day in the flames of the Auschwitz crematoria. Gina was silent about the young girl in the barracks with her at Bergen-Belsen who died just weeks before liberation, Anne Frank. And she kept inside, in the still voice of her silently screaming soul, the story about the entire family she lost to the Nazis' Final Solution.

Only in later years did Gina start telling the story of life in the camps. She hoped that her testimony to younger generations would help them to strive to live in peace and never have civilization repeat the horrors she had experienced. Ultimately, Gina felt it was important to tell more of her story with her children and testify to school groups. Pastor Bruno Linhares, a chaplain who gave pastoral comfort to Gina in the final days of her life at Jacksonville's Baptist Medical Center hospital, said, "Every time the story was told, she managed to find a little more meaning in her life."

Late in life, Gina proclaimed, that she loved all people, and they loved her. She went on to volunteer that "I don't hate, not even the

Germans," though she did add that she retained a hatred for the Nazi regime. She couldn't forgive the Nazis, yet added she hoped peace will be on this Earth! The passage of the years, when Gina relied on her deep faith, her hope for the future, a love for her adopted homeland, and the strength of family, gradually eased her hatred and bitterness. They were replaced by joy. This joy emanated from the Gina I got to know as she neared eighty years of age.

Gina had endured a crisis of faith following her experiences in the Holocaust. She could not come to grips with how, in her heart, G-d could abandon her and the entire Jewish people of Europe. "How can I believe in G-d," she said, "when he took His Chosen People and let them burn alive? I was away from my religion for a long time." She added: "It was hard. I will never adjust to [sic]. You see, I sometimes wonder how this is [that] we can be regular people, liberated, alive, after what happened to us? And to this day, 50 years, I still have nightmares." Over time, however, Gina returned to the faith of her youth, in part because the jagged edges of bitterness in her heart began to soften, and in part because she wanted her two beloved children to be of the Jewish faith.

In her later years, Gina went to Israel to remember the dead. She went to Washington, D.C., for a reunion of Holocaust survivors to commemorate the six million Jews, including her family members and friends, who perished at the hands of the Nazis and their henchmen. It was only then, in the 1980s, that she began to speak to groups about her experiences. She spoke several times to various groups in the 1980s and through the mid-1990s. Her message to young people was simple but powerful and important: "People can live in peace, and they no have [sic] to hate nobody. We live in a country where we have freedom, and you should appreciate this. To watch out for the young Nazi people, like the ... skinheads. We will have peace if we learn from the past, because history, history can repeat. G-d forbid, it will be not just me and you, it could be everybody. ... Hatred brings a lot of bad stuff."

Sadly, Gina later stopped speaking publicly when she received antisemitic threats from neo-Nazi groups in the Jacksonville area and became fearful for her safety. She spoke to my class only once and declined to return despite my repeated invitations. The pervasive fear of her youth crept back into her consciousness in her final years, and she retreated to the safety of her home.

In 1945, the rabbi of the British army, the one who gave her the wine in the hospital as she wavered between life and death, promised to keep Gina in mind while reciting the prayers of Shabbat. Fifty-five years later, a young Protestant pastor also offered a prayer for her in Hebrew as she lay dying, the only one he knew in the original tongue, from Numbers 6: 24–27, hoping that the Creator would provide her comfort and welcome. He recited, "The Lord bless you and keep you; the Lord make His face shine upon you and be gracious unto you; the Lord lift up His countenance upon you, and give you peace. So shall they put my name upon the people of Israel, and I will bless them."

After her death, as she wished while in the hospital in Lingen (Ems) so many decades before, when she thought she would not survive, she was buried in a Jewish cemetery. It was, however, 55 years later and on a different continent. In the intervening decades, despite Nazi aims, Gina Freiden had come back to life – a life well-lived in America, in Jacksonville – experiencing the blessings of raising two lovely children and seeing the fruit of two granddaughters provide a legacy that could not be squelched by the Nazis.

Her daughter, Elisa Freiden Topper, eulogized her mother after she died at the age of 83, on December 19, 2000, saying, "She was a remarkable woman and a pillar of Jacksonville. Despite all the tragedy in her life, she was such a positive person." Elisa added: "People were drawn to her, and she just had this tremendous warmth. She loved people and people loved her. Many people close to her called her 'Mama Gina.'"

Gina Freiden, the gentle, warm, and kind woman, lived 83 full years overflowing with love. In sharing with a newspaper reporter why she chose to speak with schoolchildren, Gina said, "What I do is not for me. I want this generation to know that mankind can live in peace. ...We never need to have something like this happen again. We must never, ever forget."[1] In her own small way, Gina was able to let a generation of young people in Jacksonville not forget man's inhumanity to man in the Europe of the 1930s and '40s. Her words became a legacy and will not soon be forgotten. As for me, my life will never be the same because I knew this courageous and kind woman, Gina Freiden.

Gina Freiden laying a wreath at Bergen-Belsen.

Gina Freiden after liberation.

Gina and Phillip Freiden

Gina and Phillip Freiden

7

LEONA HOCHERMAN KROHN
LODZ, POLAND

Leona Krohn, Orange Park, Florida, 1996.

When I came to know Leona Krohn, she was approaching 80 years old. I was immediately attracted to her affable warmth and winsome spirit, and I quickly came to know her to be a kind and tender soul, easy with a smile and with an effervescent sparkle in her eyes. She had a gentle, self-effacing sense of humor, a ready wit that seemed to balance the softly spoken, painful words recalling her young adulthood in Eastern Europe half a century earlier. She was born Lonea (Lea in Yiddish) Hocherman, on June 21, 1917, and was the fifth of seven children, having four brothers and two sisters. Leona grew up in Łódź – about 120 kilometers southwest of Warsaw – a city of about 665,000 people. Łódź enjoyed a large and vibrant Jewish community, representing approximately one-third of the population, about 233,000 strong. Her father, Nusen Hocherman, was one of 12 children – all of whom had grown up in Warsaw; her mother, Yetta, had a sister and two brothers, so Leona's large family included 28 aunts and uncles. Nusen had come to Łódź because of a matchmaker and married his 16-year-old bride Yetta there when he was just 18 years old. Their union produced seven children and a home full of energy and love.

Leona enjoyed a happy childhood, and she cherished wonderful memories of it all of her life. Her family was in the textile business. They were a very observant, Orthodox Hasidic family and their faith was central to their daily life. The family was close-knit, and all nine of them ate almost every meal together each day. They had the benefit of a Jewish cook, Leocia, who lived with them for 20 years to help support the large family. Leona was closest to her brother Mailech (Mila) and sister Dora, and they were almost inseparable, but all of the siblings, despite their age differences, were close. Her other brothers were Berek, Kacek, and Nuchem; her other sister was Adela. "It was a very happy family," Leona reminisced. "I have very good memories." The extended family, numbering in the dozens, included siblings, cousins, aunts, uncles, and grandparents, with memories of good times and great love.

Leona recalled late in life that, in addition to her immediate family, there were frequent visitors, particularly for meals. Her many aunts, uncles, and cousins joined them often, as did many close friends and neighbors; the dining-room table could seat 24 people and was regularly full. One can imagine the vibrant mealtime activity, filled with conversation, and the hospitality extended to friends. After dinner, evenings were often spent playing cards as the house vibrated with laughter and joy.

The Hocherman family spoke Yiddish and Polish at home. Leona graduated from public school, then continued her education at a private school for four years of teacher education, followed by six months of sewing school to learn a trade. She and her family had little to no connection with Polish Gentiles because only Jews lived nearby. Leona recalled that in public school she had a single Polish (non-Jewish) teacher. Her family lived in a spacious flat within a large apartment building housing about 100 Jewish families. The Hocherman apartment had four bedrooms. By 21st-century American standards it was perhaps cramped for a family of nine, but for Eastern European standards in the 1920s and 1930s, the apartment was spacious and grand, and the family was considered rather well off. They also had a small home in the country about an hour's train ride away. They would go there every summer to escape the heat of the city. For three years, she lived with her grandmother, whom she adored; her grandfather had passed away after suffering many years from polio. Leona recalled these times as particularly happy. Leona's father had served in the Russian army in World War I and one brother served in the Polish army in the 1930s. This brother, like Leona, survived the Holocaust, also living a long life in America after the war.

On September 1, 1939, the German army invaded Poland, and Łódź was under German control already by September 8. Leona was on "vacation" during the invasion; she and her boyfriend, Mark (Mayer), were in the countryside for a month, helping Polish farmers in their fields. Upon her return to Łódź, they discovered the Nazis had attacked, so they went into hiding in the basement to escape the German bombs. After several days, they heard on the radio that the Nazis were going to burn down the entire city and that citizens should go to Warsaw to be safe, so she and her family fled there, walking the 150 kilometers from Łódź. Her father and two brothers traveled with her, hastily fleeing, with no time to pack. Along the route, houses, barns, and various other buildings were burning from the Nazi offensive. Fighting was all around them, making for a dangerous and harrowing passage. Leona experienced nightmares for the rest of her life. "We ran and ran and thought that we would be shot and killed!" Leona exclaimed 55 years later. "I can still feel my heart beating [so fast]; I was so scared." Somehow, amid battle and their flight, Leona and her family were able to jump on a train – she was pushed onto it through one of its windows as it left the terminal.

The battle for Poland lasted just 26 days; for that entire period, there was no food or water, no change of clothes, or bathing. Many trying to flee the bombing were killed during that nightmare month. After the Polish defeat, Leona, her father, and two of her brothers made the lengthy journey back to Łódź to see what had become of their home. During the journey, one of her brothers was arrested by the Nazis and taken to a labor camp, but he was later released and came to the Warsaw Ghetto.

Though Leona and most of her immediate family were home in Łódź, they soon heard that they would be sent back to Warsaw to the newly created ghetto there. Leona and Mark had already witnessed antisemitic persecution and great devastation and decided that they would attempt to escape Łódź and not go to Warsaw. Earlier, Mark had been in Warsaw, walking down a street with his father, when a Gestapo officer stopped them, took out his knife, and cut his father's beard off with the knife. In the process, he intentionally cut much of one cheek off along with the beard. Such atrocities were common and struck terror in the hearts of the Jews. This atrocity left an indelible impression on both Mark and Leona that would not soon be forgotten.

All the ghettos in Nazi-occupied Eastern Europe were places of great suffering. Often, there was little to no water, no electricity, and severely rationed food. The Warsaw Ghetto was no exception. An eyewitness in the Warsaw Ghetto remembered: "corpses of men and animals are heaped in the streets. Men of goodwill are burying the dead where they find them: in a garden, a square, or courtyards. Famished people cut off pieces of flesh as soon as a horse fell." A Polish resistance newspaper article reported early in 1941 that "the population density [inside the Jewish quarter of the Warsaw Ghetto] is unimaginable. An average of six people live in one room; sometimes, however, there are as many as 20. ... This increased crowding has resulted in unspeakable hygienic and sanitary conditions. Hunger and unimaginable misery are now prevalent." The German governor of Warsaw gloated that the official German policy was starvation, saying, "The Jews will die from hunger and destitution and a cemetery will remain of the Jewish question."

Mark and Leona rightfully feared for their lives. Despite the conditions in Warsaw, it was better than staying in Łódź. In the end, Łódź and its environs lost 420,000 prewar inhabitants, including around 300,000 Polish Jews, which included Jews rounded up from smaller villages nearby and placed in the Łódź Ghetto. Very few of its Jews survived. When the Russian army entered the city on January 19, 1945, only 877 Jews were still alive, 12 of whom were children. Of the 223,000 Jews in Łódź before the invasion, and the 300,000 soon after, fewer than 10,000 survived the Holocaust.

Leona and Mark, fearing what seemed to be the inevitable, decided to attempt an escape 3,000 kilometers northeast to Siberia in the Soviet Union. Leona had not known Mark long, but he asked her to escape with him and get married. She received her parents' blessing and so, on the evening of November 14, 1939, they exchanged vows. The simple civil ceremony allowed them to register as husband and wife, but they did not have the privilege of enjoying a wedding ceremony due to the war and the persecution of the Jews. Wedding celebrations have been seminal ceremonies in most societies, and they have been especially so in Jewish culture for millennia. Yet Leona and Mark experienced no such special event.

The next month, in December 1939, in the shrouded darkness of early morning, they managed to get on a train heading east to Siberia. However, after they boarded, the Germans gave the order *"Alle Juden aus!"* [all Jews get off!]. Somehow, Leona and Mark were able to escape and went back to Warsaw and spent the night in her grandfather's home. Her parents, along with most of her siblings, had returned to Warsaw and lived with their parents in the ghetto. Leona and Mark decided to flee again and, taking nothing with them except a diamond ring and an expensive watch (thinking she might need them for bribes at some point), they began a long walk eastward to Siberia. After a tearful farewell, the jewelry in hand and one small suitcase apiece, their journey began. Leona never saw her family again.

Leona and Mark escaped in December in cold weather and terrible rain as they left. She suffered from bronchitis all during their trek. Leaving her grandfather's Warsaw home, they began their journey east on foot, then caught a train to Białystok to go to a sister's house. Her sister already had 20 visitors staying there, so there was no more room, even on the floor, to sleep. Leona and Mark decided to go to a nearby farm for the night. Białystok, though incorporated into the Soviet republic of Belarus during the Russian occupation, had become a popular destination for Jewish refugees from German-occupied Poland. It had a large Jewish population, growing by as much as 30 percent over the final few months of 1939 when fleeing refugees rushed in. At the farm, they stayed in a shed for a month and ate meals with the farmer and his family. Leona said years later that the hospitable Polish Christian family treated them with great kindness and adopted them "like their own children." When it was time for Leona and Mark to leave, the family cried. The couple walked the nearly six-and-a-half miles (over ten kilometers) into Białystok, said goodbye to Leona's sister, who was a nurse there, then kept going east to Siberia, spending nearly a month in a cattle car in the freezing cold winter air. The rail car had no heat and no toilets, nor any food. The journey took 27 long, cold days and nights. Exhausted, chilled to the bone, and starving, they got to Siberia with about 1,000 more Jews, were crammed into a dining hall, then assigned a room in a barracks.

Their journey took them to Chelyabinsk, in southern Siberia, where they stayed for two-and-a-half long years. Only about 300,000 Polish Jews, out of approximately 3.5 million living there prior to the Nazi occupation, survived the war. Of those who did, approximately 80 percent escaped the Holocaust by being deported by Joseph Stalin to Soviet gulag labor camps in 1940. Mark and Leon were among 40,000 to 50,000 Polish Jews who voluntarily escaped to the Soviet Union.

As cruel as the gulags were, they ultimately saved the lives of many Polish Jews. The story of Polish Jews surviving the Holocaust in Soviet gulags is a largely untold account and gives new meaning to the definitions of "survivor" and "survival." Leona and Mark's story, then, is a vitally important one to be told.

Leona and Mark were fortunate to be able to flee to the Soviet Union when they did. The migration of Jews into the Soviet-occupied zone of Poland and then farther east into the Soviet Union itself slowed down significantly in the first few months of 1940 when stricter border controls were put into place by both the Germans and the Soviets. Refugees from German-occupied Poland, however, continued to slip into eastern Poland and then the Soviet Union until June 1941, albeit in much smaller numbers, when the German army invaded the region. The refugees varied in terms of background but tended to be older adolescents, young married couples, and small groups of friends traveling into the Soviet zone together. Leona and Mark, of course, fit this profile.

Leona remembered how cold it was in Siberia. In Chelyabinsk, Mark was given factory work as a tool-and-die laborer, and Leona was assigned to assist in building more barracks. Chelyabinsk experienced rapid industrial growth during the 1930s, transitioning from a small provincial town to a major industrial city. Several important factories were built during this period, and soon afterward, during World War II, Stalin decided to move much of Soviet manufacturing to areas removed from the reach of advancing German forces. The result was new industries and thousands of workers going to Chelyabinsk, including facilities to produce T-34 Soviet tanks and rocket launchers. During the war, the city's industries produced 18,000 tanks, 48,000 tank diesel engines, and more than 17 million units of ammunition. Chelyabinsk earned the nickname of "Tankograd" ("Tank City"). There was a great need for new workers such as Mark and Leona for the war effort.

When the Krohns arrived at the work camp in Chelyabinsk, the late winter weather in Siberia was extremely cold and workers had few clothes to keep them warm. It was days before they received their first food rations. When they finally got their first meal, it was 140 grams of bread for the two of them. Their hunger continued because they had little to eat their entire time there, typically just bread and a little watery soup. One day early in their stay, Leona recalled eating Mark's bread ration before he got back from work because she was starving so badly. She immediately regretted her decision, breaking down in tears when admitting her error to Mark. More than 55 years later, she still viscerally lamented what she described as her selfishness.

Later, Leona was given seamstress duties, and so her six months at sewing school in Poland helped save her life. The hours were long and arduous, living conditions were miserable, and food was scarce – not altogether much different from many of the German slave labor camps. The primitive barracks had cold, dirt floors and no electricity; winters were brutally cold inside and out. Workers at the gulag endured hunger, disease, exhaustion, mistreatment, and unfamiliar terrain and circumstances. Outbreaks of malaria and typhoid surfaced, and extreme infestations of bedbugs and lice were common. They had to live new lives in exile and, in step with the Soviet labor camp motto, were warned to "work or die." Guards and overseers announced that "those who do not learn to live here will perish." Some died of hunger and disease; one estimate is that 10 percent of the refugees did not survive the deplorable conditions of the camps.

However, despite the conditions, the couple experienced little overt antisemitism while in Siberia because the laborers included Jews and ethnic Poles who were all in the same boat. In contrast to the situation in Nazi-occupied Poland, conditions did not specifically or exceptionally affect Jews but, to one degree or another, affected all Poles – Jewish and Christian – and, in many ways, many inhabitants of the war-torn Soviet Union. Furthermore, there were no killing centers. Workers often became sick and very weak, malnourished, and overworked, yet the survival rate, while not favorable, was markedly greater than that of the German concentration camps. While the Soviets allowed refugees and prisoners to sustain life only barely, their intent was not to eradicate their workers. Leona and Mark knew they were fortunate to be working there despite of the miserable environment. One Polish Jew, Michael Goldberg – who had been a very pro-Soviet youth but was transformed into a strong anti-Soviet adult after his experience in the gulag – nevertheless wrote after the war:

Looking back to the east, I could state to myself that the only positive note about the Soviet Union which we should never forget was that in the darkest hours of our Jewish tragedy, when the Western free world was deaf and blind to our destruction and kept all doors closed to the US, even turning back the refugees to Nazi ovens, the Soviets were the only ones who admitted hundreds of thousands of Eastern European Jews who found a place of refuge. As an eyewitness, I can state that in the worst years of hunger and misery, they shared the little they had with the refugees, and if thousands of us found ourselves in the Soviet gulags and many died, that was a product of the mad dog Stalin who destroyed the best of his own people as well.

After over two years in the Soviet labor camp, the factory in which Leona and Mark worked burned down, so they were forced to leave. The young couple was able to get train tickets to journey from the Siberian gulag to yet another destination. In late January 1942, they left on a 27-day trip to Samarkand, Uzbekistan. Initially, they stayed at her cousin's home, where they remained for two or three days, sleeping on a table. One Jewish refugee later wrote that "most living quarters were built of clay, patched together with small windows, low ceilings and doors," and "one had to bend to enter."

They had no bread for the next month, but soon both Leona and Mark were able to get jobs. They moved into a small shack, living in destitution while experiencing a great deal of antisemitism. There they stayed, struggling in poverty and fear, for nearly three more years. Memoirs of several refugees reveal that the locals in Samarkand were not particularly welcoming to the Polish refugees, particularly the Jews. One refugee noted that "the Uzbeks on our street did not talk to or look at us." Another, Moshe Grossman, presented a similar view, noting considerable hostility between the local Uzbeks and the refugees, even the Uzbek children, who were constantly throwing rocks at Jewish children. "The little Uzbeks hated Polish children because they were better dressed and received clothes and food from America," he said. Like the other Jewish refugees there, Leona and Mark felt this weight of antisemitism as well.

The couple ultimately remained in the Soviet Union for most of the war, surviving work camps in Siberia and Samarkand. Leona, though, had no contact with her family back in Poland the whole time and didn't know where they might be or even if they were still alive. So, in December 1944, as the war still raged on, she and Mark returned to Poland; the bond of blood and not knowing the fate of her many family members took precedence over their relative safety in the Soviet Union.

In retrospect, she said it wasn't necessarily a wise decision, but they were young, and emotion and aching hearts ruled over rationale. They were able to register with the Polish army to return to their homeland. After an arduous journey of more than two-and-a-half months – a total of 77 days – they finally arrived back in their homeland. Miraculously, Leona saw her brother, a Polish soldier, at the train station; she had thought he was dead. She recalled that this serendipitous meeting was a "one in a million chance."

However, she was to learn from him that her parents, brothers, sisters, grandparents, and cousins had met their deaths at Auschwitz, Treblinka, or the Warsaw Ghetto. She and one sister were the only survivors of the extended family besides the one brother, who had been hiding outside the Warsaw Ghetto with his Polish Gentile wife, most of the time deep in a chimney, to evade capture. Leona suggested that in some ways, he had a more difficult time than those who were in the concentration camps because the prisoners had each other, living in some sort of community, however barbaric it was, while he endured the war without family or social interaction. Mark's father perished in the Warsaw Ghetto, and Leona's mother was deported to Auschwitz just one week before its liberation.

By this time, the Soviet army had invaded Poland and liberated it from Nazi control, pushing the Germans back into Germany. The American and British armies were attacking and routing the German military from the west and south, and Leona and Mark, without surviving family in Poland and facing the threat of living amid the brutally dangerous invading Soviet army, escaped yet again. They hoped to go westward into Germany on the American side since the war was ending. The Poles had stolen everything from the Hocherman and Krohn families; neither family possessed a home, furniture, or any personal belongings. They stayed, however, in Lublin, Poland, for two months before being liberated by the Russian military in late 1944 or early 1945. Then they went to Łódź, where they remained for a year before finally leaving for Germany. As they escaped, several Poles made them run and then shot at them as they ran. They found many of their Polish countrymen as antisemitic and hateful as the Nazis had been, so their newfound freedom was not freedom after all.

Like most of the Polish Jews who returned, they quickly learned there was no place for Jews in the new Poland. The rejection and verbal insults they encountered were at times accompanied by major violent outbreaks; hundreds of Jews were killed in such attacks between 1945 and 1947. Most Jews, like Leona and Mark, if they still had doubts, became convinced that it would be wise for them to leave Poland as soon as they could. Thousands did – the postwar Jewish population reached its peak of around 240,000 in the summer of 1946 following the mass repatriation from the Soviet Union, but in the nine months between mid-1946 and March 1947, 140,000 left Poland for good. The Krohns were among them.

Once they decided to flee, finally reaching safety, Leona and Mark were provided a room for the night by some Russian soldiers who thought that they were Russian Jews and even bought them a train ticket to Berlin. By this time, Leona was eight months pregnant, so soon after arriving in Berlin, they went to a DP camp in Lampertheim. It was there that their daughter Irene (Irene Krohn Jaffa) was born in 1946. While in the DP camp, they began making plans to move to Paris, which seemed the most practical destination, or possibly – in their biggest dream – even the United States.

Leona and Mark lived in the DP camp for about three years until finally receiving permission to move to Paris to live with Mark's cousin. Excited to leave Germany and start their new life and raise Irene free from antisemitism and persecution, they gathered their few possessions and prepared for the move. The day they were scheduled to take the train to Paris, however, they received word that they had been granted a visa to emigrate to the United States. The opportunity to go to the United States was too good to pass up, so they quickly changed plans and, on August 18, 1948, set sail for New York City with two-and-a-half-year-old Irene.

They lived in New York for a month, "so happy to be in America," she said. But they "had nobody" and no money, "no clothes ... we had nothing." They were given clothes by an organization, but Irene was reluctant to take handouts. Soon, after just a month in New York, they settled in Detroit. New York was too large, they felt, and so west they went again. Mark got a job in the auto industry, starting at $50 a week, walking in the snow to work every day that first winter. He stayed in the job for 25 years, from 1948 until 1983, and they raised Irene and settled into American life in the Midwest, active in both Jewish and Polish-American activities. Never wealthy, Mark worked hard and was able to establish middle-class stability for his family of three, and they felt very much at home. Leona and Mark put the past behind them and poured their energy into work, family life, friends, and assimilating into Midwestern American culture. Mark, sadly, developed early-onset Alzheimer's disease and retired early at 60. In 1983, they moved south to Jacksonville, where Irene and her husband were now living. Mark died five years later, in 1988, barely past 70, his mind and body ravaged by dementia.

Leona experienced frequent nightmares for 50 years after the Holocaust. The nightmares stopped when she went to Poland for a visit in the 1990s. While there she was able to better come to terms with her past. Irene learned of her parents' experiences only when she was an adult, a common occurrence with survivors and their children. Leona spoke little of her life in the Holocaust until the 1990s, when she entered her seventies; Irene was middle-aged, and her children were around middle-school age. Irene grew up without grandparents, aunts, uncles, or cousins. She knew her parents were Holocaust survivors, but little else. With no extended family members, Irene felt different from her peers. She also felt different from many of her classmates because she grew up poor. Once Leona began sharing details of her Holocaust journey with Irene and her extended family, she began speaking with student groups about her story.

Despite the painful memories of the six years, she experienced in the Holocaust and the loss of her entire family – a past she tried so hard to put behind her – and the nightmares she experienced for decades, the Leona I came to know was a kind and loving lady possessed of an exceedingly gentle spirit. She spoke to my Holocaust Studies class several times, and I had the privilege to interview her and Irene. Leona exuded a warmth, humility, and tenderness that made one want to be in her presence. There was not one ounce of pretentiousness and, despite the deep pain of her past, she never exhibited anger or bitterness. Her sight gradually deteriorated as she grew older and she grew blind in later years, yet she never lost her sense of humor or zest for life. Always ready with a smile or a joke, including self-deprecating humor to help others enjoy life, she brought smiles to everyone she met. One joke she shared often in her old age, always with a twinkle in her eyes and laughing at the end, was: "Two old ladies were sitting on a bench. One said to the other, 'Remind me again who died yesterday, you or your sister?'"

She lived more than four months past her 97th birthday, an amazing feat considering the physical and emotional trauma of her youth. Leona's life was not merely long, however. It was a life well lived, with a contagious joy and an eager humor, and filled with new-found faith and pride in her Jewishness. Her beautiful and kindhearted daughter is a testament to her mother's life marked by human flourishing, a life that also produced three grandchildren – Laura, Daniel, and Andrew – along with great-grandchildren, all of whom provide testimony that Hitler and the Nazis were unsuccessful at eradicating G-d's Chosen People.

Leona's grandchildren described both Leona and Mark as grandparents who were always helping people. Grandson Andrew recalled that they gave a "communal feeling," making everyone they knew feel welcomed and loved. They passed on to their whole family the love of helping others. They cared little for material possessions or great personal comfort, constantly thinking of others first. They both greatly valued hard work and self-discipline and passed these qualities down to Irene and the grandchildren. The grandchildren told others that their grandparents were frugal and instilled in them the discipline of savings and prudence. Irene, for instance, recalled that her parents never threw out bread. I witnessed Leona's passing a legacy of generosity, hospitality, hard work, and gracious kindness to her daughter and grandchildren.

She and Mark wrestled with their faith after surviving the Holocaust. Mark, though he had trained in his youth to be a cantor, ultimately settled on atheism since he could never quite come to grips with the question of how G-d might allow the sufferings of the Jews. Leona was raised in the Orthodox tradition, and her wrestling match was a bit more ambivalent – she remained somewhat a skeptic until the end and did not regularly practice her faith. Irene, however, along with her husband, developed a deep appreciation for the traditions of Judaism and, ultimately, became a deeply faithful conservative Jew. Leona's one granddaughter has returned to her family roots and is a practicing Orthodox Jew. Regardless of any personal faith journeys, Leona endowed a heritage of compassion for others and a profound love for people that still runs through the veins of her progeny. Her mark on her family and all those she encountered in her long, rich life will not be forgotten.[1]

Leona and Mark Krohn after liberation.

Leona Krohn's daughter, Irene Jaffa, and family.

8

LT. COL. JOSEPH WILLIAMS
FRONT ROYAL, VIRGINIA

Lt. Col Joseph Williams. Credit: arlingtonparkfuneral.com

Unlike the others spotlighted in this book, Joe Williams was not born in Europe and was neither a victim of the Holocaust nor a rescuer of Jews, yet he witnessed firsthand the tragic results of the Nazi regime and their inhumane treatment of those Europeans they considered "life unworthy of life." His story comes from a vastly different vantage point, one that is important to share, nonetheless. Williams's narrative provides a different sort of glimpse into the lives of the Nazi perpetrators in the immediate aftermath of the Holocaust and the Nazi crimes against humanity, and he shared his fascinating testimony with my classes in a way that helped put additional pieces of the Holocaust puzzle together. What follows is his riveting journey.

Joseph Haley Williams, son of Joseph "Willie" Williams and Nanie Smedly Williams, was born April 24, 1921, in Front Royal, Virginia. Joe, a child of the Great Depression, grew up in relative poverty on a Virginia farm in the foothills of the Blue Ridge Mountains. His mother died when Joe was just three, and he was raised by his father and his stepmother, with whom he had a rather stormy relationship. He described her as a stern, unbending woman who did not have any great love for children. The family owned a boardinghouse on the outskirts of the small town of 3,000 residents, with its rolling hills and farmland, and not much money.

Joe's older sister had married, and left home and his older brother had done likewise, so as the only child left home, Joe had to perform schoolwork and farmwork, along with being required to help in the boardinghouse under his not-so-kind stepmother's reproving eye. Joe was close, though, to his aging grandmother, who filled his head with stories from her youth during the Civil War, and Joe became fascinated with history and the world around him. Growing up, Joe longed for adventure and excitement, things he felt he was unable to find in the rural area of the Shenandoah Valley. In 1936, at just 15, Joe enlisted in the US Army, lying about his age so he could find both opportunities and new challenges serving his country, leaving the confines of Front Royal and his stepmother for a new world. Little did he know as a young teenager in 1936 what awaited around the corner.

The unsophisticated country boy from the mountains of rural Virginia embarked on an army career that would transform his life, growing and refining him as an infantryman around the United States and on the battlefields of North Africa and Europe during World War II and long afterward. Williams became a highly decorated soldier in both World War II and the Korean War, earning a Silver Star for his extreme gallantry during the battle of El Guettar in Tunisia in 1943. Soon after, he was awarded a battlefield commission as a second lieutenant from none other than Lt. Gen. George S. Patton. Williams served a total of 22 years in the army.

When Joe was just a teenager dreaming of living a life of adventure in exotic places, halfway around the world, Adolf Hitler and his Nazi henchmen had come to power in Germany and begun preparing their quest to conquer and rule all of Europe. The Nazi Party, officially the National Socialist German Workers' Party, was led by Hitler, who had risen to head the German government on January 30, 1933. Almost immediately, its members, growing daily by scores who bought into the Nazi ideology, began to silence those who challenged the authority of the new government or who were perceived as a threat to a new way of life. Included among these were people who did not fit the mold of an "aryanized" new Germany – the Jews of Germany were a primary target. A decade later, the divergent paths of young Joe Williams and the German military would collide in ways that would forever alter Williams's life.

Williams, after gaining valuable experience in the peacetime army, was shipped to Europe in 1943 to fight and help liberate Europe from the German stranglehold. For two long years serving with the 47th Infantry Regiment, 9th Division, he engaged in combat, earning a battlefield commission from Patton's unit for his notable leadership, professionalism, and gallantry in combat. His regiment had a total of 15,000 soldiers pass through its ranks; of those, it counted about 9,000 wounded and 1,300 dead during the war, according to Williams. The 9th Division suffered a total of 4,581 killed. Williams certainly knew about the hardships of warfare and death and the bloodiness of combat in the trenches of Europe firsthand.

However, as the war was nearing its close, on April 28, 1945, Lieutenant Williams, who had just turned 24 years old but already had nine years of military service and several years of combat experience under his belt, stumbled onto a site that even a combat veteran like himself could not fathom.

About 30 kilometers northwest of Munich, adjacent to a pleasant-looking village of the same name, was Dachau concentration camp. Several of the subjects of this book, whom you have met in earlier chapters, passed through the barbed wire of Dachau as prisoners, each of them near death by the time they were imprisoned there. Williams and his unit could not believe what they found. As they entered the camp, they observed the skeletal remains of hundreds upon hundreds of rotting corpses. In addition, they witnessed the walking dead, much like skeletons themselves, and thousands more barely alive. All around them was the stench of death. Adding to the foulness was the repulsive odor of these filthy, malnourished, diseased prisoners. There were lice and maggots everywhere in the barracks, on the feeble bodies of those still alive, and eating away at the rotting corpses. Many prisoners were stricken with typhoid or dysentery; all the living were starving. There at Dachau, Williams also saw the wounds and scars of prisoners who had been badly tortured and beaten. Williams would never forget his experience liberating this hell.

Established in March 1933, Dachau was the first concentration camp erected by the Nazis in Germany. It remained in operation for 12 years, until April 1945, when it was liberated by the American soldiers. The camp was located on the grounds of an abandoned munitions factory on the edge of the medieval village of the same name. Dachau served as a prototype and model for other Nazi camps that followed. In its first year of operation, the camp held about 4,800 prisoners, but by 1937, the number had grown to 13,260. Initially, the prisoners were primarily Communists and other political opponents of the Nazi regime. Later, however, other groups were also interned there, including Jehovah's Witnesses, Roma and Sinti people (Gypsies), and homosexuals, as well as repeat criminals. Early on, relatively few Jews were interned at Dachau unless they belonged to one of those groups.

In 1937, prisoners were forced to construct a large complex of additional buildings, significantly increasing the size of the camp. The number of Jewish prisoners began to rise after Kristallnacht in November 1938, which took place in towns and cities throughout Germany as angry mobs, unofficially sanctioned by the stormtroopers, destroyed synagogues, shops, and stores owned and operated by Jews, and killed 91 of them. Immediately afterward, thousands of German Jews were rounded up and deported to Dachau and other German concentration camps. Dachau also served as a central camp for Christian religious prisoners. By the advent of the war, physicians there had begun to conduct all sorts of notorious, inhumane medical experiments on prisoners, particularly the Jewish ones, as more and more came into the camp. The guards conducted all kinds of torture in other nefarious ways. Prisoners were also used as slave laborers, primarily for construction projects around the camp and, during the war, to work in a local armaments factory.

As the war neared its end in late 1944 and early 1945, conditions at Dachau went from bad to worse. As Allied forces advanced toward Germany – the Americans and British from the west and south and the Russians from the east – the Germans began to move concentration camp inmates who were close to the front to camps more centrally located. Dachau was one of these camps and received nearly nonstop transports of evacuated prisoners from other camps, in filthy cattle cars or from long, arduous forced marches, arriving after days of travel with little food or water, exhausted, and often near death. Many prisoners entering Dachau in the last months of the war were Jews evacuated from other camps. Richard Friedemann, the clever young man from Kraków from a previous chapter of this book, was one of them, as was Gina Freiden. With overcrowded quarters, poor sanitary conditions, insufficient rations, and weakened, malnourished prisoners, a typhus epidemic ran through the camp in the spring of 1945. In just the last three months or so of operations, more than 15,000 prisoners died, and 500 Soviet soldiers were executed.

When US military forces approached Dachau in late April 1945, there were 67,665 registered prisoners alive at the camp – 22,100 of them Jews. Just 48 hours before a long-awaited liberation, Nazi guards forced 7,000 prisoners, mostly Jews, on a death march from Dachau to Tegernsee, about 44 miles [72 kilometers] to the south. Many of those prisoners died enroute from hunger or exhaustion, and those unable to keep up were shot. On April 29, the American forces of the 42nd Infantry Division, accompanied by some companies from the 47th Regiment, liberated Dachau. First Lieutenant Williams served as one of the liberating officers; he was company commander of L Company in the 47th Regiment.

As he and his fellow soldiers neared the camp, they found more than 30 cattle cars filled with bodies that had been brought to Dachau, all in an advanced state of decomposition. Williams and his compatriots found 32,000 prisoners alive, though most were barely so, with 1,600 crammed in each of 20 barracks that had been designed to house 250. "There our troops found sights, sounds, and stenches horrible beyond belief, cruelties so enormous as to be incomprehensible to the normal mind," one fellow officer reported.

Williams echoed such comments, and he remarked half a century later that he would never forget the stench that forever remained in his nostrils, nor the walking dead with the emaciated skeletal remains of the newly liberated prisoners. Williams said that in the large rooms adjacent to the Dachau gas chamber, "bodies were stacked to the ceiling. ... It was obvious from these bodies, other bodies on the lorry, and those strewn around the campgrounds, that the daily death rate far exceeded the daily capacity of the crematory." And 50 railroad boxcars had been jammed with about 100 prisoners each. "Approximately 3,000 of the prisoners were dead, yet many others were still alive – barely." The ashes from the cremated bodies, Williams said, were buried in holes dug all over the crematory yards. After liberation, a group of Polish-Christian ex-prisoners built a large stone cross near the crematory entrance to commemorate the more than 200,000 who perished there. "Under the cross alone are the ashes of 20,000 former inmates," he said. While tens of thousands at Dachau had died and ten million more all over Europe in the Holocaust, in just a little more than a decade, Williams and his fellow soldiers were able to save at least some of the near-dead prisoners. The Americans were seen as saviors of the liberated – and indeed they were.

Though the war was finally over, Williams's work in Germany was not finished. While he and his liberating compatriots had a part in ending the tragedy soon known as the Holocaust, saving thousands of lives, he had an even more important role to play. The US Army determined he was a valuable asset and should remain in the newly occupied country of Germany as the Allies made decisions about the future of Nazi war criminals – the perpetrators of the Holocaust and leading instigators of World War II. The top Nazi officials who had been captured were charged and tried for war crimes in the German city of Nuremberg, in what became known as the Nuremberg Trials. Hundreds of lower-level functionaries were tried at Dachau, which had been transformed into holding cells for SS officers, and then imprisoned at Landsberg Prison, about 50 kilometers away. Landsberg, ironically, was the same prison where Hitler had been imprisoned in 1924 for his unsuccessful Beer Hall Putsch in Munich. US Army brass designated Williams as the assistant commandant of Landsberg Prison in May 1945. Among his duties was to command the executioners, who were tasked to carry out the death sentences handed down on Nazi war criminals in the postwar trials.

The city of Landsberg rests at the southern tip of Lichfield, in the Bavarian foothills of the Alps in southern Germany. In 1945, it was a picturesque Alpine village along a winding river, the medieval Bavarian Gate, a Gothic church, and its Renaissance city hall, all beneath the steady gaze of the forbidding ancient fortress prison of Landsberg. Landsberg Prison was completed in 1881, ten years after the unification of Germany. It was built on a high bluff overlooking the Lech River, about one mile south of the city of the same name. It was three stories with a steep roof of clay tile, housing four cell blocks with three tiers of cells, with one tier for each of its three floors. Most of the cells housed prisoners in solitary confinement, except for a few communal cells for some female prisoners. Each cell was a room with four plastered walls and a ceiling and a single window to the outside with eight vertical one-inch steel bars encased in concrete. A heavy oak door fortified with steel was the single entrance and exit to each cell. The furniture consisted of a metal bunk bed with a hard straw-filled mattress and one three-legged short wooden stool. Rooms were heated with coal and a large boiler, each with its own radiator. Since coal was in such short supply, many rooms were quite cold; some prisoners even suffered from frostbite. Each prisoner was issued a "night pail" for bathroom use, collected each morning by the guards. Meals consisted of fresh fruits and vegetables, but like coal, food was rationed due to short supply, so the prisoners had to get by with meager portions. Despite relatively limited rations, food was nutritionally healthy and certainly adequate, far exceeding the starvation allocation provided by the Germans in the ghettos and concentration camps.

In the early days of the American administration of Landsberg Prison, the camp commandant was Major Carlson. He had a German mistress, to whom he devoted much time, energy, and black-market activity to maintain a lavish lifestyle for the two of them. Carlson was soon relieved of his command and replaced by Maj. George T. Scheiner. Scheiner was a far more professional, no-nonsense officer than his predecessor. Born in Germany, he immigrated to the United States with his family when he was just a youngster. The major had served 30 years in the US Army, rising through the ranks, a hardened veteran who had no sympathy for the Germans of his original homeland.

On one occasion, ten condemned war criminals from the Mauthausen concentration camp were brought into Scheiner's office at Landsberg headquarters to be read their sentences by Williams. The ten felons had been sentenced to death, but their sentences were being commuted to life in prison. Williams read each order in English, while an interpreter translated it into

German, with the last line of each order reading: "... is hereby commuted to life imprisonment." Each of the ten prisoners, Williams said, fainted upon hearing the news and later were so overjoyed they "were dancing, hugging one another, and crying."

Williams served at Landsberg for three years. During this time, more than 250 war criminals were sent, "hands tied behind their backs, to their execution," Williams said. Their executions were carried out by a firing squad or at the end of a noose. Williams cited that as many as 22 Nazi war criminals were executed in a single morning during his time there. The scaffolds used for the hangings were, appropriately, constructed at Dachau, and among Williams's more important responsibilities was the oversight of the transport of those gallows to Nuremberg or Landsberg for the executions.

Williams submitted that from August 1946 until the summer of 1949, more than 1,000 prisoners had been tried and sent to Landsberg Prison. Most were convicted and sentenced from three years to life, but about 250, or 25 percent, met their fate with the executioner. Their crimes included the mass murder of some six million Jews and millions of others deemed undesirable by Hitler and his Nazi henchmen. Nuremberg Trials Chief Prosecutor Justice Robert Jackson, on leave from the US Supreme Court, argued, "The wrongs which we seek to condemn and punish have been so calculated, so malignant and so devastating, that civilization cannot tolerate their being ignored because it cannot survive their being repeated." Jackson added, with great moral clarity: "That four great nations, flushed with victory and stung with injury stay the hand of vengeance and voluntarily submit their captive enemies to the judgment of the law is one of the most significant tributes that Power has ever paid to Reason." Roberts further said, "The real complaining party at your bar is Civilization. ... It asks whether law is so laggard as to be utterly hopeless to deal with crimes of this magnitude."

In November 1945, the trials began, marked by a statement: This was the century's most "heroic attempt to achieve justice without vengeance – heroic because the victors of World War II had every reason to destroy the vanquished without pity. Heroic because they ultimately resisted the temptation to impose on the Germans what Nazis had imposed on their victims – collective guilt." The Allied judges presiding over Nuremberg and ensuing war crimes trials granted the captives "a presumption of innocence" and conducted the trials to determine any personal responsibility. Williams, now a seasoned combat veteran yet still a young junior officer, had boots on the ground in those unprecedented trials, going face to face with many perpetrators, arguably among the evilest men in modern history.

Williams met Hermann Goering, the second-highest ranked war criminal to be tried at Nuremberg, commander-in-chief of the Luftwaffe, creator of the Gestapo secret police, and the mastermind behind the concentration camp system. During the Nuremberg Trials, an American documentary film company was chronicling the liberation of Dachau's concentration camps, with other camps at Bergen-Belsen and Buchenwald, permeating a dark courtroom with "ghastly images of skeletal survivors, stacked cadavers, and bulldozers shoveling victims into mass graves," historian Robert Shnayerson reported.

Hans Frank, who served as head of the German government in Poland, the duties of which included overseeing four of the death camps, was convicted of war crimes and crimes against humanity. Soon to be sentenced to execution by hanging, he returned to his cell that night, bursting out: "To think we lived like kings and believed in that beast!" Goering, on the other hand, offered merely: "It was such a good afternoon, too – and then they showed that awful film and just spoiled everything."

Goering, like Frank, was charged and convicted of war crimes and crimes against humanity. He was sentenced to die by hanging. Goering insisted on being executed by firing squad instead, considered a more noble way to die as a soldier rather than as a common criminal, but the court refused. Goering, ever the coward, took his own life instead. Williams met and spoke with Goering in his cell on at least one occasion and found him arrogant and unrepentant to the end. Williams said he was standing a few feet from Goering when the Nazi swallowed cyanide, apparently smuggled into his cell in a fountain pen. Williams was one of only a handful of people to see Goering take his last breath.

Sepp Dietrich, Hitler's personal chauffeur, and bodyguard before 1929, later the highest ranking Waffen-SS officer, was another important Nazi imprisoned at Landsberg. Williams met him when assistant commandant. Dietrich commanded the 6th Panzer Army during the Battle of the Bulge, in which he was responsible for the Malmedy massacre in Belgium – the murder of 750 American prisoners of war in December 1944. He was convicted of war crimes at the US Military Tribunal at Dachau in the summer of 1946 for his responsibility in ordering the execution of POWs at Malmedy and in the Ardennes. These murdered American soldiers – unarmed prisoners of war, their hands raised overhead – were shot in cold blood. Williams described his first encounter with Dietrich:

Dietrich entered the visitor's room quietly, smiling broadly as his eyes darted around the large room. He stopped abruptly when he saw me and drew himself up. *"Guten tag, Herr Oberleutnant!"* he rasped, saluting briskly. I could not help but make a mental comparison of the falsely jovial, little man before [me], whose creased, mobile face could have belonged to a Hollywood movie thug or to a waiter in a *Gasthaus* [small inn] to the photographs I had seen of Dietrich in other times. Then he was a preening peacock, in bemedaled SS black, standing arrogantly beside his beloved Führer Hitler and ... Reichsführer SS Heinrich Himmler. Dietrich was a different man now, wearing his wrinkled prison uniform, a caricature of his former self. Williams ignored the salute and had Dietrich sit down at the opposite end of the long visitor's table. Williams watched Dietrich as he sat nervously at the table, examining his fingernails, smoothing down his thinning hair, and grinning like a mischievous little boy.

In the end, however, Dietrich was among the more fortunate Nazi prisoners. He had originally been sentenced to life in prison, but he eventually was granted a shortened sentence, 25 years at Landsberg Prison. He was released on parole in 1955 after serving a mere ten years. He lived until 1966, dying of a heart attack at age 74. Six thousand people, including many former SS officers and men, attended his funeral – a vile war criminal allowed to live his final decade as a free man, unrepentant to the end. Dietrich's sadistic war crimes ultimately netted him a mere slap on the wrist.

During the initial Nuremberg Trials, 199 defendants were tried, generally all high-level Nazis in the German government. Of these, 161 were convicted and 38 were sentenced to death. The remaining convicted Nazi criminals were given prison sentences, typically ranging from three years to life. After the Trial of Major War Criminals, 12 additional trials were held between December 1946 and April 1949, grouped as the Subsequent Nuremberg Proceedings. Prisoners were charged with one or more of three crimes: crimes against peace, war crimes, and crimes against humanity.

They differed from the first trial in that they were conducted before US military tribunals rather than the international tribunal that decided the fate of the major Nazi leaders. Growing differences among the four victorious Allied powers made other joint trials nearly impossible. The subsequent trials were held in the same location – the Nuremberg Palace of Justice. By August 1946, more than 1,000 prisoners were serving sentences at Landsberg under the supervision of Assistant Camp Commandant 1st Lt. Joseph Williams, with sentences ranging from three years to death by hanging or firing squad. Many of these inmates had been concentration camp guards and administrators at Buchenwald, Dachau, Mauthausen, Kaufering, and numerous other concentration camps. Inmates included a group of approximately 20 medical doctors found guilty of conducting inhumane and grotesque medical experiments, most often on Jewish prisoners. Hitler's personal physician, SS Gen. Karl Brandt, and Himmler's physician were among the group serving sentences at Landsberg.

Williams said there were over 300 SS and concentration camp leaders imprisoned, many of them at Landsberg under his supervision. In addition to his duties as assistant commandant, Williams directly oversaw the executioners. For those serving on the firing squads, each shooter loaded six live rounds and two blanks so that no one would know for certain who was directly responsible for each execution. Williams recalled that with each execution, whether by hanging or firing squad, "we tried to use as much dignity as possible." There were exactly 13 steps for each prisoner to clear as he was marched up to the gallows. While death by firing squad was considered a more honorable form of execution, it was up to the judge(s) to determine the type of fate each prisoner would receive. Williams mentioned that in some weeks, there would be three or four executions, and then sometimes there would be a couple of months between executions.

Williams took the responsibilities of his job seriously, especially since he had seen firsthand the horrors on the battlefield and the horrific results of the concentration camps. He was the consummate professional officer, and most of his subordinates were US Army noncommissioned officers also exhibiting the highest degree of professionalism and sense of moral duty. One executioner, however, a hangman called by the pseudonym of Master Sgt. Lee Forrest (or Sergeant Wood in his class testimony), had to be relieved of his duty in August 1946. Forrest, from Texas, who later was killed in combat in Korea, was "a small man, in his late thirties," who was a "loud, boisterous, little man who tried to equalize his size with the importance of his unique job." He was appointed, Williams reported, the chief executioner of the US 1st Military Command Area.

The first war criminals executed were a group of Nazi killers from Dachau concentration camp. Forrest performed his duties with pride and precision. Williams wrote that the hangman's job requires precision – he had to know the weight and height of each of the condemned prisoners and cut the hanging ropes accordingly. The rope was then stretched until there was no more elasticity and tested until the hangman was satisfied that it was just right. Finally, the convicted felon was ushered to the scaffold over the trapdoor, his hands and feet bound, and the sentence read to him one final time. The hangman placed a black hood over the head of the criminal, the noose secured around his neck. The hangman made the final adjustment to the knot so the rope would break the prisoner's neck rather than strangle him. Then, finally, he stepped back, pulled the small lever, and the prisoner immediately plunged to their death.

Forrest continued to perform his role professionally until he was called upon to execute the "Big Ten" from the Nuremberg Trials: the top Nazi hierarchy. That evening, after the hangings, Forrest got drunk at the Non-Commissioned Officers' Club, mouthed off, and challenged Williams when he was called to settle Forrest down. Word of Forrest's actions leaked to the media, and he was relieved of his responsibilities and shipped back to the States. Confidential information about executions was slipped to the press, and *Life* magazine ran a detailed article on the executions, presumably information provided by Forrest. At least two more hangmen followed Forrest during Williams's tenure, serving with greater distinction than had their predecessor. Williams and his assistant were present at every one of the executions during the assistant commandant's three-year tour of duty overseeing them.

Nuremberg and Landsberg prisons were the only two prisons in the American zone of occupation in Germany where war criminals were executed between 1946 and 1952. The first executions that took place at Landsberg were in April 1946 and included a group from Dachau. The next executions occurred in October 1946 at Nuremberg and included the group of ten top Nazis. All other executions in the US zone took place at Landsberg.

Also at Landsberg, along with German war criminals, were 54 former concentration camp inmates who had been tried and convicted under the charge of "common design." These were typically prisoners who served as *kapos* or in other positions of authority over other prisoners and committed atrocious acts against their fellow prisoners. A third group of prisoners awaiting execution included Greeks, Poles, and various Eastern Europeans who were former concentration camp prisoners who took revenge after liberation, roaming parts of Germany and indiscriminately robbing, raping, and murdering.

A batch of prisoners from that third group was sent to Landsberg in February 1947 for execution by firing squad. The squad consisted of eight volunteers from the US 508th Military Police Battalion out of Munich. Lieutenant Colonel (later Major General) Smith, 3rd US Army Provost Marshal in Heidelberg, came to Landsberg on February 14, 1947, to command the firing squad. A firing range had to be constructed. Williams was responsible for overseeing its construction. Large oak timbers went in deep holes and were cemented in place. Bolts were fastened on the timbers so the prisoner's legs could be secured to the bottom of each timber; a rope was placed under each arm and latched on a top metal hook. The prisoner's hands were tied with rawhide straps or rope around and in the back of the timber. About 200 sandbags were stacked two deep and ten feet tall behind the timbers. Thus, the firing line was complete, awaiting only the prisoner to execute.

Williams was responsible for bringing the condemned prisoners to the place of execution. Williams was accompanied by a US military chaplain and a civilian pastor or priest, depending on the prisoner's religious affiliation. US Army guards were posted in front and back of each prisoner. For the final 24 hours of the convicted prisoner's life, he was guarded around the clock by a special guard. The evening before the execution, each prisoner was given his last meal. On execution morning, Williams escorted prisoners to their execution posts and directed the guards to fasten the straps through metal rings. The prisoners were given a choice: have a black hood placed over their heads or not. Then they were asked if they had any final words.

One prisoner, a Greek concentration camp survivor who had been sentenced to execution by firing squad because of his postwar revenge, was Dimitrious Kosturos. Kosturos declined the black hood and gave his last words in German, which were translated into English to everyone present. His words were touching:

> I am a Greek prisoner of war who fought in frontline action against Italian fascism and Nazi Germany. The English and Americans are well informed about the catastrophe which was brought upon Greece by Fascism and Nazism. It is a pity that the Americans are to shoot on this St. Valentine's Day such a prisoner of war who has been imprisoned five years in a Nazi concentration camp. But I am not afraid of the bullets which are going to hit me, for I am going to see my brother, Engel, and my father God the Greek.

These last words were read in English by Williams to those assembled. Once Williams had read the translated words, the command of "ready" was given, followed by "aim," and finally "fire!" Death came quickly to the brave Greek, much as it had to the others executed by firing squad. Others followed Kosturos, each with their own unique story. The Nazis were successful in turning the world upside down and blurring the lines of human morality and depravity.

Williams reported that of all the former SS men imprisoned at Landsberg, none were more brutal or sadistic than Jurgen Stroop. Stroop had been an SS major general and police chief of Warsaw in 1943 when his forces destroyed the Warsaw Ghetto. Later, he committed crimes against Greek nationals and partisans and in 1944 and 1945 ordered the murder of several American pilots. Largely for these latter crimes, he was tried, convicted, and sentenced to death by an American military tribunal. In early 1947, orders were given to prepare Stroop for execution by firing squad. Preparations were made to be carried out at Landsberg Prison.

Stroop was given his last meal. Just before the moment of execution, though, orders came in from the US Third Army Headquarters in Heidelberg that the execution was not going to be held. The new Polish government had requested Stroop be turned over to their government to stand trial for atrocities he had committed against Poles and Jews in Warsaw in 1943.

Before the Nazi invasion of Poland in September 1939, Warsaw had the second-largest Jewish population of any city in the world, behind New York City, with more than 350,000 Jews out of a population of 1.3 million, about a third of the total population. German troops entered Warsaw on September 29, shortly after its surrender. A year later, on October 12, 1940, the Germans ordered the establishment of the Warsaw Ghetto, requiring all Jewish residents of Warsaw to move into a designated area, which was then sealed off from the rest of the city. The ghetto had a wall more than ten feet tall, topped with barbed wire and carefully guarded to prevent movement between the ghetto and the rest of Warsaw. The ghetto population quickly swelled to nearly 450,000 Jews as those in nearby towns and *shtetls* were forced into the 1.3-square-mile area, with an average of 7.2 people per room.

Conditions in the Warsaw Ghetto deteriorated rapidly, with several families crammed into tiny apartments designed for one family, with little to no heat or water, poor hygienic conditions, and nearly starvation food rations. Rations were about 300 calories daily, with no medicines, and as many as 50,000 Jews were dying each year. One diary entry of a ghetto resident read: "The hunger in the ghetto was so great, was so bad, that people were laying on the streets and dying, little children went around begging."

Between 1940 and mid-1942, 83,000 Jews died of starvation and disease, many of them children. Then, in a seven-week period from July to September 1942, the Germans deported about 265,000 Jews from the ghetto to the Treblinka death camp while killing another 35,000 Jews in the ghetto itself.

In January 1943, the SS and Gestapo returned to the Warsaw Ghetto with the intent of liquidating the remaining 70,000 to 80,000 Jews through deportation to Treblinka. The Jews, knowing their potential fate, began to resist, and after deporting about 5,000 Jews, the Nazis temporarily halted operations and withdrew. On April 19, 1943, the SS soldiers returned with the full intent to deport the remaining Jews by all means necessary. The Jews had smuggled in a variety of weapons, improvised additionally with homemade weapons, and were determined to fight to the death. The Warsaw Ghetto Uprising ensued. The fighting lasted nearly four weeks – longer than it had taken the German army to successfully conquer all of Poland. The Jewish resistance fighters in the ghetto were about 1,500, mostly young men who were convinced it would be better to revolt against the Nazis to fight and die, taking some Germans down with them. More than 7,000 Jews died fighting in the ghetto, and about 42,000 were deported to Majdanek in Lublin, Poland, and another 7,000 to Treblinka. As many as 20,000 Jews, however, survived and remained in hiding on the Aryan side of the ghetto.

Stroop had been a World War I veteran and was 48 years old when he arrived in Warsaw in April 1943. A loyal Nazi and an ardent antisemite, he was assigned by Himmler as the right man to solve the "Jewish Problem" in the Warsaw Ghetto. Despite ferocious fighting by Jews willing to fight to their deaths and numerous casualties for the SS troops, Stroop's brutality, aggressiveness, and overwhelming numerical and firepower superiority led to an SS victory. And Stroop's orders were certainly brutal. One example came when several of Stroop's subordinate commanders were concerned about what to do with captured Jewish infants. Stroop's response was, "You men don't seem to understand that Jewish infants grow up to become Jewish monsters; therefore, the infants must be destroyed." "Take the infants to the wall, hold them by their feet and legs, and smash their heads against the wall." Stroop's men also took target practice on Jewish children or impaled them on spikes as they tried to jump from windows and ledges to safety. He recommended that a sharpshooter who made a hit with every shot receive a decoration. The final blow came with the blowing up of Warsaw's Great Synagogue.

Stroop surrendered to American troops in early May 1945. When his execution was canceled at the last minute, he was extradited to Poland in 1951 and, on March 6, 1952, hanged in Warsaw Central Prison. Stroop was yet another high-level Nazi whom Williams met and escorted to meet his executors, though his death was delayed.

Another prisoner under Williams's authority was Ilse Koch, a female SS guard at Buchenwald, infamously known as "The Bitch of Buchenwald." She and 30 other guards and administrators from Buchenwald were under Williams's supervision at Landsberg Prison. Williams recalled her as the most notorious. Williams and his wife attended Koch's trial proceedings in the Dachau courtroom and saw the evidence exhibits, including lamp shades, handbags, and other articles made from the human skin of Jewish prisoners, which she was infamous for collecting.

For nearly six years, Koch lived at Buchenwald; she was the wife of the camp commandant. Dozens of former inmates, in the short space of time from April 1945 to April 1947, accused her of innumerable atrocities. Her husband, Karl, had been executed by the SS just a week before the end of the war for murder and embezzlement. Ilse escaped the wrath of her fellow Nazis and the occupying Allies. She was finally arrested in October 1945 and sent to join the Dachau War Crimes group to await trial with the 30 other Buchenwald defendants. Initially, she was convicted and sentenced to life in prison, but a review board commuted the sentence to only four years; she was released in October 1949. Shortly after her release from Landsberg though, the West German government had Koch arrested and charged with the murder of 35 Germans and crimes against an additional 135 German inmates at Buchenwald. The German court sentenced her to life at a Munich women's prison. In 1967, at age 60, she committed suicide.

Williams's duties at Landsberg included not only making the necessary arrangements for executions but notifying the next of kin for final visits, being in charge of prison supplies and transportation, supervising 17 prison workshops and keeping them operating with prison labor and German civilians; and conducting routine spot checks of all cells to ensure there were no unauthorized articles or homemade weapons, particularly after Goering committed suicide in 1946. When making his cell checks and hospital visits to prisoners, Williams was careful not to display any overt signs of either friendliness or hostility.

Another infamous prisoner Williams encountered at Landsberg was SS *Obersturmführer* [Lt. Col.] Joachim Peiper. Peiper had been convicted of the mass slaughter of American soldiers from the 30th Infantry Division near Malmedy in December 1944. Earlier, in 1943, near the city of Kharkiv, Peiper gave the order to set fire to a village of around 800 people and eliminate all life in the village. Soon afterward, in Kursk, Russia, Peiper's soldiers used flamethrowers to burn innocent women and children to death. There were other alleged atrocities committed or ordered by Peiper as well. Peiper was sentenced to death. Williams met with him in his cell not long before his execution. Williams described his meeting with Peiper:

"The heavy wood and steel door clanged shut behind [me]. Walking down the corridor ... I could sense the piercing eyes of these hardened Nazis as they individually peered out ... through the small, single openings in their cell doors. Each now awaited a final review of his sentence before execution. It was almost hopeless, but as long as each lived, they hoped and, in many cases, hated.

Williams approached the cell door, stopped, and saw the white three-by-five card affixed to the door, which read: 'DEATH Joachim Peiper.' Williams unlocked the door and walked in. The cell was empty except for a stool and a wooden bunk attached to the wall. Peiper was sitting on the three-legged stool, reading. He immediately rose, moved quickly to the corner of the cell, and stood at attention with his back to Williams, as inmates were required to do. After a long hesitation, staring at Peiper's back and pondering what kind of evil monster was before him, Williams finally gave the prisoner the commands of 'At ease!' and 'About face!'"

As Peiper turned and faced Williams, the German stared straight ahead. Williams described him as having "piercing, dark eyes, and an intelligent expression on his face that bore no evidence of resentment or hatred. There was an air of dignity about him that even the drab prison garb could not disguise." Williams introduced himself and Peiper responded in kind with "excellent English." After Williams left the cell, he wondered what had been going through the mind of that barbaric soldier. Yet, he pondered, there was something about Peiper that made Williams wonder if in another place and time, they might have been friends. "But," he quickly thought, "there would be no other times, or other places. [We] are of two different worlds."

After the cell visit, Williams and Peiper, along with Peiper's former adjutant, Hans Grule, met often over the next two years while the two Germans were imprisoned. They discussed combat tactics at great length, comparing their experiences. In late 1946, Williams had Peiper and Grule write down their combat experiences on the Russian front and in the Ardennes offensive and Malmedy massacre. Williams found Peiper arrogant but fascinating. Peiper expressed to Williams his contempt for those Nazi political leaders who, defeated, were denying everything they had once supported.

On July 16, 1946, the court found 73 men involved in the Malmedy massacre guilty, with 43 sentenced to death by hanging, 22 to life in prison, and the remaining eight prisoners sentenced to terms ranging from ten to 20 years. Peiper was sentenced to death. In 1948, US Gen. Lucius Clay reviewed some of the sentences, including Peiper's, and commuted Peiper's sentence to life in prison. He was released in 1956, however, having served fewer than 11 years behind bars. He lived until 1976, when anti-Nazi arsonists set his house on fire, killing Peiper in the process.

Williams finally left his assignment in Germany, returning to the United States in 1949, where he continued serving his country as an army officer on various assignments for the next decade. Following his distinguished military career, including combat duty in the Korean War and various global assignments, Williams retired as a lieutenant colonel in 1958 at only the age of 37. He then graduated from Florida State University in 1960 and earned a master's degree from Georgia Southern University in 1967 and a doctorate in education from Nova University. In Florida, he embarked on a second career, working 25 years as an educator, starting as a history teacher at Jacksonville's Terry Parker High School. Williams retired from teaching in 1984. He was known as a wonderful storyteller, which served him well in that capacity, and later as the author of *Captor-Captive*, his memoir on his experiences at Landsberg.

Williams passed away on February 10, 2017, just shy of his 96th birthday. He was preceded in death by his beloved wife, Dorothy Girtman Williams, from Hazelhurst, Georgia, and is survived by his son, Joseph H. Williams Jr., and daughter, Linda O'Neal, along with their spouses, and grandchildren Haley and Patrick O'Neal. Williams was truly a part of the American "Greatest Generation," earning that distinction as a child of the Great Depression who fought courageously in both World War II and the Korean conflict, helped to liberate Dachau, and served notably with great distinction at Landsberg Prison, assisting in the process of bringing to justice many of the most brutal Nazis.

Williams spoke humbly, often deflecting the significant impact of his role in bringing perpetrators of the Holocaust to justice as he told his stories of his life in Germany in an engaging fashion. He spoke several times to my Holocaust Studies class in Orange Park. Since the students and I were enthralled by his accounts, I couldn't help but wonder how very fortunate his students had been during his two-and-a-half decades of teaching history, a part of which he had such a significant role. The atrocities committed by the barbarians who implemented, led, or took part in the Holocaust can never be undone. The ten million innocent victims murdered at the hands of the Nazis and their henchmen cannot be brought back to life, and the trauma suffered by the survivors, the stories of a few of whom I have shared with you in this book, was never erased from their hearts and minds. And yet men like Joe Williams were true American heroes who did their part in executing justice and helping ensure that the lessons of the Holocaust will never be forgotten.[1]

Lt. Joseph H. Williams, deputy commandant of the Landsberg prison, poses next to a sign marking the site of the crematorium in Dachau. It reads: "'This area is being retained as a shrine to the 238,000 individuals who were cremated here. Please don't destroy.'" Dachau, Germany, 1946. Credit: Captor Captive, Girtman Press.

Exterior of Landsberg prison, where German war criminals were interned during the subsequent Nuremberg trials, Landsberg, Germany, circa 1946. Credit: Captor Captive, Girtman Press.

9

ERNST TRIER-MØRCH, M.D., PH.D
SLAGELSE, DENMARK

Noble be man, merciful and good! For that alone sets him apart
from every other creature on earth. – **Goethe**

Whoever saves a single life, saves an entire universe.–**Mishnah,
Sanhedrin, 4:5**

Rescue those who are being taken away to death; hold back those
who are stumbling to the slaughter, oh, hold them. – **Proverbs 24:11**

Dr. Ernst Trier-Morch in the author;s classroom holding up his medals, 1995, Orange Park, Fl.

On a cool winter afternoon outside Callahan, on a farm in northeast Florida, the week before Christmas 1995, I attended the funeral service for a man I had come to know over the previous 18 months. He had lived a long, fruitful, and fascinating life, touching the lives of countless people, many of whom he would never know, from Denmark to Chicago to Florida. Ernst Trier-Mørch, M.D., Ph.D., was a captivating and charming gentleman, already in his mid-eighties when I first met him, a retired anesthesiologist and town deputy sheriff who drove a red convertible sports car. Frequently described by others as a character, Dr. Mørch was charismatic, a bit flamboyant, and small in stature in his later years but large in both personality and intellect. He led a life filled with extraordinary accomplishments, including a career as a renowned scientist and physician. Just one of his many medical accomplishments was developing one of the first ventilators, which ultimately saved innumerable lives. Perhaps most extraordinary of all was when, as a young Danish physician in Copenhagen during the Nazi occupation from 1940–45, he was instrumental in saving thousands of Jewish lives by ingenious and heroic measures, the likes of which were regrettably rare in Nazi-occupied Europe. I invite you, as you read the following pages, to take a glimpse into Mørch's life of adventure, accomplishment, and heroism.

On the morning of April 9, 1940, seven months after starting the World War II, the Nazis invaded their small neighbor to the north, Denmark. The battle that followed was brief because Denmark's modest military forces were small and used antiquated arms and equipment. Within 24 hours, with fewer than 50 combat deaths combined suffered by both sides, Denmark surrendered, knowing it had no chance against the vastly superior German military machine. Denmark was one of the steppingstones in Nazi Germany's attempt to conquer all of Europe. It was important to Germany's war strategy for several reasons. Though a small nation, Denmark provided railroad lines to transport Sweden's war materials to Germany. Sweden was neutral and a trading partner with Germany and served as a geographic buffer between Great Britain and Germany. Maybe most importantly, Denmark's rich farmland was vital for feeding millions of Germans their butter, pork, and beef as they increasingly ramped up their war efforts throughout the continent. One other reason to invade Denmark was to seize its air bases, necessary for the invasion of Norway. The Nazis wanted a "peaceful occupation" in Denmark to save their assets for more difficult conquests while gaining the nation's strategic advantages.

In the preceding years, the Danish coalition government formed by Social Democrats and Social Liberals had undertaken a policy of neutrality, knowing well that keeping up with German rearmament and eventually defending the small, flat country against aggression from their powerful neighbor to the south would be impossible. After a few skirmishes on that fateful day in April 1940, the Sovereign in Council quickly decided to halt fighting the superior German forces and engage in talks with the Germans. The Germans glibly assured the Danish government and King Christian X that they would respect Denmark's political independence and allow them to keep their government intact. The Danish leaders thought that resuming fighting would only bring about the destruction of the nation and wanted to believe the assurances from the Nazis. No fewer than two hours after the invasion, the Danish government agreed to Germany's terms, and the king ordered a ceasefire. For the first time in nearly a millennium, Denmark was no longer a free and independent nation.

The early years of German occupation were not particularly terrible for the Danes, including their sizable Jewish population, in comparison to most other countries that had fallen under Nazi domination. Hitler and Nazi leaders considered Danes more aryanized than much of Europe and tended to favor a softer approach to the occupation. Hitler went so far as to describe Denmark as "a model protectorate" and allowed the occupied nation to retain its king, parliament, and judicial system. Despite Nazi efforts to wreak genocide on European Jews, Danish Jews at first found less interference from the occupiers in Denmark. Moreover, the Danish government, in concert with its citizens, pushed back against Nazi demands that Denmark establish anti-Jewish legislation. The Danes, unlike most of their European counterparts, considered Jewish people no different than their non-Jewish citizens and refused to capitulate to the German demands. Mørch recalled Jews "had always behaved as good Danes and therefore there were no antisemitic feelings in the population." And so a strong Danish underground resistance movement sprang up almost immediately, covertly pushing back against Nazi occupation. Mørch had an important role in the resistance movement from its inception.

When Germany began its occupation of Denmark in the spring of 1940, the Jewish population was roughly 7,500, about 0.2 percent of the nation's total. About 6,000 of those Jews were Danish citizens; the rest were German and Eastern European refugees who had fled to Denmark since the Nazis rose to power in 1933. Most of the Jews lived in Copenhagen, the capital and largest city in Denmark, with the rest scattered around the small country.

Unlike in other occupied European nations, the Danish Jews were not required to register their property and assets or give up their homes and businesses, and they were not issued Jewish identification papers. Also, initially, they were not required to wear the yellow Star of David badges or armbands. Danish authorities, led by King Christian X himself, refused to discriminate against the Jews. Their resistance efforts against the occupying Nazis, combined with the Germans' relative tolerance of the Danes in those early years, led to a somewhat peaceful existence for the Jews.

By 1943, however, the Germans began to take a more severe approach toward Denmark, including toward the Jews. In August, the Germans dissolved the Danish government and two months later ordered the deportation of the nation's Jews to Nazi concentration camps, signifying a likely death sentence. The Danish resistance quickly began to double down on its efforts to resist Nazi domination, working together with many other Danish citizens to save their Jewish brothers and sisters. One man who played an active role in the resistance and helped save thousands of Danish Jews was Dr. Ernst Trier-Mørch.

Mørch was born May 14, 1908, in Slagelse, Denmark, and lived his first ten years in the nearby small Danish village of Nykøbing. It was a pristine setting – a "lovely landscape geographically, but completely uncivilized," Mørch said. His mother, Gudrun Trier Mørch, was an artist; his father, Ejvind, was an architect and carpenter who had also been the administrator of a hospital for the insane. With nine children, the family was close, living in a three-room apartment with indoor plumbing. They owned a lively, high-spirited Icelandic pony that would often wander inside the home, sometimes even into the kitchen. In describing his childhood days, Mørch said, "All of my sisters and brothers stuck very closely together." Mørch never knew his grandparents; they had died when he was very young. He counted 60 first cousins, though, so he had a large extended family in addition to his eight siblings. They grew up formally as Lutherans, as did most Danes of the day, but they did not practice the faith, and Mørch never considered himself a religious man.

When he was five years old, Mørch had tonsillitis, resulting in a tonsillectomy without the benefit of anesthesia. It was such a traumatic experience that he vowed then and there that he would become a physician so he could work toward making surgery less painful. He did indeed go into medicine when he got older, graduating from the University of Copenhagen Medical School in 1935 and, undecided in which area of medicine he wanted to specialize, he accepted residencies in psychiatry, genetics, obstetrics, pathology, and surgical training. After a decade, he became more involved in administering anesthesia, particularly in the practice of thoracic surgery, a new field. "I was drawn to anesthesia because it is the most dangerous field in medicine, therefore the most important," he once said with a bit of bravado and a grin. "You can find good surgeons all over the world, but it doesn't help the surgeon if the patient dies from anesthesia."

In addition to his medical degree and residencies, Mørch went on to earn a Ph.D. at the University of Copenhagen in 1942, writing his dissertation on chondrodystrophy (a cause of dwarfism) in Scandinavia; his research was the first to document the frequency of mutations in humans. Immediately after World War II, the US Atomic Energy Commission used Mørch's dissertation research on dwarfism to study the genetic damage caused by the atomic bombs that fell on Hiroshima and Nagasaki.

When Mørch began working as an anesthesiologist, it wasn't even a specialty field in Denmark. "Anesthesia was administered by the intern or nurse who had not hidden fast enough," Mørch sardonically said. "Oxygen and artificial airways were not used. They never used an intravenous line. Blood pressure was taken before and after surgery, but not during. We had no electrocardiograph machines. The mortality rate was incredible." Chloroform or ether was typically given to patients by hand, he said, "breathing for them for hours. We never operated on old people, and in those dark days, old people were defined as those over 50." Mørch's good reputation grew quickly; even Denmark's royal leader, King Christian X, asked Mørch to anesthetize his favorite horse in 1937. It was the first time a horse had ever survived anesthesia.

Mørch would invent a piston-type artificial ventilator that would breathe for the patient, allowing for easier thoracic as well as other types of surgeries. It was, essentially, the first practical respirator. He developed his makeshift "piston contraption" by combining part of a Copenhagen sewer pipe, a piston, and some hardware he was able to scrounge. This prototype for modern ventilators is used today in respiratory care and anesthesiology. Mørch described his respirator as "elegant in its simplicity," wryly saying, "it was so simple even a doctor could operate it." His ingenuity continues to save countless lives, most recently during the COVID-19 pandemic.

He improved his respirator after immigrating to Chicago, where he became head of the University of Chicago School of Medicine. It replaced the iron lung that had been used by polio victims for years. Mørch claimed that he never made much money from his inventions. Nonetheless, he was proud of them and showed them off whenever he could. Indeed, as his friend and former colleague Dr. Geraldine Light once joked, "He showed them off too much and got beat to the market."

Although Mørch accomplished more as an anesthesiologist, it was his role in the Danish resistance efforts during the Nazi occupation that he described "as the most exhilarating time of my life." He risked his life time and again in attempts to defy the Gestapo, striving to maintain the dignity of the Danish people. He played a key role in saving thousands of Danish Jews from almost certain death.

Soon after the Nazi occupation of Denmark in 1940, Mørch began an instrumental role in the growing underground resistance movement. Along with a network of other Danish physicians – about ten individuals in all – he quickly published and distributed illegal newspapers with news covertly gathered from the BBC about the true status of Allied military actions, revealing information that ran counter to the German propaganda being communicated by the occupiers who controlled mainstream Danish press. As part of these efforts, he helped smuggle reports to Great Britain concerning German plans to send bombing missions over Denmark to London. In addition, Mørch took part in stealing paper and ink, which were rationed by the Nazis and thus in short supply, printing papers on stolen presses in various hidden locations. Circulation soon reached 1,000. Mørch recounted more than half a century later, "This was great fun and satisfaction, especially in a time where we could not buy a typewriter, so we had to steal one. It was such fun to steal for a good purpose!" The ever-ingenious Mørch often distributed the illegal newspapers around Copenhagen in the baby carriage of his two-year-old daughter. Placing the newspapers under the toddler right after she dirtied her diaper reduced the likelihood of Gestapo officers getting too close and discovering them.

Life in occupied Denmark took a turn for the worse in 1943. By that summer, the Soviets had attacked the Germans from the east and the Americans and British had come from the west and south. With the increase in fighting over a broader area, the Germans, in need of more war materials and food, began to plunder the Danish land. Danish agricultural products went to Germany while Danes went hungry. The Germans plundered Danish supplies of coal, petroleum, and other items, and the defiant resistance movement responded by trying to thwart the Nazis in more violent ways. They began to blow up railroad tracks to prevent the Germans from using them. They set fire to trucks carrying supplies for German soldiers. Danish workers making products for the Germans began to boycott their factory jobs. Finally, the Danish government refused to help catch or punish any saboteurs, much to the anger of the occupying Germans. There were two acts of sabotage in 1940, 12 in 1941, and 59 in 1942; in 1943, that number mushroomed to 816.

One of the most critical factors in the Danish attitude change was the notable shift in the tide of the war. Not only did the Allies invade German-occupied territories, but they also gained significant victories at El Alamein in Egypt in November 1942 and at Stalingrad in Russia in January 1943, which led to Winston Churchill's powerful "End of the Beginning" speech. Throughout Europe, including Denmark, people began to rethink the war's likely outcome.

In mid-1943, Jews finally were faced with the same consequences that the rest of Europe's Jews had been: roundup, deportation to camps, and extermination. Legions of Danes immediately began to act courageously to save their Jewish countrymen. When the occupying Germans, led by the Gestapo and SS soldiers stationed in Denmark deployed to keep the Danes in check, began to intensify their persecution of Danish Jews in 1943, the Danish resistance movement stepped up efforts to help safeguard their Jewish citizens. Unlike many European counterparts, the Danes had little antisemitism by the 1930s and '40s and considered Danish Jews as fellow citizens whom they fought hard to protect. King Christian led the charge of resistance, defying Nazi orders at every opportunity. However, he implored Danish citizens not to resort to violence and go as far as killing Nazis. Otherwise, he asserted, reprisals would be too great. So Mørch complied and happily joined his countrymen in blowing up factories, ships, and railroads and continued to help publish and distribute the illicit newspaper, broadcasting intelligence from the Allies, and even hiding Jews. Mørch and other doctors even pioneered bizarre attempts to reverse circumcisions in an attempt to prevent Jewish men from being discovered.

"The Gestapo, when they found a suspicious fellow, would tell him to drop his pants," he said. "If he was circumcised, they shot him. Danes normally were not circumcised, only Jewish Danes. So, our Jewish friends asked us to 'uncircumcise' them, and that was a hell of a job. We had to transplant little strips of skin and stitch them, and it was a real mess. It took several operations and looked really terrible. But it confused the Gestapo enough that at least they would not shoot them on the spot. ... Our patients, though, became terribly embarrassed. When their wives and sweethearts saw our work, they'd point their fingers and laugh: 'What is that?' Many men became impotent. They finally decided they'd rather risk the Nazis. So, we stopped uncircumcising them."

In 1943, the Nazis finally ordered the Danish Jews to wear the odious yellow armbands with the Star of David emblazoned on them, as their brethren had been ordered to do throughout Nazi-occupied Europe. Legends arose that King Christian, so protective of his nation's Jews, immediately began to wear the Jewish armband himself, particularly when he made his morning ride on his beloved horse around Copenhagen each day. But while the king was supportive of the Jews and the nationwide resistance movement, the story is merely legend, not fact. Mørch himself, however, wore a yellow Jewish armband around the city, he asserted years later, in solidarity with his Jewish brethren.

Mørch also assisted in the distribution of weapons to resistance fighters in case armed resurrection was necessary. In 1943, his three-year-old son, Claus, was recruited by his father to sit silently in a car atop a stash of illegal weapons covered by a blanket. The smuggling operation was successful, but when the "chubby, blond, and cute" toddler later bragged to his friends about "his guns," his parents rushed to a local toy store to purchase all the toy guns they had so any inquiring German soldier might be satisfied with the toy story.

Finally, on September 28, German shipping attaché Georg Duckwitz informed a handful of Danish Social Democratic Party leaders of an *aktion* planned against the Danish Jews within 72 hours. Danish political leaders got to work, using their extensive network of contacts and warning as many Jews as possible. Most of Denmark's Jews were warned soon enough.

The Danish resistance leaped into action, as did nearly the entire country as if to say, "This will not happen here!" Ordinary citizens, often led by physicians, began to hide their Jewish friends and neighbors from the German roundups. Mørch, like many of Denmark's 2,000 physicians, eagerly embraced the little country's resistance against the Nazis. At one point, Mørch said, a bounty of $500,000 was put on his head, "with or without the shoulders," he said.

"We stashed [the Jews] in homes, churches, and especially in hospitals, under typical Danish names like Hansen, Petersen, and Sorensen," Mørch said. Numerous public institutions opened their doors to provide temporary refuge. A key player was one of the largest Copenhagen hospitals, Bispebjerg, which quickly became the center to house many of the refugees. Physicians and medical students connected to the underground would let the Jews from Copenhagen and the surrounding areas know about the imminent danger and help coordinate, using Bispebjerg as a rallying point. One of the students was 17-year-old Robert Pederson, who said the following:

I went from house to house in the streets of the neighborhood. Whenever I saw a nameplate that indicated a Jewish family, I rang the doorbell and asked to talk to them. Sometimes they did not believe me. But I succeeded in persuading them to pack and come with me to Bispebjerg Hospital, which had been turned into a gathering place for Jewish refugees. I merely turned them over to the receptionist. After that, the doctors and nurses took care of them. And then I went back to my neighborhood and collected more Jews.

The central figures in this rescue operation were Dr. Karl Henry Koester, head nurse Signe Jansen, Dr. Stephan Lund, and Professor Richard Ege, and his wife, Vibeke. Once the refugees were gathered at Bispebjerg, they were dispersed to various other smaller hospitals or homes and given fictitious Danish names and diagnoses. As many as 200 or more Jews were held in Bispebjerg on any given day, and the hospital was surrounded by German soldiers, but not once did the Germans penetrate its walls. One morning, 200 Jews were escorted from the hospital in a ruse – a funeral procession. Though Mørch was not a key leader in this covert operation, he was one of the physicians who quietly played a supportive role.

The Danish Gentiles were not the only ones to exhibit great courage and resilience. The Jews also acted bravely and swiftly. As historian Robert Delong wrote:

> In many cases, decisions had to be made by family units involving family members from the most elderly to the very young. The required family discussions and decisions are nearly unimaginable. Nearly all earthly possessions, no matter how treasured, would have to be left behind. Family members too old or too sick to flee would have to be left behind to their fate at the hands of the Germans. Jobs and income, neighbors, the physical and emotional comfort that one's home had provided for years – all left behind on a moment's notice with absolutely no certainty of ever being able to return. In many cases, the warning was received too late to allow for the gathering of personal financial assets. The decision to flee was often also a decision to be destitute. In cases of mixed marriages, especially if the non-Jewish spouse was employed, impossibly difficult decisions had to be made about whether to split up the family. There was uncertainty about the degree of risk to either spouse in a mixed marriage. Those families with children that decided that the non-Jewish spouse would remain in Denmark then had to decide whether the children would flee or stay. Additionally, as has been documented most recently in Sofie Lene Bak's *Ikke noget at tale om* [*Nothing to Speak of*], some parents, out of fear of the dangers and uncertainties of being on the run from German authorities, made extraordinarily difficult and heartbreaking decisions to leave very young children in hiding with foster parents in Denmark.

The next problem was what to do with 7,000 hideaways. The Danes arranged to secretly get the Jews out of the country. Nearby neutral Sweden, separated from Denmark by only a few miles of sea, was the planned destination. The plan, Mørch said, was to build false decks on fishing boats – a second deck about five feet from the bottom – to hide the Jewish cargo, "and at night we'd sail out to the middle of the Øresund, the narrow water between Denmark and neutral Sweden. Then the people would be transferred to Swedish boats."

The maneuver worked until the Gestapo began using bloodhounds to search the boats. After an atrocity in which several people were murdered, Mørch and a young pharmacist friend, Oluf Hubner, considered how to conceal the human cargo more safely. "We discovered," Mørch later recalled, "that if we took a rabbit's blood and dried it, this created a lovely brownish powder that Oluf's cocker spaniel couldn't resist. He licked it, sniffed it, rolled in it. To this, we added cocaine, a 10 percent mixture." Oluf's dog, Mørch said, "couldn't smell a pizza if he was standing on it. But the dog ended up as a cocaine addict and soon died."

Mørch and Hubner determined that their plan would be successful and confiscated large quantities of rabbit blood and cocaine from the medical university laboratory so they could make mass amounts of the concoction to distribute to the dozens of fishermen and boat captains who had agreed to ferry the Jews to Sweden. Fishermen and boatmen placed the powdery substance in handkerchiefs and, if the Gestapo came on board the boats with their dogs sniffing for human cargo, a crewman would pretend to sneeze, emptying the contents of his handkerchief onto the boat's deck.

"This cocaine-blood mixture [was] then sprinkled on the decks of our fishing boats," Mørch said. "The next Gestapo dog that came along loved and sniffed and licked and reported back to his master that he couldn't smell anything ... because he *couldn't* smell anything. His nose had a good local anesthetic. ... As you can see, it very often was a great advantage to be an M.D. in the resistance movement."

To add to this exotic concoction and its unique scent, the fishermen were instructed to have dozens of rotting fish on the boat deck as well, which further confounded the dogs. Mørch said spreading rotten fish made "it less attractive for detailed examination."

Keeping hidden babies and small children from discovery was another challenge. "If they should start crying in their dark, hot, wet quarters, everybody could get killed," he said. "So, we gave the parents barbiturate suppositories, and they'd knock the kids out – actually put them in life-threatening comas. Then when the Swedes took over, doctors would quickly revive them." Mørch quickly developed one of the near-fatal barbiturate suppositories for distribution to parents with infants and toddlers, anticipating the need for a dose that was strong enough to put the young children to sleep for up to 12 hours or more, a "near-lethal dose," but not strong enough to endanger their lives. Leo Goldberger, a 13-year-old Jewish refugee at the time, remembered his three-year-old brother being given sleeping pills to keep him quiet, one of other various, quick but effectively thought-out ways to keep the evacuees quiet and safe.

Once the evacuated Jews reached the shoreline, various Swedes helped usher the new refugees into their new home. Carl Palm, a Swedish police commissioner of Helsingborg, was one of those who greeted arriving Jewish refugees in his country. "There were about 200 of them," he recalled, "and among them were dozens of women with babies in their arms. ... The babies and the children were so still that I was sure they were dead. I couldn't believe it. Why were all the grownups alive and all the children dead? You see, I didn't know at the time that the children had been given injections to make them sleep. I couldn't help myself. I started to cry."

One challenge facing the rescue organizations ferrying Jewish refugees to Sweden was funding for the operation. Initially, when transportation was organized privately, the cost ranged from 1,000 to 10,000 Danish kroner per person (approximately $3,000 to

$30,000 in today's US dollars). The amount was cost-prohibitive for all but the wealthiest refugees, so the Danes began raising funds to assist those who could not afford the transport. They also negotiated with the boat captains to lower the price for the trip to about 500 kroner.

Hanne Kaufmann, 16 years old, was on one of the fishing boats with her twin brother, her older sister, and her mother. The boat was leaving just before 11 p.m. on October 8, 1943. Joining them were two members of the resistance movement, two elderly women, and two babies. Hanne, hiding below deck, was frightened as they journeyed in the blackness of night. Suddenly, there was an eerie silence; the boat's motor had stopped. A German patrol boat was passing nearby, and the captain of the boat in which Hanne was hiding quelled the engine to escape detection. Successful, he turned the motor on again, only to have to quickly stall it again so he could navigate the boat around a mine just a few feet away.

At 5:53 a.m., after seven hours on the water, the motor stopped a third time. This time, though, it was because they were safely in Swedish waters, just off the coast of the mainland. The hiding refugees came up on deck when, suddenly, one of them turned, facing his homeland in the distance, and began singing the Danish national anthem: "There is a beautiful country with broad bays and a wide seacoast. With hills and dales, the home of Freia, and its name is Denmark." Soon, the others joined in, with their faces looking to their homeland behind them. They then sang the Swedish national anthem, turning and facing their new home – their safe haven.

The motor started up once again. They were now in the Trelleborg Harbor, the banks of which were packed with people despite the early morning hour, to welcome and receive the Danish refugees. Afterward, Hanne wrote, "In this moment, I was offered life. And I accepted it with gratitude. As the gift it always is." Danish citizens like Mørch made this gift possible for Hanne and thousands of others.

About 300 fishing boats were used in the clandestine operation of transporting at least 7,220 Danish Jews and 680 non-Jewish families to Sweden. They set sail from more than 50 points of embarkation along the coast of Denmark – from Gilleleje in the north of the island of Zealand to Asnæs in the south, as well as from the islands of Møn and Falster. In October and early November 1943, as many as 1,000 crossings took place. For some, the journey lasted fewer than 60 minutes; others spent as many as 24 hours at sea, battling elements, mines, and German patrol boats. Ultimately, about 90 percent of the Danish Jews were successfully evacuated to Sweden.

On October 1, 1943, the second day of the Jewish New Year, the Germans found fewer than 500 Jews left in Denmark. Only 481 Danish Jews were eventually arrested by the Gestapo. Most were deported to Theresienstadt in Nazi-occupied Czechoslovakia, of whom 423 were saved. All told, more than 95 percent of the Danish Jews survived the Holocaust. Jews from Denmark deported to Theresienstadt were not forgotten, though, by their government or their fellow Danish citizens during the internment. Almost immediately after their deportation, the Danish chargé *d'affaires* in Berlin requested permission from the German Foreign Ministry to visit the camp and send them packages. By November 1943, permission was granted for other organizations and family members to send clothes and letters to Danes in Theresienstadt, which the Danish Red Cross quickly began doing. Additionally, the Danes inundated the German occupation authorities with thousands of inquiries about the health and location of their fellow Jewish and non-Jewish citizens. Meanwhile, neighbors of those deported were encouraged by the Danish government to regularly clean the homes and water the plants of the Jews no longer occupying their homes. Most Danes had the attitude that their friends and neighbors would return.

Leo Goldberger, a Danish Jew who was a child during the evacuation operation, wrote that the operation in 1943 "has been rightfully recognized throughout the world as an example of moral courage under fire. Whether the Danish act is characterized as altruistic, compassionate, humanitarian, or heroic, and no matter what contextual complexities scholarly research may ascribe to it, the deed speaks for itself. ... Almost all Jews, about 7,200 out of some 7,800, were rescued from the clutches of the Nazis by a massive effort of other human beings who risked their own safety, and in some instances their very lives."

By the close of 1944, there were thousands of Scandinavian prisoners in German concentration camps, including approximately 6,000 Danes and 8,000 Norwegians. Most of them were not Jewish and had been arrested by the Germans on trumped-up charges. Additionally, resistance members, several thousand Danish police, and other Danes determined to be undesirable were deported to Dachau, Buchenwald, Sachsenhausen, Neuengamme, and several smaller labor camps in Germany. Of the Danes imprisoned as slave laborers in the German camps, at least 10 percent perished, though this figure included both Jews and non-Jews. Ultimately, all but 481 of the nation's 7,500 Jews escaped the Gestapo and deportation and it is estimated that only 58 Danes perished at the hands of the Nazis.

Discussions had begun by the fall of 1944 concerning just how the Danish and other Scandinavian prisoners would be freed from the camps. Frants Hvass of the Danish Foreign Ministry initiated a series of diplomatic negotiations in the fall and winter of 1944 with various German authorities to obtain the release of prisoners not engaged in "acts of war." One early mediator was Felix Kersten, the personal masseur of Heinrich Himmler, one of Hitler's top adjutants and the Nazi in charge of the Final Solution to annihilate all of Europe's Jews. A native of Finland, educated in Berlin, Kersten lived in neutral Sweden and commuted to Berlin to care for his infamous patient.

While early negotiations began between Hvass and Kersten, more serious discussions soon involved Count Folke Bernadotte, a nephew of King Gustaf V of Sweden and vice president of the Swedish Red Cross. On February 12, 1945, Bernadotte obtained permission from Red Cross Chairman Prince Carl to fly from Stockholm to Berlin to negotiate with German authorities for the release and rescue of Scandinavian prisoners to Sweden. Kersten had greased the skids to arrange a meeting between Bernadotte and Himmler. The negotiations began at a time when American and British planes had destroyed several German cities and Allied forces had crossed into Germany. The Germans had refused time and time again to let foreign observers conduct even the most cursory investigations of concentration camps, and the Geneva Convention did not cover political prisoners there, so the odds were stacked against successful negotiations. Bernadotte was negotiating without any help from the Allied powers, meaning he was proceeding down this nearly impossible road alone.

First, however, Bernadotte had to arrange a meeting with Himmler, one of the few in the Third Reich who still held any sway with Hitler. Though Himmler remained loyal to Der Führer, he was a realist – he knew the war was lost. He was cunning enough to know he needed to earn some capital with the invading Allies. On February 17, 1945, just outside Berlin, Bernadotte was able to get an audience with *Obergruppenführer* Ernst Kaltenbrunner, Himmler's number two man in the Gestapo, who was directly in control of the killings at the concentration camps. *Brigadeführer* Walter Schellenberg, head of the German Foreign Intelligence, joined them. Bernadotte informed Kaltenbrunner and Schellenberg that he wanted them to arrange a meeting for him with Himmler so that he could obtain the release of Scandinavian concentration camp prisoners married to Germans – concealing his plan to rescue *all* Scandinavian prisoners. This meeting was followed by one with German Foreign Minister Joachim von Ribbentrop, in which Bernadotte argued his case again.

Amazingly, not one of these men – Kaltenbrunner, Schellenberg, or Ribbentrop – stood in the way of Bernadotte. In fact, on Monday, February 19, 1945, Schellenberg personally picked Bernadotte up and drove him 120 kilometers north of Berlin to Hohenlychen, a secluded lakeside setting just five miles from Ravensbrück concentration camp. It was there that Bernadotte came face to face with Himmler, describing him as "one of the most complicated people I ever met."

Bernadotte had to be patient in his negotiations with Himmler. That Himmler would even agree to meet was an unprecedented miracle. Bernadotte told a friend, Major Sven Frykman: "It would be futile to ask the Germans to open their concentration camps and allow us to take their inmates away immediately. ... We must proceed by stages. First, we must get the Scandinavians assembled in one place in Germany near the Danish border so that we can keep an eye on them in case of a breakdown of the Nazi regime and ... succor the sick and try and reduce the liquidations. ... The next step must be to get the Scandinavians over the border into Denmark and eventually to Sweden."

Himmler questioned the motives behind liberating Scandinavian prisoners. When Bernadotte suggested that the Swedish Red Cross enter the camps, Himmler feared they would discover the deplorable conditions there. He finally acquiesced, with restrictions. Bernadotte and his Red Cross team would be allowed to corral the Norwegian and Danish prisoners into a single camp. They would then be allowed to segregate the sick and elderly among the Scandinavian prisoners and send them home. Finally, he would be allowed to send all Swedish women who were married to Germans but were now widowed back to Sweden – with their children.

Himmler agreed to allow imprisoned Scandinavians at various camps, including many of the Jews at Theresienstadt, to be pulled out and amassed at a "collection center" – Neuengamme concentration camp, outside of Hamburg, in northern Germany. It was the camp closest to Denmark. Despite last-minute efforts from various Himmler underlings to thwart the plan, the project went off without a hitch. The convoy consisted of three platoons of buses, each with 12 vehicles, along with one platoon of 12 trucks. Personnel of the rescuers was limited to no more than 300 Swedish soldiers, doctors, and nurses. They were deployed to Germany to collect any Scandinavian prisoners they could and bring them back to the collection point, a sort of holding center, at Neuengamme.

In March, the Danes were able to negotiate participation in the Swedish scheme, and from March 12–21, 1945, the Danes rescued 262 of their prisoners. Once out, the prisoners were to await the Swedish Red Cross, assisted by several Danish citizens, including Mørch, to collect them and take them across the border into Denmark. Initially, the buses were painted in camouflage, with red crosses and Swedish flags on the sides and roofs. But just before departure, at the insistence of British authorities, all vehicles were painted white so the Allies could distinguish them from enemy vehicles. Consequently, the rescue henceforth was known as the "White Buses." (Once the convoys began the trip, the Germans painted several of their own military trucks white with red crosses to try to trick the Allies into not bombing them as well.)

The Scandinavian buses were in danger throughout their travels despite the precautions with their appearance. They were often fired on by Allied planes and many times had to pull over to the side of the road so passengers could scramble off and take cover in roadside ditches.

In March 1945, the Swedish buses and ambulances drove to Sachsenhausen on a new operation, dodging bombings and air raids. They were able to rescue 2,176 Scandinavian prisoners from the camp, taking them north to Neuengamme. Another group was responsible for collecting prisoners from camps in southern Germany, including Dachau and Mauthausen. It was much riskier because the camps were farther away; Dachau was 800 kilometers south of the Danish border. The first convoy left on March 19, 1945, and arrived at Neuengamme on March 24.

The first transport rounded up 550 prisoners. Most were sick from infection, starvation, malnourishment, severe diarrhea, and abuse. "You wouldn't believe the brutality," Mørch said. "It was absolutely lawless, ruthless bestiality, which is impossible to understand for normal human beings." He said that in addition to physical abuse, the mental torture was in some ways even worse. "There was no dignity," Mørch said.

By early April, most of the Scandinavian prisoners were now at Neuengamme. The concentration camp was overflowing with prisoners when the White Buses arrived. Countless prisoners died before the camp closed, and the crematorium was in operation around the clock. About 120 buses and ambulances, driven by Danish volunteers, left Denmark to go to Neuengamme to evacuate prisoners as quickly as they could. Reportedly, some of the buses rushed across the border into Germany before the white paint on their vehicles could even dry.

On April 5, nearly half of the Swedish rescue contingent returned to Sweden, and the Germans allowed them to be replaced by Danes. The Danes used 33 buses, 14 ambulances, seven trucks, and four private cars for this expedition. They were led by Hvass, and Mørch accompanied them. After April 8, the White Buses were a mixed Swedish-Danish operation, with the Swedes in command. The Danish vehicles, like those of the Swedish, were also painted white, but with the Danish flag prominently displayed instead of the Red Cross.

Mørch described his involvement in the White Bus expedition, reporting that it was a two-week round trip from Copenhagen to Neuengamme, about 100 miles. He made several trips, leaving every third week. He described the prisoners as weak, sick, and malnourished. "We couldn't give them much food or they would die," Mørch said. Instead, they gave rescued prisoners little glasses of beer, providing a near-constant stream to infuse their depleted systems with liquid to treat dehydration and with calories for strength. "We stole the beer because we were unable to buy it," he said. Some prisoners were beyond help, though, dying from dehydration, starvation, or disease soon after rescue.

After picking up about 1,000 prisoners from Neuengamme, the convoy left the camp, heading north to Denmark. First, it had to pass through Hamburg. The British were bombing the city, so the convoy could not proceed; earlier convoys had been hit by stray bombs, with one driver and some prisoners killed. "We were cheering on the Allied bombers," Mørch said, "but we had several hundred patients on buses who were dying from typhus, typhoid fever, tuberculosis, and other diseases. They had no time to wait."

Mørch had an idea. They went to a payphone. "I gave Bernadotte a dime and asked him to call his [uncle], who happened to be King Gustav V of Sweden, and ask him to call his cousin, who happened to be King [George VI] of England, and ask him to call [American Supreme Commander] Gen. [Dwight] Eisenhower, who happened to be in charge of bombing Hamburg, and ask him to hold things up for a few minutes," Mørch said. "It worked! The bombing ceased. In disbelief, we dashed through the burning city. Then the bombing started right up again." Mørch, 52 years later, at 87 and close to death, exuberantly recalled that he was among the only ones who, if but for a brief period, "stopped ... World War II!"

While the White Buses program was first aimed at saving Scandinavian citizens, both Jews and non-Jews, it ultimately expanded to include those of other countries. In recent years, there has been criticism from some that the rescue operation did not do more to save others, but it truly was a massive, heroic undertaking. According to the Swedish Red Cross the operation rescued a total of 15,345 prisoners from concentration camps; of these, 7,795 were Scandinavian and 7,550 were non-Scandinavian.

For Mørch's humanitarian and courageous contributions to the Danish resistance movement, the evacuation of Jews to Sweden, and the White Bus campaign, he was decorated after the war by the kings of Denmark, Norway, and Sweden.

In 1953, the Israeli government established the World Holocaust Remembrance Center in Jerusalem at Yad Vashem. One item on their agenda was to begin recognizing the Righteous Among the Nations, or Righteous Gentiles. Mindful of the Talmudic admonition to "Remember the evil and do not forget the good," those honored by Yad Vashem are "non-Jews who took great risks to save Jews during the Holocaust. Rescue took many forms and the Righteous came from different nations, religions, and walks of life. What they had in common was that they protected their Jewish neighbors at a time when hostility and indifference were the norm – the wrong thinking prevailed."

Sadly, throughout most of Nazi-occupied Europe, attitudes toward Jews largely ranged from indifference to overt hostility. All too often, Europeans in nation after nation watched as their Jewish neighbors were rounded up, deported to concentration or death camps, or killed before deportation. Some collaborated with occupying Nazis, and many benefited from expropriating Jewish property. All too many were indifferent. However, in a world turned upside down, where moral collapse was the norm, there was a tiny minority who demonstrated extraordinary courage by risking their lives to hide, save, or otherwise rescue their Jewish neighbors. These were the Righteous Among the Nations. As of 2021, out of the 1930s European population of nearly 300 million, 27,921 people had been named Righteous Among the Nations.

If only more had helped. In the Nazi-occupied nations, most Jews were murdered. Poland had Europe's largest Jewish population in 1933 at 3.3 million. By 1950, it was only 45,000 – more than 90 percent of the Polish Jews had been murdered. Similarly, 85 percent of Lithuanian Jews were killed, 73 percent of those in the Netherlands, 91 percent in Greece, 73 percent in Czechoslovakia, 69 percent in both Germany and Hungary. And the list goes on. Miraculously, the results were different in Denmark.

In July 1995, fewer than six months before Mørch's death, I was studying in Poland and Israel on a teacher's fellowship. In Jerusalem, while taking classes at Yad Vashem, Israel's Worl Holocaust Remembrance Center, I made an appointment to speak with a gentleman who directed the Department of the Righteous at Yad Vashem (I believe it was Mordecai Paldiel), who oversaw collecting information on candidates for selection as a Righteous

Gentile. When meeting with him in his office, I informed him that I had a friend in Jacksonville worthy of selection. When I told him the name of Dr. Ernst Trier-Mørch, he looked in his files and responded that, like most of the Danes participating in the resistance (including those who participated in the White Buses operation), Mørch had refused recognition. While Mørch exhibited a fair degree of pride in being recognized by the kings of Denmark, Sweden, and Norway, glowingly showing me his three medals, he said in an earlier interview, "Naturally I was flattered and happy for the recognition. But it's always a little sad that they couldn't give out 20,000 medals, because we couldn't have done it without the help of thousands of others."

Mørch said it was not his efforts, but his country's collective deeds, and he didn't want to take individual credit by being named a Righteous Gentile. His attitude was prevalent throughout the Danish resistance forces. When asked if he was a hero, Mørch responded, "No, I am no hero. I did what any human being should do."

However, later in the day when I spoke with the Yad Vashem historian, I was deeply moved as I walked along Yad Vashem's Avenue of the Righteous, where carob trees are planted to commemorate the Righteous Gentiles, each tree marked with a placard identifying by name every one of the nearly 28,000 now recognized. Among others, I saw Oskar Schindler's tree and placard, Corrie Ten Boom's, and those of other rescuers' names I recognized. And there along the long and winding path, lined with the trees and individual names recorded, was an olive tree adjacent to a Danish fishing boat. The placard simply read: The Danish Resistance.

After the war, an Oxford fellowship was bestowed upon Mørch to study anesthesia with two leading experts, Sir Robert Macintosh and William Mushin. Following his fellowship, he returned to Denmark as the top man in his field. He tried to start a school for the study of anesthesia at the University of Copenhagen, but the faculty was reluctant, so Mørch and his family emigrated to the United States in 1949, first to Washington, D.C., then briefly moving to Kansas City, before settling in Chicago, where he began work at the University of Chicago. Four years later, he became the anesthesia department head. In 1959, he became the chair at one of the nation's largest hospitals, Cook County Hospital in Chicago.

From 1967 to 1978, he served as an anesthesiologist at Presbyterian St. Luke's Hospital in Chicago until reaching the mandatory retirement age of 70. Altogether, Mørch spent 24 years in Chicago before moving south in 1979 to Florida, where he accepted a position as head of anesthesia and chief of the medical staff at Nassau County Hospital in Fernandina Beach, close to Jacksonville. He worked there until 1988, past his 80th birthday. Remarkably, he also served as the town's deputy sheriff for a season. Divorced in 1962, after 22 years of marriage, Mørch moved to Fernandina alone, his four children – Claus, Sys, Ibi, and Peter – having grown and scattered.

Mørch remained a colorful personality throughout his life. He had myriad passions outside his professional career. One of them was flying airplanes. He earned his pilot's license and flew for both enjoyment and professional reasons. He frequently would maneuver his plane around the United States to deliver his now-famous respirator to hospitals without one so that he could save the lives of patients in distant locations. He once was forced to make an emergency landing in the Pacific Ocean and was rescued by boat. When he worked late in life at Nassau General Hospital, Mørch discovered the staff was anxious when the local sheriff brought in a rowdy, handcuffed convict for treatment. From then on, he went to where the prisoners were instead, becoming a part-time jail doctor. The sheriff was both impressed and grateful and deputized him as an official deputy sheriff, giving Mørch a badge. The sheriff also gave the good doctor the right to carry a firearm.

With a home at the beach and a small farm in nearby Callahan, Mørch stayed active until he died of lung and throat cancer on

December 13, 1995. He continued to drive his red sports car until age 86, often motoring to see his sweetheart, Louise. He was a gentleman farmer in his eighties, remaining busy, energetic, and until the end, retaining his engaging sense of humor. He spoke to my Holocaust Studies class in nearby Orange Park twice, the last time just weeks before his death. He was quite weak from cancer, so his daughter, Sys, did much of the speaking for her father at that last visit. Mørch was also interviewed by Steven Spielberg's Shoah Foundation at about the same time in November 1995.

Mørch remained buoyant until his final moments. As he approached his final days, he went to stay with Sys at her apartment in New York City. Not long after his arrival, as Sys pushed her dying father in his wheelchair for his daily "walk" through nearby Central Park, Mørch turned to her and told her to take him back up to the apartment so he could die. Sys, inheriting her father's robust sense of humor, scolded him, responding that it would be quite rude for him to die before his nurse came that afternoon, as the nurse would have a wasted visit. Mørch agreed, so Sys took him back to her apartment, and soon the nurse made her daily trip to tend to the great man. Moments later, the nurse came out of the room and told Sys, "Your father said to come get you as he is now ready to die." Sys entered her father's room, they told one another that they loved each other, and Mørch passed out of this life. This man who knew the human body so well knew when his own life was over.

An award Mørch received in 1985 from the University of Illinois had an appropriate quotation from Charles de Gaulle inscribed on it: "Nothing great will ever be achieved without great men, and men are great only if they are determined to be so." Ten years later, in the spring of 1995, as he spoke to my class in Orange Park, Florida for the first time, I had coincidentally written a quotation on my chalkboard (I selected different ones for each class day) that read "The deed is everything, the glory nothing," from Johann Wolfgang von Goethe. The selection was not planned but most fitting in describing our speaker that day. Six months later, in the fall of 1995, shortly before his death and speaking for one final time, my quote of the day was also coincidentally from Goethe: "Noble be man, merciful and good." Yes, Mørch was indeed a noble man, merciful and good. Had there been more in Europe like Dr. Ernst Trier-Mørch and the Danish resistance, perhaps more would have been saved from the Holocaust.[1]

Doctor Mørch before the German occupation of Denmark.

Dr. Ernst Trier-Mørch, showing his medals awarded to him by the kings of Denmark, Norway, and Sweden; t. Taken in the author's classroom, Orange Park, Florida, 1995.

Sys Trier-Mørch, the author, and Dr. Ernst Trier-Mørch just before he gave a talk to students at St. Johns Country Day School in Orange Park, Florida, in 1995.

One of the Danish fishing boats that was used in the evacuation of Danish Jews to the neutral nation of Sweden. Credit: Yad Vashem, Jerusalem.

One of Dr. Mørch's early respirators. Credit: Wood Library Museum.

NOTES

Introduction

1. Irene Butter, "I Witnessed the Rise of Nazism Firsthand." CNN, January 27, 2021. cnn.com/2021/01/26/opinions/holocaust-fascism-un-capitol-riots-butter/index.html.

1. Ella Lucak Rogozinski

1. Information for this chapter come from the following sources: Ella Rogozinski, Shoah Foundation testimony, November 24, 1996; Ella Rogozinski, class testimony, Orange Park, FL, November 1995; Melissa Ma, "Hillel at FSU hosts Holocaust survivor story for International Holocaust Remembrance Day," *FSU News*, February 2, 2020; Patrick M. Nolan, "The Survivors: Stories of Transition." unpublished class research paper, 1992, 42–43, 45–52 ; Ella Rogozinski interview by Patrick Nolan, February 5, 1992, 3, 5–7, 9, 11, 18–20, 22; Peleg 2005, 14, 588–91; Liebert Online 2009; Mason 1998, 1, 14; "Death Marches" n.d.; "Liberation of Bergen-Belsen" n.d.; Harriet Sherwood, "'The Horrors I Saw Still Wake Me at Night.' The Liberation of Belsen 75 Years On," *Guardian*, April 12, 2020, https://www.theguardian.com/world/2020/apr/12/the-horrors-i-saw-still-wake-me-at-night-the-liberation-of-belsen-75-years-on; Knoch, Habbo 2010; Dan Scanlan, "A Holocaust Survivor Tells Students about Freedom and What It Means," *Florida Times-Union*, April 11, 2009; Sam Rogozinski and brothers, personal interview, October 2020, Jacksonville, FL.

Josef Mengele served Auschwitz as ranking physician, in charge of making brief, usually ten seconds or fewer, physical "exams" on newly arrived prisoners to determine if they should stay in the camp to do slave labor for as long as they were physically able and needed or be selected for immediate murder in the notorious Auschwitz gas chambers. Those deemed unable to work and help the German cause – the very young, the old, the infirmed, the weak – were sent to the gas chambers. Mengele was responsible for sending more than 900,000 Jewish prisoners to their death. He performed many medical experiments on prisoners, largely Jewish ones, including experiments on twins – without anesthesia. Mengele had an M.D. and a Ph.D. in physical anthropology. He had completed significant coursework toward a doctorate in dentistry; he was well educated and intelligent – perhaps even brilliant – but he used his intellect and knowledge for evil, earning the nickname "The Angel of Death." After the war, he avoided capture and fled to South America, living in Paraguay, Argentina, and Brazil, before drowning in 1979 at the age of 67, forever eluding capture and dodging justice for the Holocaust victims.

2. Carla Nathans Schipper

1. Information for this chapter come from the following sources: Shirat Devorah, "Against All Odds: Carla's Story," from Stacey Goldring, *On Wooden Wheels: The Memoir of Carla Nathans Schipper,* blog post, April 19, 2012; Goldring *On Wooden Wheels: The Memoir of Carla Nathans Schipper,* Xlibris Corporation, 2006, 51–53, 56–59, 62, 65–67, 70–75, 79–82, 84–88, 93–96, 102–4, 106–8, 110–12, 114–23, 129–32, 135–39, 141–45, 148–50, 154, 175, 179–80, 201–7; Chana Arnon, "Jews Rescued Jews During the Holocaust," presentation at Yad Vashem Conference, June 2004; Jackie Headapohl, "Holocaust Survivor Gains Righteous Among the Nations Status for Three Rescuing Families" *Jewish News.* January 24, 2019; Carla Schipper, class testimony, Orange Park, FL, winter 1996; Carla Schipper, personal interview, Orange Park, FL, winter 1996; Paldiel 1993.

3. Rene Goldstein Jakob and Leslie Jakob

1. Information from this chapter comes from the following sources: Susan Clark Armstrong, personal interview, Jacksonville, FL, Fall 1995; Rene Jakob, Shoah Foundation interview, February 7, 1997; Leslie and Renee Jakob, class testimony, St. Johns Country Day School, Orange Park, FL, winter 1996; Bezwinska 1973; Frost 2022; author's interview of Leslie's children and grandchildren, St. Augustine, FL, September 2020; Anna Jakob Sussman phone interview, December 2020; interview with Leslie and Rene Jakob, Orange Park, FL, fall 1995; interview with Tina Jakob Hart and son Jason Hart, St. Augustine, FL, October 2020; Salmen Gradowski, qtd. from *Amidst a Nightmare of Crime,* Oświęcim: Auschwitz State Museum Publication, 1973; Natasha Frost. "Horrors of Auschwitz: The Numbers Behind WWII's Deadliest Concentration Camp." history.com. Jan. 21, 2020, updated: Jan. 5, 2022.

4. Richard Friedemann

1. It is ironic so many survivors remember Mengele as being tall when he was only five-feet, eight-and-a-half inches.
2. Information for this chapter comes from the following sources: Patrick M. Nolan, The Survivors: Stories of Transition (unpublished paper), 1992, 73, 75, 77–88, 90, 92; Friedemann 2017, published only in Polish, from the unpublished English version, 28–31, 34, 43–47, 53–55, 66–67, 69, 97, 120–22, 160–63, 171–72, 183, 185, 192–93, 240–41, 265, 271, 276, 314–15, 335, 343, 347, 350–54, 362, 364, 370–71, 394–95, 398–99, 405–7, 414, 439–41, 460, 465, 489–90, 494, 511–18, 528–30, 587–88, 602–3, 626; Richard Friedemann, class testimony, Orange Park, FL, 1996; Ariel Schiller, "Tallahassee man remembers father, a Holocaust survivor, on International Holocaust Remembrance Day," WXTL ABC News, Tallahassee, FL, January 29, 2023; Beth Dalbey, "Holocaust Survivor Kept Secret, Fearing 'History Might Repeat,'" Patch: Across America, September 10, 2019; James Call, "A Holocaust Survivor's Incredible Life and Escape: 'The Indomitable Spirit' of Richard Friedemann, *Tallahassee Democrat,* September 4, 2019; Mark Friedemann,

personal interview, Tallahassee, FL, October 2020; Mark Friedemann's notes, obtained from his father, Richard Friedemann, in an email to the author, April 25, 2023; Richard Andrew Friedemann obituary, dignitymemorial.com/obituaries/tallahassee-fl/richard-friedemann-8828827; Richard Friedemann, personal interview, Orange Park, FL, winter 1995; Richard Friedemann testimony, Shoah Foundation, February 7, 1997.

5. Rose Mibab Goldberg

1. Information for this chapter comes from the following sources: Muzychenko translated by Marta Daria Olynyk, *Jewish Ludmir: The History and Tragedy of the Jewish Community of Volodymyr-Volynsky, A Regional History*, Academic Studies Press, Brighton, MA, 2016, xxv–xxvii, 83–84, 114, 116–18, 125, 129, 132; Zucker 2019; Rose "Roza" Mibab Goldberg obituary; Anita Mibab Goldberg, class testimony, Orange Park, FL, 1996; "Rose Mibab and Carl Goldberg: The Holocaust Quilt: Commemorating Charleston Survivors," College of Charleston, Addlestone Library, Jewish Studies, https://holocaustarchives.cofc.edu/about/index.html; Yahil 1987, 331–35; Bauer 1982, 193–99; "We Won't Survive Anyway: Rose Mibab Goldberg's Story," *Holocaust Remembrance Supplement*, told to Lilly Filler by Anita Goldberg Zucker, April 26, 2019; Lukin 2010; "Perry Mibab," Frisch Family Holocaust Memorial Library https://jacksonvilleholocaustmemorial.com/perry-mibab/; Eva Goldberg Lipman obituary, *Atlanta Jewish Times*, November 25, 2020; Erin Davis, "My Nana Rose – Shabbatness," blog, March 4, 2020; Lilly Fuller, MD, email exchange with the author, June 15, 2021; "The Original Ms. Rose's Fine Foods and Cocktails," msroses.com, July 5, 2021; Elizabeth Bush, "Anita Zucker Shares Family Story Steeped in Survival, Love, Hard Work and Charity," *Daniel Island News,* September 16, 2015.

6. Gina Sculz Freiden

1. Information in this chapter comes from the following sources: Linhares 2008, 169–172; Fawn Germer, "Holocaust Survivor: Jacksonville Resident Tells of the Horror," *Florida Times-Union*, April 18, 1983; "Włocławek" 2014, holocausthistoricalsociety.org.uk/contents/ghettoss-z/wloclawek.html; "Gina Freiden," Shoah Foundation testimony, 1996; Patrick Nolan, 1992, *The Survivors, Stories of Transition*, unpublished class research paper, 30–39; Patrick Nolan, "Gina Freiden: Oral History Transcripts," January 30, 1992, 1–2, 27; Saul Freiden, personal interview, October 2020; Schulz 1967, 2–3; Dobroszycki 1984; Rosenfeld 1993, 57–59; History.com 2001; Gina Freiden obituary, *Florida Times-Union*, December 22, 2000; Chris Webb, Wloclawek," Holocaust Historical Society, 2014. https://www.holocausthistoricalsociety.org.uk/contents/ghettoss-z/wloclawek.html.

7. Leona Hocherman Krohn

1. Information in this chapter is from the following sources: Leona Krohn, class testimony, Orange Park, FL, January 1995; Leona Krohn, Shoah Foundation testimony, 1996; Mazzeo 2016, 33; "Lodz" n.d.; Slawomir Grünberg and Robert Podgursky, 2016, "Saved by Deportation: An Unknown Odyssey of Polish Jews," https://logtv.com/deportation/"; Leona Krohn obituary; Leona Krohn, personal interview, Orange Park, FL, January 1995; family interview, Jacksonville, FL, October 2020; Irena Krohn Jaffa, personal interview, October 2020; Garrels 2016, 43–45; Goldberg n.d., 117–18; Edele et al. 2017, 1–2, 5–6, 10, 36–37, 49, 60, 73, 103.

8. Lt. Col. Joseph Williams

1. Information for this chapter has been obtained from the following sources: Joseph H. Williams obituary, https://obits.arlingtonparkfuneralhome.com/obituary/williams-joseph; Williams 1986 (Is the full citation of book title not necessary??), 12–15, 30, 44–45, 53, 55, 57–59, 61–63, 67–70, 97–98, 100–5, 110–11, 115, 130–32, 134, 137–39, 150–51, 156, 178–81, 183–84, 188–89, 210–13, 220–26, 290–95; Joseph Williams, class testimony, St. Johns Country Day School, Orange Park, FL, spring 1995, 1996, and 1997; Joseph Williams, personal interview, Orange Park, FL, spring 1995; Wood 2008; "Dachau concentration camp: history and overview," n.d.; "Warsaw" n.d.; Robert Shnayerson, "Judgment at Nuremberg," Smithsonian, October 1996, 125–26, 134; Snyder 1994; "Nuremberg Trials" n.d.; Holocaust Encyclopedia, The US Holocaust Museum (encyclopedia.ushmm.org/content/en/article/warsaw); Louis Snyder, Encyclopedia of the Third Reich. Da Capo Press, 1994; The US Holocaust Museum, encyclopedia.ushmm.org/content/en/article/warsaw; Jens Westemeier, Joachim Peiper: A Biography of Himmler's SS Commander, Schiffer Publishing, 2007.

9. Ernst Trier-Mørch, M.D., Ph.D

1. Information in this chapter comes from the following sources: Dan Lewis, "How Dead Rabbits and Cocaine Saved Thousands of Lives," Now I Know blog, June 17, 2020, https://nowiknow.com/how-dead-rabbits-and-cocaine-saved-thousands-of-lives; "Denmark" n.d.; Levine 2000, 2–5, 122–23; Sarah Bottoms, "Fernandina's Own Schindler," Fernandina News-Leader, Fernandina Beach, FL, July 20, 1994; Peter Gorner, "A Mind for Mankind," Chicago Tribune, August 1, 1985; Stephen 1996; Meier and Cadogan 2021; Ernst Trier-Mørch, Shoah Foundation testimony, November 14, 1995; Byers 2012, 12–15; Kirchoff, Lauridsen and Trommer, cited in DeLong 2016, 50–76; Claire Bessette, "Son of a WWII Hero Relays Events to Norwich Students," The Day, February 22, 2016, https://www.theday.com/local-news/20160222/son-of-danish-wwii-hero-relays-events-to-norwich-students; Werner 2002, 49–50, 61–62, 68, 80–81, 85, 108, 116–17; Ernst Trier-Mørch, personal interview, Orange Park, FL; Sys Mørch, personal interview, Orange Park, FL; Mørch, ET interview, KJXT-TV, Jacksonville, FL, March 1988; Gorner, Peter, "A Mind for Mankind," chicagotribune.com/

newsctzpm-1985-08-02-8502200595-story.html); Wikberg 2000; "White Buses," military-history.fandom.com/wiki/White_Buses; Emling 2019, 122, 132–33, 137–42, 145–49, 132, 150–51, 157; Goldberger 1988; Gilbert 2003, 221; Leo Goldberger, who became a psychologist in the United States, wrote of the rescue of Danish Jews. He indicated he wasn't aware of Gestapo dogs sniffing for hidden Jews on fishing boats, though he said it was plausible (email exchange, 2012); Lois Lowry, author of the highly acclaimed historical novel, *Number the Stars*, wrote about Mørch's concoction of rabbit's blood and cocaine used to deter Gestapo dogs, yet with no reference to Mørch. She said she found information while doing research for the novel, including on Mørch's work (email exchange, 2012).

ACKNOWLEDGMENTS

There are many people to thank for this labor of love. My late grandfather, Charles Jones, inspired in me a love of history at a very young age; my mother, Rosemary Jones Cox, nurtured that love of history along with a devotion to reading good books and developing a pursuit of lifelong learning. She also encouraged me to follow my passions wherever they might lead.

Many excellent teachers along the way fostered my love of history, including Drs. Lisa Sarasohn, Darold Wax, and Don McIlvenna at Oregon State University, and, in particular, Dr. Paul Kopperman for his inspiration and encouragement to study the Holocaust in greater depth. John Iorii from Jacksonville was a significant source of help as I began to develop my Holocaust course in 1993–1994 and introduced me to several of the subjects in this book. I am forever indebted to him. I sincerely thank the second- and third-generation survivors of my book focus: Elisa Freiden Topper; Saul Freiden; Jason Hart; Tina Hart; Anna Jakob Sussman; Irene Krohn Jaffa; Sam, Chaim, and Abraham Rogozinski; Mark Friedemann; Sys Trier-Mørch; and Anita Goldberg Zucker.

I would also like to thank Stacey Goldring, who was invaluable in her sage advice, assistance, and encouragement, along with my pro bono editors Susie Armstrong and Marlene Dryden, who devoted countless hours reading, editing, suggesting, prodding, and encouraging me.

Of course, I also thank my wife, Erin Bobel Cox, for her constant source of strength and encouragement for all my various and assorted whims, including the many hours devoted to this book.

BIBLIOGRAPHY

"About the Righteous." Yad Vashem. n.d., https://yadvashem.org/righteous/about-the-righteous.html.

Bak, Sofie Lene. *Ikke noget at tale om* [Nothing to Speak of], 2010.

Bauer, Yehuda. *A History of the Holocaust.* London: Franklin Watts, 1982.

Bezwinska, Jadwiga. *Amidst a Nightmare of Crime: Manuscripts of Prisoners in Crematorium Squads Found at Auschwitz.* New York: Publications of State Museum at Oświęcim, 1973.

Byers, Ann. *Rescuing the Danish Jews: A Heroic Story from the Holocaust.* Berkeley Heights, NJ: Enslow Publishers. 2012.

"Dachau Concentration Camp: History & Overview." Jewish Virtual Library. Accessed January 21, 2021, https://www.jewishvirtuallibrary.org/history-and-overview-of-dachau.

"Death Marches." *Holocaust Encyclopedia,* United States Holocaust Memorial Museum. n.d., encyclopedia.ushmm.org/content/en/article/death-marches-1.

DeLong, Robert, ed. "The Flight of the Danish Jews: 'Rescue' or 'Escape.'" *Scandinavian-Canadian Studies/Études Scandinaves au Canada* 23 (2016).

"Denmark." *Holocaust Encyclopedia.* United States Holocaust Memorial Museum. n.d., encyclopedia.ushmm.org/content/en/article/Denmark.

Dobroszycki, Lucjan, ed. *The Chronicle of the Lodz Ghetto, 1941–1945.* Translated by Richard Lourie, Joachim Neugroschel, et al. New Haven, CT: Yale University Press, 1984.

Edele, Mark, Fitzpatrick, Sheila, and Atina Grossmann, eds. "Shelter from the Holocaust: Rethinking Jewish Survival in the Soviet Union." Detroit: Wayne State University Press. 2017.

Emling, Shelley. *A Forgotten Hero: Folke Bernadotte: The Swedish Humanitarian Who Rescued 30,000 People from the Nazi.* Toronto: ECW Press, 2019.

Frost, Natasha. "Horrors of Personal Auschwitz: The Numbers Behind WWII's Deadliest Concentration Camp." history.com. January 21, 2020, updated January 5, 2022.

Garrels, Anne. *Putin Country: A Journey into the Real Russia.* New York: Farrar, Straus and Giroux, 2016.

Gilbert, Martin. *The Righteous: The Unsung Heroes of the Holocaust.* New York: Henry Holt & Co., 2003.

Goldberg, Michael. "Memories of a Generation." United States Holocaust Memorial Museum, RG-10.120. Qtd. From Mark Edele, Sheila Fitzpatrick, and Atina Grossman, eds. *Shelter from the Holocaust: Rethinking Jewish Survival in the Soviet Union.* Detroit: Wayne State University Press. 2017.

Goldberger, Leo, ed. *The Rescue of the Danish Jews: Moral Courage under Stress.* New York: New York University Press, 1988.

Goldring, Stacey. *On Wooden Wheels: The Memoir of Carla Nathans Schipper.* Bloomington, IN: Xlibris, 2006.

History.com, ed. "Auschwitz." December 15, 2009. history.com/topics/world-war-ii/Auschwitz.

Knoch, Habbo. ed. *Bergen-Belsen: Wehrmacht POW Camp 1940–1945, Concentration Camp 1943–1945, Displaced Persons Camp 1945–1950.* Catalog of the permanent exhibition, Wallstein, 2010.

Levine, Ellen. *Darkness Over Denmark: The Danish Resistance and the Rescue of the Jews.* New York: Scholastic, 2000.

"Liberation of Bergen-Belsen." United States Holocaust Memorial Museum. n.d., https://encyclopedia.ushmm.org/content/en/timeline-event/holocaust/1942-1945/liberation-of-bergen-belsen.

Linhares, Bruno Mattos Jr. "Nevertheless I Am Continually with You: A Cosmopolitan and Theopoetic Reframing of Pastoral Theology." Unpublished dissertation. Princeton, NJ: Princeton Theological Seminary, 2008.

"Lodz." United States Holocaust Memorial Museum, n.d. https://encyclopedia.ushmm.org/content/en/article/lodz

Lopez, Agnes. *The Faces to Remember Project,* n.d., https://www.thefacestoremember.com/portraits/ella-rogozinski/

Lukin, Benjamin. "Volodymyr Volyns'kyi." *The Yivo Encyclopedia of Jews in Eastern Europe,* Yivo Institute for Jewish Research, Translated by I. Michael Aronson. 2010, yivoencyclopedia.org.

Marwell, David G. *Mengele: Unmasking the "Angel of Death."* New York: W. W. Norton & Co., 2020.

Mazzeo, Tilar J. *Irena's Children: A True Story of Courage.* New York: Gallery Books, 2016.

Meier, Ciselle, and Mike Cadogan. "Ernst Mørch." Medical Eponym Library. September 29, 2021.

Muzychenko, Volodymyr. *Jewish Ludmir: The History and Tragedy of the Jewish Community of Volodymyr-Volynsky: A Regional History.* Translated by Marta Daria Olynyk. Boston: Academic Studies Press, 2015.

"Nuremberg Trials." History. n.d., history.com/topics/world-war-ii/nuremberg-trials.

Paldiel, Mordecai. *The Path of the Righteous: Gentile Rescuers of the Jews during the Holocaust.* Hoboken, NJ: KTAV Publishing House, 1993.

Peleg, Roni. "Gisella Perl: A Jewish Gynecologist in Auschwitz." *Journal of Women's Health* (2005): 588–91.

Rosenfeld, Alvin L., ed. *Fifty Years Ago: Revolt Amid the Darkness.* United States Holocaust Memorial Museum, Washington, D.C. 1993.

Schulz, Natan. "The Figure of a Fighter." *Museum of the Combatants and Partisans,* Tel Aviv. From Chaim Lazar. *Masada of Warsaw.* Translated by Shalom Oak. 1967.

Snyder, Louis. *Encyclopedia of the Third Reich.* New York: Da Capo Press, 1994.

Stephen, C. R. "E. Trier-Mørch, MD – Inventor, Medical Pioneer and WWII Freedom Fighter." *Bulletin of Anesthesia History* 14, no. 2 (1996).

"Warsaw." Holocaust Encyclopedia, United States Holocaust Memorial Museum. n.d, encyclopedia.ushmm.org/content/en/article/warsaw.

Webb, Chris. "Wloclawek." Holocaust Historical Society. 2014, https:www.holo-causthistoricalsociety.org.uk/contents/ghettoss-z/wloclawek.html.

Werner, Emmy. *A Conspiracy of Decency: The Rescue of the Danish Jews During World War II*. Boulder, CO: Westview Press, 2002.

Westemeier, Jens. *Joachim Peiper: A Biography of Himmler's SS Commander*. Lancaster, PA: Schiffer Publication, 2007.

Wikberg, Martin, ed. "The White Buses: The Swedish Red Cross Rescue Action in Germany during the World War II." Translated by Anita and Peter Hodgson. Swedish Red Cross. 2000.

Williams, Joseph H. *Captor, Captive*. Jacksonville, FL: Girtman Press, 1986.

"Wloclawek." Holocaust Historical Society. n.d., http://holocausthistoricalsociety.org.uk/contents/ghettoss-z/wloclawek.html.

Wood, Angela Gluck. *Holocaust: The Events and Their Impact on Real People*. New York: Dorling Kindersley, 2008.

Yahil, Leni. *The Holocaust: The Fate of European Jewry*. Oxford: Oxford University Press. 331–335, 1987.

Zucker, Anita Goldberg, as told to Lilly Filler. "We Won't Survive Anyway: Rose Mibab Goldberg's Story." Holocaust Remembrance Supplement, Columbia Holocaust Education Commission, April 26, 2019.

ABOUT THE AUTHOR

Samuel Cox is a retired US Army Reserve officer, an educator for four decades, and a lifelong student of the Holocaust. He taught various history courses for many years, including courses on the Holocaust, and served as a K–12 private school headmaster in Virginia and North Carolina for more than 20 years.

He holds a B.S. from Wake Forest University, a B.A. from Oregon State University, an M.S. from the University of South Carolina, and an M.A. from The College of William & Mary, along with additional graduate coursework at several other universities.

From 1994 to 1999, he taught a Holocaust class at St. Johns Country Day School in Orange Park, Florida, where he came to know the ten friends he writes about in this book. Sam resides in Greensboro, North Carolina, with his wife, Erin, and has three grown children.

AMSTERDAM PUBLISHERS
HOLOCAUST LIBRARY

The series **Holocaust Survivor Memoirs World War II** consists of the following autobiographies of survivors:

Outcry. Holocaust Memoirs, by Manny Steinberg

Hank Brodt Holocaust Memoirs. A Candle and a Promise,
by Deborah Donnelly

The Dead Years. Holocaust Memoirs, by Joseph Schupack

Rescued from the Ashes. The Diary of Leokadia Schmidt, Survivor of the
Warsaw Ghetto, by Leokadia Schmidt

My Lvov. Holocaust Memoir of a twelve-year-old Girl, by Janina Hescheles

Remembering Ravensbrück. From Holocaust to Healing, by Natalie Hess

Wolf. A Story of Hate, by Zeev Scheinwald with Ella Scheinwald

Save my Children. An Astonishing Tale of Survival and its Unlikely Hero,
by Leon Kleiner with Edwin Stepp

Holocaust Memoirs of a Bergen-Belsen Survivor & Classmate of Anne
Frank, by Nanette Blitz Konig

Defiant German - Defiant Jew. A Holocaust Memoir from inside the Third
Reich, by Walter Leopold with Les Leopold

In a Land of Forest and Darkness. The Holocaust Story of two Jewish
Partisans, by Sara Lustigman Omelinski

Holocaust Memories. Annihilation and Survival in Slovakia,
by Paul Davidovits

From Auschwitz with Love. The Inspiring Memoir of Two Sisters' Survival, Devotion and Triumph Told by Manci Grunberger Beran & Ruth Grunberger Mermelstein, by Daniel Seymour

Remetz. Resistance Fighter and Survivor of the Warsaw Ghetto, by Jan Yohay Remetz

My March Through Hell. A Young Girl's Terrifying Journey to Survival, by Halina Kleiner with Edwin Stepp

Roman's Journey, by Roman Halter

Beyond Borders. Escaping the Holocaust and Fighting the Nazis. 1938-1948, by Rudi Haymann

The Engineers. A memoir of survival through World War II in Poland and Hungary, by Henry Reiss

The series **Holocaust Survivor True Stories**
consists of the following biographies:

Among the Reeds. The true story of how a family survived the Holocaust,
by Tammy Bottner

A Holocaust Memoir of Love & Resilience. Mama's Survival from
Lithuania to America, by Ettie Zilber

Living among the Dead. My Grandmother's Holocaust Survival Story of
Love and Strength, by Adena Bernstein Astrowsky

Heart Songs. A Holocaust Memoir, by Barbara Gilford

Shoes of the Shoah. The Tomorrow of Yesterday, by Dorothy Pierce

Hidden in Berlin. A Holocaust Memoir, by Evelyn Joseph Grossman

Separated Together. The Incredible True WWII Story of Soulmates
Stranded an Ocean Apart, by Kenneth P. Price, Ph.D.

The Man Across the River. The incredible story of one man's will to survive
the Holocaust, by Zvi Wiesenfeld

If Anyone Calls, Tell Them I Died. A Memoir, by Emanuel (Manu) Rosen

The House on Thrömerstrasse. A Story of Rebirth and Renewal in the
Wake of the Holocaust, by Ron Vincent

Dancing with my Father. His hidden past. Her quest for truth. How Nazi
Vienna shaped a family's identity, by Jo Sorochinsky

The Story Keeper. Weaving the Threads of Time and Memory - A Memoir,
by Fred Feldman

Krisia's Silence. The Girl who was not on Schindler's List, by Ronny Hein

Defying Death on the Danube. A Holocaust Survival Story, by Debbie J. Callahan with Henry Stern

A Doorway to Heroism. A decorated German-Jewish Soldier who became an American Hero, by Rabbi W. Jack Romberg

The Shoemaker's Son. The Life of a Holocaust Resister, by Laura Beth Bakst

The Redhead of Auschwitz. A True Story, by Nechama Birnbaum

Land of Many Bridges. My Father's Story, by Bela Ruth Samuel Tenenholtz

Creating Beauty from the Abyss. The Amazing Story of Sam Herciger, Auschwitz Survivor and Artist, by Lesley Ann Richardson

On Sunny Days We Sang. A Holocaust Story of Survival and Resilience, by Jeannette Grunhaus de Gelman

Painful Joy. A Holocaust Family Memoir, by Max J. Friedman

I Give You My Heart. A True Story of Courage and Survival, by Wendy Holden

In the Time of Madmen, by Mark A. Prelas

Monsters and Miracles. Horror, Heroes and the Holocaust, by Ira Wesley Kitmacher

Flower of Vlora. Growing up Jewish in Communist Albania, by Anna Kohen

Aftermath: Coming of Age on Three Continents. A Memoir, by Annette Libeskind Berkovits

Not a real Enemy. The True Story of a Hungarian Jewish Man's Fight for Freedom, by Robert Wolf

Zaidy's War. Four Armies, Three Continents, Two Brothers. One Man's Impossible Story of Endurance, by Martin Bodek

The Glassmaker's Son. Looking for the World my Father left behind in Nazi Germany, by Peter Kupfer

The Apprentice of Buchenwald. The True Story of the Teenage Boy Who Sabotaged Hitler's War Machine, by Oren Schneider

Good for a Single Journey, by Helen Joyce

Burying the Ghosts. She escaped Nazi Germany only to have her life torn apart by the woman she saved from the camps: her mother, by Sonia Case

American Wolf. From Nazi Refugee to American Spy. A True Story, by Audrey Birnbaum

Bipolar Refugee. A Saga of Survival and Resilience, by Peter Wiesner

In the Wake of Madness. My Family's Escape from the Nazis, by Bettie Lennett Denny

Before the Beginning and After the End, by Hymie Anisman

I Will Give Them an Everlasting Name. Jacksonville's Stories of the Holocaust, by Samuel Cox

The series **Jewish Children in the Holocaust** consists of the following
autobiographies of Jewish children
hidden during WWII in the Netherlands:

Searching for Home. The Impact of WWII on a Hidden Child,
by Joseph Gosler

Sounds from Silence. Reflections of a Child Holocaust Survivor,
Psychiatrist and Teacher, by Robert Krell

Sabine's Odyssey. A Hidden Child and her Dutch Rescuers,
by Agnes Schipper

The Journey of a Hidden Child, by Harry Pila and Robin Black

The series **New Jewish Fiction** consists of the following novels, written by Jewish authors. All novels are set in the time during or after the Holocaust.

The Corset Maker. A Novel, by Annette Libeskind Berkovits

Escaping the Whale. The Holocaust is over. But is it ever over for the next generation? by Ruth Rotkowitz

When the Music Stopped. Willy Rosen's Holocaust, by Casey Hayes

Hands of Gold. One Man's Quest to Find the Silver Lining in Misfortune, by Roni Robbins

The Girl Who Counted Numbers. A Novel, by Roslyn Bernstein

There was a garden in Nuremberg. A Novel, by Navina Michal Clemerson

The Butterfly and the Axe, by Omer Bartov

To Live Another Day. A Novel, by Elizabeth Rosenberg

A Worthy Life. Based on a True Story, by Dahlia Moore

The Right to Happiness. After all they went through. Stories, by Helen Schary Motro

The series **Holocaust Heritage** consists of the following memoirs by 2G:

The Cello Still Sings. A Generational Story of the Holocaust and of the Transformative Power of Music, by Janet Horvath

The Fire and the Bonfire. A Journey into Memory, by Ardyn Halter

The Silk Factory: Finding Threads of My Family's True Holocaust Story, by Michael Hickins

Winter Light. The Memoir of a Child of Holocaust Survivors, by Grace Feuerverger

Hiding in Holland. A Resistance Memoir, by Shulamit Reinharz

Stumbling Stones, by Joanna Rosenthall

The Unspeakable, by Nicola Hanefeld

Hidden in Plain Sight. A Journey into Memory and Place, by Julie Brill

The series **Holocaust Books for Young Adults** consists of the following novels, based on true stories:

The Boy behind the Door. How Salomon Kool Escaped the Nazis. Inspired by a True Story, by David Tabatsky

Running for Shelter. A True Story, by Suzette Sheft

The Precious Few. An Inspirational Saga of Courage based on True Stories, by David Twain with Art Twain

The Sun will Shine on You again one Day, by Cynthia Monsour

The series **WWII Historical Fiction** consists of the following novels, some of which are based on true stories:

Mendelevski's Box. A Heartwarming and Heartbreaking Jewish Survivor's Story, by Roger Swindells

A Quiet Genocide. The Untold Holocaust of Disabled Children in WWII Germany, by Glenn Bryant

The Knife-Edge Path, by Patrick T. Leahy

Brave Face. The Inspiring WWII Memoir of a Dutch/German Child, by I. Caroline Crocker and Meta A. Evenbly

When We Had Wings. The Gripping Story of an Orphan in Janusz Korczak's Orphanage. A Historical Novel, by Tami Shem-Tov

Jacob's Courage. Romance and Survival amidst the Horrors of War, by Charles S. Weinblatt

A Semblance of Justice. Based on true Holocaust experiences, by Wolf Holles

Dark Shadows Hover, by Jordan Steven Sher

Amsterdam Publishers Newsletter

Subscribe to our **Newsletter** by selecting the menu at the top (right) of amsterdampublishers.com or scan the QR-code below.

Receive a variety of content such as:

- A welcome message by the founder
- Free Holocaust memoirs
- Book recommendations
- News about upcoming releases
- Chance to become an AP Reviewer.

Made in United States
Orlando, FL
03 May 2024

46446352R00157